EFFECTIVE STUDY

EFFECTIVE STUDY

Fourth Edition

FRANCIS P. ROBINSON

Professor of Psychology
Ohio State University

HARPER & ROW, PUBLISHERS

New York, Evanston, and London

To SIDNEY L. PRESSEY

A pioneer in many fields,
one of his earliest being
work on study skills.

Contents

Preface

Efficient work skills are necessary in college, as in any occupation, so students may make effective use of their time and be able to select and understand the important ideas in their lessons. Although not every individual can become an outstanding student, a training program can show each student how to work to his full capacity. The responsibility of the college must go beyond merely providing courses; it must also show the student how to take full advantage of his opportunities.

Hundreds of colleges and universities have how-to-study programs; one of the oldest and most successful is the one at Ohio State University. As a result of an extensive research program, a great deal of useful training material has been developed. This book represents a coordination of these diagnostic and training materials and should be of use in other similar courses.

Since the beginning of how-to-study work in the early 1920s, there have been changing emphases as new ideas and needs became evident. Previous editions of this book have presented these developments. In the early decades of how-to-study work, emphasis was placed on working in a noncredit program with failing and probation students, and attention was given to diagnostic and remedial work with skill disabilities and personal problems. The first edition of this book contained two major sections devoted to remedying disabilities in the three Rs and to helping with distracting personal problems; it was entitled *Diagnostic and Remedial Procedures in Effective Study* (Harper & Row, 1941).

Later in the 1940s it became obvious that practically all students needed student personnel assistance, and the slogan of the times became "guidance for all." This meant that not only weak but also average and superior students needed help. Good students were found to have not only skill disabilities and personal problems but also inefficient study methods. Their academic success was a result of brilliance rather than good study methods. Psychologists discovered that self-taught skills in every field were always inefficient, *e.g.*, self-taught swimmers or typists could not compete with persons taught the best methods. The psychologists also found in the study-skill field that, as with swimming and typing, research results could be used to design new, higher-level study skills that are more effective than any that even the best students use. Another slogan developed: "The best is none too good."

A special need during World War II gave particular impetus to the discovery of higher-level study skills. Some soldiers had to be trained quickly for specialized positions; and although the soldiers selected were very bright and had excellent student records, they were found to be extremely inefficient in work methods. As a result of these findings, educators designed and taught them various new higher-level study skills. The initial presentation of some of these new skills, *e.g.*, the SQ3R method of study, was made in the second edition of this text (*Effective Study*, Harper & Row, 1946). This study method, or some variation of it, has been included in most how-to-study books since that time and is one indication of the importance of higher-level study-skill instruction. How-to-study work in the 1940s also continued to do remedial work and to help with distracting problems.

Later, continuing research showed still more effective methods of learning and a need to design study skills to fit differing study situations. The next edition (*Effective Study*, revised edition, Harper & Row, 1961) had a separate chapter on variations of the SQ3R method of study for handling assignments in different kinds of courses and with different kinds of materials. The topics of motivation, distracting problems, and foreign language study were also given expanded treatment in separate chapters.

In the 1961 edition major emphasis was placed on helping all types of students to learn higher-level study skills and to clarify and develop more mature motivational patterns. Remedial work took a secondary role. Whereas how-to-study work was once seen as a penalty treatment for the inadequate, by 1961 it was seen as an opportunity for all. It was an accentuation of the positive as well as an elimination of the negative.

In considering needed changes in the present edition, it was found that the 1961 emphasis on higher-level study skills still prevails; it is now widely accepted in college how-to-study programs and other published manuals. However, there has been a tremendous upsurge in new research studies that provide a basis for further refinements in study methods and a further demonstration of their importance—for instance, 70 percent of the references are new in this edition.

Some particular changes in terms of new material and changing emphasis have occurred: The chapter on motivation no longer simply emphasizes the sources of negative motivation, *i.e.*, distracting problems, but dwells at some length on characteristics of the achiever and overachiever that are of interest to even more students. Further, recent studies of student activists may indicate that the superior students are not only mature, conforming persons, but also many active students protesting slowness in academic development; and both types of students may be our future community leaders. The upsurge in research findings suggests new refinements in study methods and the need to adjust these methods to differing courses and to differing student personalities. Various attempts are made to show how this individualization may be carried out.

Early how-to-study textbooks (and some current books still follow this approach) consisted entirely of advice on how to study; the personal relevance of any particular point was left completely to the reader. However, research findings show that a person has such little insight into his own difficulties that mere reading of advice can do little good. Every edition of this text has included diagnostic tests so the reader could discover his profile of abilities and determine specific areas in which he needed to work. These tests, with some additional refinements, are contained in this edition, and practice exercises are included for use while reading this text. It is important in learning study skills that the student practice them as quickly as possible after reading about them and that he has measures of progress as he does so. The majority of the chapters are written so that measures of work rate, note-quality, and comprehension accuracy can be obtained as the student studies each chapter. Some of the longer chapters are divided into two exercises so that a particular exercise can be completed within a class period. It is hoped that this innovation will assist students in learning these study methods. It must be emphasized, however, that additional practice of these skills on outside lessons is also necessary if these new study skills are to be fully mastered.

A program to develop effective study habits in students also has other characteristics that have served as guideposts in the preparation of this book.

1. A how-to-study program must be individualized to each student's needs. Students have different programs of courses or needs and they have different ability patterns and methods of learning. Even in the field of higher-level study skills, in which few have any initial competence, the program must be individualized as a student progresses in learning a skill, much as coaching in golf takes individual instruction. For this reason it is important that a student have some means provided for determining his level of skill and, if there is a difficulty, some knowledge of its nature. As he makes progress in learning a skill, he needs evidence of the nature of his improvement and of what is needed next.

2. How-to-study work has to go beyond helping a student discover what is wrong or giving him information—through reading or lecture—on how to study efficiently. As is true of most skills, the mere desire to improve and the gathering of information on how to do it will not guarantee that correct procedures will be used. How-to-study training demands actual practice under supervision until the best skill is obtained and fixed.

3. To develop maximum motivation and to increase transfer of skills to actual studying, this work should be allied as closely as possible to a student's lessons in his other courses. Artificial exercises may produce gains on similar tests, but these gains do not transfer as well to actual studying as when the how-to-study suggestions are made in terms of the student's methods on other courses and his gains measured there. For this reason much of the student's practice and application must be done outside this book. This book acts as an introduction, a basis for diagnosis, a presentation of study techniques, and provides some practice—but

much more practice will have to be carried on with other materials, preferably the student's actual textbooks.

4. Finally, this training in study methods can be of little value unless the student realizes its importance and believes it worthwhile to expend some effort toward improvement. The instructor's cajoling, giving assignments, and threatening grade penalties have little place in such work. The student must of his own volition do the work. The chapters are so arranged that he can select those of interest; the specific directions make it possible for him to go ahead on his own. These factors free the instructor so that he may become a counselor or coach rather than a taskmaster. The purpose of this book is to provide a working aid for the student and teacher, which will increase the efficiency of classroom and counseling sessions.

The arrangement of the chapters and the emphasis on self-direction permit the use of this book either in a course or in conferences. At Ohio State University many sections of a class meet daily for a full quarter in an informal laboratory. Various chapters and tests are also used in the counseling of individuals who want help but are not registered in the class.

Effective Study is the product of the writer's experience in how-to-study work over a period of 40 years. In this work the writer has been fortunate in having colleagues who have willingly and capably experimented with possible teaching methods and materials. The diagnostic and training materials included here are an outgrowth of many research adventures in personnel work; many persons have had their part in shaping the program and their help has been much appreciated. Tests that are not original with this program are used by permission of their authors and acknowledgments are made in the proper places.

FRANCIS P. ROBINSON

January 1970

EFFECTIVE STUDY

CHAPTER 1
Introduction

Research indicates that each succeeding generation of young adults is improving in achievement and ability because of increasingly better diet, family care, schooling, and intellectual emphasis. For instance, men inducted into the armed forces in World War II scored two years higher in mental age than those inducted during World War I (386).[1] The World War II group also averaged two more years of schooling than the World War I group. A test of General Educational Development was constructed carefully after World War II to measure the broad educational development of returning veterans. Norms were developed by testing seniors in 814 high schools in 1943, but by 1955 a retesting of seniors in 834 comparable high schools showed that the later testing consistently ran about five percentiles higher (40). As a result of these intellectual gains and improved economic conditions the emphasis on intellectual pursuits has increased. For instance, annual surveys by the publishing industry show that the dollar volume of sales increases about 10 percent *each* year and that a greater and greater proportion of the sales are for nonfiction books in science, education, sociology, and economics (1).

This increasing intellectual emphasis has put greater demands on students' study skills. However, in spite of high levels of achievement, objective analysis of students' behavior shows that students at all levels of ability lack effective study methods (63, 77). As a result, when college students are asked to list their problems they mention difficulties with their studies more often than any other type of problem (202).

A nationwide survey made by college reading specialists (329) shows that the majority of entering freshmen need formal reading instruction, not as compensation for inadequate elementary education but as a regular part of high school and

---

[1] References are listed in the Bibliography, pages 211–227.

college instruction. Several studies (167, 260) have found that college students are surprisingly inflexible in their method of reading different types of material with different directions, e.g., they read third-grade and college-level material at the same rate and read much the same when asked to read three different times for the general idea, for detail, and for criticism. Perry (281) has found that whereas all freshmen at Harvard University read above the 85th percentile on a reading test, their actual methods are so inadequate that he has dropped the term "remedial" and now provides a developmental reading program for all interested students. Perry has found that "out of 1,500 of the finest freshmen readers in the country, only one hundred and fifty even claim to take a look ahead during a twenty minute struggle with a chapter. And the vast majority of these seem to have looked ahead only to determine how long the assignment was" (281, p. 197). Perry concludes that college students lack flexibility and purpose in using reading skills, read each selection straight along, and are good only at answering questions concerning detail. He has found only 15 students who can write a short statement of what a chapter is about. Other studies (180, 310) have found that even good students seldom make use of headings in textbooks or newspapers.

Our purpose is not to ask you to study like grade-A students because they, too, are often inefficient in their study methods (96, 299). As a matter of fact, Williamson (418) has found that good students study no more—usually slightly less—than poor students; they just use their time somewhat more effectively. As Edgar Dale (94, p. 2) has said, "Plan not to work harder but to work smarter!" Ineffectiveness may be due to inefficient study skills and to distractions caused by worries or outside interests. Of most importance, and an aspect that will be emphasized in this book, is the advantage to be gained from learning some specially designed, higher-level study skills.

Research on learning and remembering has been used to design new, higher-level skills that can be of benefit to all types of students. These methods are more efficient than any typically used by even the best students. However, as Berg and Rentel (30, p. 346) point out, "students do not learn study skills automatically; they need guidance and direction." Thus, this book will not only describe these study methods but also will provide diagnostic tests to help describe your present strengths and difficulties. The instructor in your present course will help further with this personal application.

THE VALUE OF A HOW-TO-STUDY PROGRAM

Colleges are sincerely interested in helping students "make the grade." Hundreds of colleges have how-to-study programs whose function is to help interested students work to their full capacity (132, 189, 225, 226, 328).[2] Although many programs were started in the 1920s to help students on probation, training in techniques for efficient study can help any student, since every person is somewhat inefficient. There is evidence that the brighter the student is the more he gains

---

[2] Training in improved reading work methods has proved useful in other countries (289), in government organizations (109, 357), and in industry (189, 278, 279).

from such training. An analysis of the records of several hundred students who have taken the how-to-study course at Ohio State University shows that an almost normal distribution of intelligence (median percentile is 47 with slightly less than one-fourth of the number in either the bottom or top quartile) and grade-point averages ranged from .00 to 3.93 before the course was taken. The students with above-average grades are among the ones who have gained the most.

How-to-study programs have met with notable success. Measures of student progress have shown increased reading ability, greater skill in organizing work, better use of educational facilities, and more satisfactory personal and social adjustment. Further concrete evidence of improvement has been shown through significantly better retest scores even two years after training and through higher grade-point averages (95, 97, 119, 273, 274, 280, 302, 303, 409).

Some actual results over a period of years in such a course at Ohio State University may be of interest. Pressey (291) gave how-to-study training to 50 probationary students but not to another matched group. She found three-and-one-half years later that 58 percent of the trained group had maintained passing grade averages or had left college with satisfactory grade records but only 18 percent of the control group did as well. Twenty percent of the trained group, but none of the control group, were graduated.

A later experimental evaluation of this same how-to-study course, but with all types of students enrolled in it, shows that the students taking this course improved a great deal on various determinants of scholastic success (331). Figure 1 summarizes some of these results. For instance, the students in the how-to-study program, as a result of this training, improved 24 percentiles on a test of English skill, 34 percentiles in reading rate, 9 percentiles in comprehension accuracy, and 24

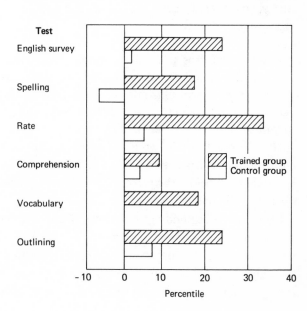

Figure 1. Changes in test percentiles after a how-to-study course, compared to those of a matched control group measured after the same period of time. (Adapted from 331.)

percentiles on an outlining test. A control group taking and retaking these tests over a comparable period of time showed very slight gains. The students in the how-to-study course received 17 percent more As and Bs on a term paper in another course than the control group with comparable background. Fewer of the trained students than students in the control group withdrew or were dropped from the university, and the grade-point average of the trained students was .15 grade points higher for the year than that of the control group. Several aspects of the students' personal and social adjustment also showed improvement.

THE APPROACH TO IMPROVEMENT OF STUDY SKILLS

It takes more than knowledge to improve study skills. Not only must the student know what effective study skills are like but also he must practice patiently until he has acquired them. He can quickly learn enough to tell someone else how to study, but he will have to use continued effort in order to develop study skills himself.

The program obviously has to be individualized to fit each student's needs, since each student progresses at a different rate and varies in the number and kind of errors he makes while learning new skills. Methods that are of value in dealing with one student's problems may be of little use to another student. More than other courses, this program demands a highly individualized laboratory approach (101). And unlike other courses, the subject for study is the student himself.

The teaching of a how-to-study program is analogous to coaching in athletics. In teaching a swimmer the crawl stroke, a coach presents it as a new method and not as a patchwork modification of the dog paddle. Further, it takes more than one explanation or trial, since continuing practice is necessary to develop a polished stroke, but practice alone is not enough because the swimmer does not recognize his errors; a coach, on the other hand, can spot difficulties and make definite suggestions. Similarly, in study-skill training higher-level work skills are demonstrated and, then, through the aid of tests and observation of work further training suggestions are made (212). The student can gain little without such diagnostic aid.

Another aspect of study skills, which is also analogous to coaching in athletics, concerns the importance of motivation in improvement. The attitude of a golfer toward his game will illustrate this point. Although the course of his ball may be likened to the meanderings of a child's tiddlywink, he does not see any great need to improve his game, or he does not want to take the trouble to work at it. In such a case, no coach in the world could do much good. To state this principle in a positive form, it has been found that the student sincerely must desire to improve his study skills before the project can be of much assistance. Mere exposure to such a program will not help him.

Some interesting findings have been discovered concerning the types of students who gain the most from how-to-study courses. Students who are brighter, who *desire* and *expect* to improve (153, 277, 383), who are self-critical and desire to do the right thing (130), and who do not believe that luck and fate determine grades (42) gain more than the less bright, the less motivated, the less hopeful, the less conforming, and the believers in the importance of luck and fate. Basically this means that those who think they can improve and who realize that improvement depends upon their own efforts make the most gains.

Finally, it is obvious that emphasis should be placed on developing effective skills, not just on finding out about them. Much of this book is devoted to helping the student discover his difficulties and learn what to do about them. Some practice exercises are included, but much of the actual practice should be done in his other courses. The student should get his practice by actually doing his work more effectively during study hours, in other classes, while reading at the library, and so on. Evaluation of achievement should be based on how much progress a student makes toward remedying his problems rather than on how much he knows in comparison to others.

SELF-INSIGHT WITH REGARD TO STUDY SKILLS

Does the typical student know how good his various traits are; or how poor his others are? Doubtless he feels that by the time he is in college he ought to know himself well. Of such traits as height and weight, of which he has had frequent measurements and has seen tables of norms, he probably does have a fairly accurate notion; but everyday life provides few opportunities for objective measures of abilities and other personality traits that affect school success. A person must be able to determine whether or not he needs help in developing study skills, so the question of how accurately a student estimates his own abilities becomes important in a how-to-study program.

The discussion of this topic will have greater interest and meaning for the reader when he fills out the following check list. Checks can be lightly made and erased later; no one will ask to see the results. Ratings should be frank and honest. Later in the book, tests are provided for some of these traits; the reader may be interested in seeing how accurately he can estimate his relative standing.

	In my school, I'm in the		
	Top 20 percent	Middle 60 percent	Bottom 20 percent
Speed of reading			
Ability to understand textbooks			
Vocabulary			
At ease with persons of own sex			
Honesty			
Note-taking ability			
Spelling			
Grammar			
Ability to recite in class			

How do you compare with the other students in your college in each of the checklist traits? If you feel that you are in the top fifth (20 percent) on a given trait, put a check in the first or left-hand column; if you feel that you are in the bottom fifth on that trait, put a check in the third or right-hand column; if you feel that you are in the middle 60 percent on that trait, put a check in the middle column.

Interesting results have been obtained from high school and college students who have used this type of rating sheet. In several schools the entire junior or senior class was asked to fill out such a sheet; since each student compared himself to the rest of the class and everyone in the class answered, the distribution of rating in the three levels should have been 20, 60, and 20 percent, respectively. Every effort was made to get estimates as accurate as possible; the students were told that they would not be asked to sign their names and that the data were to be used only as part of a research project. The actual results indicated a marked tendency to overrate. For instance, only 11 percent rated themselves in the bottom fifth. Only 1 percent felt they were in the bottom fifth in honesty, whereas 59 percent felt they were more honest than the top 20 percent of their classmates. Only 3 percent felt they were in the bottom fifth in being at ease with their own sex, but 45 percent felt they were more at ease than the top fifth of their classmates. Only 8 percent felt they were in the bottom fifth in ability to understand textbooks, and 37 percent felt that they were in the top fifth (428).

Such overrating is in part a product of (1) an unwillingness on the part of a person to admit to himself that he might be deficient, and (2) a normal tendency to view oneself through rose-colored glasses. It is little wonder that a lecture or an assignment on how to improve usually does so little good if the advice seems to apply so much more to someone else than to oneself.

Is a person's self-rating on a trait related to his score on a standardized test that measures the same trait? Various studies indicate that it is not. In one study in which students were asked to estimate how intelligent they were in comparison to other college students, only 40 percent placed themselves within the fifth in which they actually belonged; 41 percent overestimated and 19 percent underestimated grossly (324). In another study students' estimates of how many words they knew predicted their actual test scores only 14 percent better than would a blindfolded man by pulling numbers from a hat (26). Other studies of ability, attitudes, interests, and spatial localization have shown similar results (17, 83, 355). This small relationship between estimate and score indicates that students may actually be strangers to their own relative abilities.

The function of this discussion is to point out the need for the use of diagnostic tests in how-to-study training. Such testing, however, is not to be used in grading; it is solely for the information of the student. To assure the reader of this fact, the keys for all tests in the book can be found in Appendix III (pp. 281–302).

One of the first goals of how-to-study work is to help a student discover his profile of abilities and skills. Such self-discovery is of value in itself and shows where training is needed. Feelings of security in schoolwork are promoted by knowledge of areas of competence, and energy can be focused where it will do the most good when specific difficulties are pointed out. A student with such knowledge will not need to feel, as some do, that he is altogether "dumb." Because diagnostic tests show what skills need to be worked on, a "rifle" rather than a "shotgun" approach can be used to eliminate specific problems. Finally, a testing program before and after training provides concrete proof of gains.

HOW TO USE THIS BOOK

1. Organization of the text. This book is designed to assist a student in learning how to secure the most from his college life: in the classroom, in his individual study, and on the campus. The chapters will assist him in analyzing the effectiveness of various determinants of his success at college and in selecting suitable steps for improvement. The chapters are presented in two general groupings: Part One concerns higher-level work skills, and Part Two treats educational deficiencies. The chapters in Part One discuss specialized work skills developed as a result of research in techniques of learning, *i.e.*, "The SQ3R Method of Studying," "Effective Examination Skills," "Skills in Attack and Concentration," "Classroom Skills," "Preparing Reports," and "Foreign-Language Study." Moreover, since study skills are so intimately related to the attitudes of the student, Chapter 6 in Part One discusses motivation to study and suggests techniques for analysis and clarification of one's motives. The three chapters in Part Two deal with deficiencies in reading, writing, and arithmetic that are surprisingly frequent among college students. These chapters may be read in whatever order most interests a student. Some may wish to work on different sections of the book at the same time. For instance, while working on the SQ3R method in Chapter 2, a student may wish to work on reading rate in Chapter 10. Each member of a how-to-study class may also wish to give different emphasis to chapters since they differ in relevance to his needs. In Chapter 13 the student is given an opportunity to evaluate his progress in all of these areas.

As we have said, the topics discussed in this book have been selected as a result of research in the study problems of college students. However, you, the reader, will be more interested in the diagnosis and treatment of your particular problems than in a general discussion of student problems. Therefore, within the text the author has included (1) quizzes and questionnaires to help you evaluate your present skills, (2) concrete suggestions for improvement of those skills, and (3) practice materials to enable you to continue to improve. Additional material for testing your individual skills is provided in appendixes at the back of the book. Appendix I consists of quizzes for Chapters 2 through 7. Appendix II includes tests of reading rate and comprehension; special reading skills; and skills in grammar, capitalization, punctuation, sentence structure, and spelling. Appendix III consists of answer keys to the tests.

With the help of the materials named in (1) and (2) in the preceding paragraph, you should be able rather quickly to evaluate your skills and diagnose your problems. However, since constant application is necessary for improvement, the practice materials (3) are the most important part of each chapter. Additional practice materials could not be included in this text because of space limitations and because practice must be carried on in your actual courses if you are to obtain the best results. This is not a program of reading but of practice. Furthermore, as you work on improving your skills, you will need continuing diagnosis to point out what still needs to be done to develop such skills fully.

The text has been written to provide some practice in using some of the higher-level study skills described in the book, *e.g.*, the SQ3R method and skills in examination preparation and taking. Most of the following chapters direct you to do several things so that practice in study skills and measures of progress will be obtained. First, you will be asked to note how much time you take to read a section or a chapter in order to provide a measure of rate. Second, you will be asked to take notes as you read so that eventually a much more efficient note-taking system can be learned. (And the notes will be useful in later review.) Third, each section will be followed by a quiz so that you can check your comprehension, see how quizzes are made, and learn how to analyze examination questions. Even though seven measures are provided in the following text, additional practice will have to be carried on outside, but these practice sessions will help make the text more meaningful.

2. The instructor as a coach-counselor. As mentioned earlier, how-to-study training is in some respects similar to learning to swim: An observer or coach can see what needs to be worked on and make suitable suggestions; furthermore, more effective suggestions can be made if a student's actual studying can be frequently observed. For these reasons, how-to-study training is done most effectively in a laboratory situation with the aid of a coach-instructor. A student can benefit from working with this book without outside assistance, but he will be helped more if another person analyzes his study methods, notes, examinations, and papers and then makes suggestions. Most colleges provide such help through how-to-study counselors or through laboratory courses on how-to-study. The exercises in each chapter are oriented to help the reader make effective use of this individualized help.

In some areas attention also has to be given to thinking through certain topics, *e.g.*, what you hope to gain from going to college, what your vocational plans are, what some better possibilities for study conditions are, how to handle personal problems that make studying difficult, and so on. Although a student can attempt to make these evaluations on his own, it is much more effective to have someone with whom to think them through. In this case the instructor has a counseling role, but whether he is a coach or a counselor, he should make every effort to individualize this work to each student's needs.[3]

3. Use of diagnostic tests. This text contains many tests in order to give you a picture of your study abilities. If as many of these as possible are completed early, a basis is provided for planning a training program. The instructor can also be more helpful if he has such test information and any further data that you feel will help explain your study difficulties.

---

[3] Since it is difficult for an instructor to participate in all of these individualized activities with each student, some colleges supplement the efforts of the instructor in a course of this type with the help of additional persons in conferences (308).

The materials necessary for using a test are included in the book: the directions for taking the test, the key for correcting the responses, the norms for interpreting results, and specific exercises for correcting errors. This arrangement enables you to take tests at the times you need them most (except in a few instances where you will need assistance in timing a test); it also permits you to score a test immediately so that you may go on with a minimum of interruptions.

The following procedure is used in correcting tests. After you have completed a test, tear out its key from the back of the book. Fold the key so that the column of correct answers may be placed close to your column of answers and mark those that are incorrect. It is also useful at this time to write in the correct answer to any questions you may have answered incorrectly. Also, write in the symbol for the rule that was violated if it is designated on the key. Place your score (usually the number of correct items) in the place designated on the test.

The next step is to find out what the test result means. An attempt has been made in this text to include only items that test important skills in college work and that cover important topics that a student should learn. For instance, the items in the English Survey Test are not merely a sampling of all grammar rules. They are, rather, designed to test your knowledge in areas in which students make the most frequent major errors in writing. Similarly, the library and dictionary tests contain only items that are essential to effective study. Well-educated persons should know or learn the answer to every test item listed.

In addition to the general importance of the individual test items, the tests themselves tend to be of two types: (1) those difficult enough to spread out student scores so that some comparison to the skill of others can be made (these test scores are interpreted by percentile ranks), and (2) minimal essential tests consisting of items so basic that every item should be answered correctly.

Most college students are familiar with the term "percentile rank," *i.e.*, the percent of the norm group against which one is being compared who make the same score as you do or make a lower score than you do. Thus, the 25th percentile would mean that one-quarter of the norm group scores at or below your score and three-quarters of the norm group scores above you. It is important to note the norm group—college freshmen—against whom you are being compared and against whom you are now competing. They are a more select group than those with whom you worked in high school. For example, a person in the 10th percentile in intelligence for college freshmen is still above the average on this trait in comparison to the general population in the United States.

The minimal essential tests (100 percent accuracy expected) may be somewhat unfamiliar to many students, since power tests are so commonly used in high schools. These minimal essential tests may seem deceptively easy, but remember that their purpose is not to spread out student scores but to show what *every* student ought to know. Even if you get 90 percent of the items correct, your score is still inadequate; at this stage in your education you should be able to get 100 percent correct and, therefore, should study every item missed. Although it can be expected that an occasional error will occur as a result of hurried misreading of a test item and not because of ignorance, do not lightly pass over items missed; each has been shown to be important in determining effectiveness of college study.

Those incorrect test items you have noted should give direction to your study, so that you can direct your effort toward improvement in areas in which improvement is most needed. At various times during, or at the end of, the school term these same tests or additional forms will be given in order to measure the gains that you have made.

In order that your instructor can get to know you better and in order that you can get a better picture of your own problems and background, you may also be asked to fill out some questionnaires indicating what courses you took last term, what difficulties you seemed to have, how well you did in your high school courses, what courses you are now taking, what your main areas of interest are, and so forth. Some printed questionnaires available in this field, *e.g.*, a problem check list, may be used to facilitate your giving this information. Such information is for use in this course and will be considered confidential.

Summary

So far we have discussed how all types of students may benefit from learning more effective study methods, the individualized laboratory approach that is necessary in learning these skills, the importance of testing in this learning process, and how this text is organized. Reading about study skills is a first step, but much practice will be necessary if full progress is to be made. The introduction to Part One (pp. 11–13) describes how some new, higher-level study skills to be discussed in the chapters following have been designed from scientific research. Note particularly the special directions on page 13 which will help measure your progress as you go through this text.

PART ONE
Higher-Level Work Skills

Years ago many persons were taught to swim by being thrown into the water. After their initial terror they were forced to try to propel themselves toward the shore while still thrashing the water to stay up. The result of such self-instruction was commonly known as the "dog paddle" and eventually permitted the swimmer to feel reasonably safe in the water and to enjoy it. Some dog-paddlers undoubtedly became known as the best swimmers in the county, but in present-day competition would be left far behind. Modern methods of swimming have not been found by comparing good and poor dog-paddlers; they are based on scientific research on how to reduce the resistance of the body in the water and on how to obtain the most powerful forward push with the least effort. As a result, highly efficient swimming methods, such as the crawl, have been designed and taught. Because of further research and expert coaching, new swimming records are constantly being set.

Present and possible future study techniques furnish an analogous picture. Students have to learn to study as best they can, but such trial-and-error methods result only in a hodgepodge of inefficient techniques. Since everyone is almost equally inefficient, however, a student could maintain his place in class on the basis of intelligence and effort. What if this student could learn an "Australian-crawl" method of studying? His work would seem much easier, and his performance would be much better.

As noted earlier, even good students have bad study habits; some illustrations will be helpful. Several studies of Phi Beta Kappa and honor-roll candidates have shown that their rate of reading is typically little above that of other students and that they have quite inefficient study habits and skills (96, 138, 299). In World

War II soldiers assigned to the Army Specialized Training Program were a highly select group in terms of intelligence, previous scholastic record, and present knowledge, but their study skills were no better on the average than those of other college students (307). Inquiry brought out that, being brighter than their classmates, they had been able to get by in high school with their wits and personality. Other studies show that good students pay little attention to boldface headings in books, *i.e.*, they read as well when such headings are omitted, and they know few of the shortcuts in writing term papers. Of course, some people like to do things the hard way, but others—because they are lazy or want to finish sooner or want to do better—like to learn easier and more efficient ways of doing things.

The chapters in Part One describe a series of higher-level work skills that have been devised from scientific analysis of how persons learn and of the nature of school materials. They are called "higher level" because they represent an entirely different approach to studying than the one that you have been using.[1] Just as the best way to teach the crawl is to teach it as a whole skill rather than as a modification of the dog paddle, so these higher-level work skills will be taught as new methods and not as an attempt to patch up your present techniques. Evidence as to the efficiency of these higher-level work skills will be brought out in each chapter. Chapters 2, 3, and 4 take up problems in learning in the sequence of selecting and comprehending the essential ideas and of remembering and demonstrating knowledge on examinations. The next five chapters in Part One discuss skills in attack and concentration, skills in motivation, skills in the classroom, skills in preparing reports, and skills in foreign-language study.

---

[1] The idea of higher-level work skills is not new nor is it limited to swimming and study skills (325). Time and motion studies of expert bricklayers have revealed many inefficiencies and, when new work arrangements and new techniques have been taught, output has increased 192 percent. Similarly, candy dippers have been helped to increase their output 88 percent and have seemed, therefore, to others to work less hard than regular candy dippers. Experiments have been carried out in which persons have been taught methods of pitch discrimination, puzzle solving, and card sorting with resulting performance distinctly above what they have been able to do before. Finally, some experiments have been carried out in teaching persons techniques of analyzing problems with resulting improvement in the quality of their answers and the speed with which those answers have been obtained (309, chap. 10).

Directions for Studying the Following Chapters

As noted earlier, we plan to have you measure and practice your reading skills as you read this text. The early measures provide a basis for diagnosis and for determining the nature of your later gains. In order to obtain these measures you are directed to do these things in the following chapters:

1. Note the exact time when you start to read a selection and the time when you complete it. The number of words in a selection is indicated at its end, so you can easily compute your rate of studying.

2. After reading a selection, answer the corresponding quiz provided in Appendix I. In order to make this a fair test of your comprehension, look at it only after you have read a selection.

3. Since note-taking will later be shown to be an important study skill, you are asked to take notes as you read each selection. Although many students dislike the slowness usually involved in note-taking, you will learn a more efficient method and will need an early measure for diagnosis and later comparison.

Time started to read 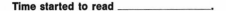 _____ .

(Be sure to take notes as you read; you will later have a quiz on this material.)

CHAPTER 2
The SQ3R method of studying

Have you ever noticed how students study? Everyone has his own technique, and most of these techniques are not very efficient. The following description (possibly somewhat exaggerated) may remind you of some of the ways your friends—or even you—study.

TYPICAL STUDENTS

Let us for the moment skip over the difficulties of getting to the library, finding a suitable place to study, looking around at people, finding out what the assignment is, and getting settled down; these are discussed in a later chapter. Once started, how do typical students go about studying? Having found the first page of the assignment, what do they do next? They probably look for the last page, hold the assignment up to see how thick it is, and then leave a finger at the end of the lesson as a goal indicator. Have you ever noticed students who, after reading a while, hold up the part read and the part to be read in order to compare their relative thickness; or students who, when asked what the lesson is about, look at the length of the lesson and say "About 30 pages."

Note how many students follow the lines with their fingers as they read. One gets an impression that they dutifully are following each line so that the next day they can truthfully say "I don't remember, but, honest, I read every word." Some so carefully mark with the cadence of their eyes that their fingernails seem to be plowing each line under. Not all are "line plowers," but, certainly, few reach the stage of using headings and context clues.

Most readers feel that they understand the material as they read; the trouble comes later when they try to remember it. Thus, as they read along they may continually murmur "mmhm," "uhhmm," as they understand each idea, much as a mirror passing over the book may clearly reflect what is printed. On finishing, they

Figure 2. Students often develop their own individual ways of studying. (Used with permission of Dr. E. M. Fuller.)

may push the book aside with a sigh. To an inquiry into what ideas have been discussed, these readers have a nebulous feeling that there is much they have understood but now it is jumbled. Rather than dwell on this discomforting fact, they prefer to say, "Well that's done! Now for the next lesson."

HOW EFFECTIVE ARE TYPICAL STUDY METHODS?

So much for caricatures of typical students. What are the facts concerning the outcomes from such study methods? When several thousand high school students were tested immediately after reading a selection, they averaged only 53 percent correct on the quiz (353). Other experiments also show that the average student remembers only about half of the ideas asked on an immediate quiz.

Since probably every student feels that he understands each of the ideas as he reads a selection, what can be causing this difficulty? A similar problem is found when a series of numbers, such as 8 9 4 1 6 5 8 7 3 5, is read once; each number is readily recognized as it is read, but somehow by the end of the series the whole list is mixed up.

Furthermore, what little is learned seems to be forgotten rapidly. The solid line in Figure 3 shows how rapidly the several thousand high school students mentioned above tend to forget what they have learned from a single reading. (The conditions that permit memory to persist, as shown by the broken lines in Figure 3, will be discussed later.) Thus, at the end of two weeks the average student can recall only 20 percent of what he knew immediately after reading; and this, it will be recalled, is only 53 percent correct.

Some conscientious students try rereading their lessons in order to raise the level of their comprehension accuracy and to retard forgetting. But simply rereading a lesson several times in one sitting does not help comprehension accuracy very much; thus, in one experiment the average reader got 69 percent correct on an easy test after one reading of the text and only 74, 75, and 74 percent correct with two,

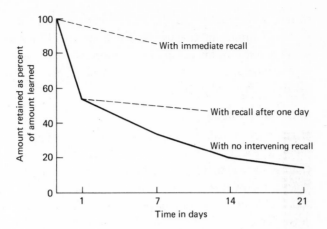

Figure 3. Curves of retention obtained by having equated groups read a selection and take tests at different time intervals. The solid line shows how forgetting takes place when there is no review before the test. The broken lines show the effect on retention when review follows either immediately after or one day after reading. (Adapted from 353.)

three, and four immediate rereadings, respectively (118, 316). (Later it will be shown that reading and then rereading at a later time is more effective.)

What then can be done? Is there a more efficient method of studying than reading and rereading a lesson? It is evident that the average student, through trial-and-error learning, has not found an efficient way. Some further experiments illustrate this point and indicate one source for building a better reading technique. In these experiments it has been found that a superior group of students do not read faster or more accurately when a selection is printed with headings than they do when reading an equivalent selection without any headings (82, 310, 248). They fail to realize that these headings indicate the subject of the text that follows and can be used to call to mind what is already known, to provide clues as to what will be said, and, as one reads on, to help indicate what is important and unimportant.

Rather than analyze the skills of good students and suggest that poor students emulate them, educational psychologists more recently have been conducting experiments to discover possible bases for devising more efficient study methods. New methods have been invented and their worthiness as study methods tried out. One of these specially designed, higher-level methods of study will be presented later in this chapter.

Now, however, it seems best to review the two types of evidence used in devising this method: (A) cues provided by the way textbooks, lectures, and quizzes are prepared, and (B) new learning techniques discovered through extensive experimentation.

A. Cues in Course Materials

Rather than being simply line after line of print, textbooks are organized with definite cues, either through typography or a writing style, to point out what is important. One tends to read fiction straight along, but nonfiction is usually written so that the expert reader can know what the main idea is even as he starts to read a section and so that he is able to skim, skip, or study in the appropriate places. Training in the use of these cues will enable a student to speed up his reading, improve his comprehension of essential points, and predict quiz questions.

The three sources of these cues—textbook, classroom lecture, and previous quizzes —will be discussed in turn.

1. TEXTBOOK CUES

Textbooks usually include many cues indicating what is important. If sensitive to them, a reader can readily increase his reading efficiency. An author in writing a chapter in a textbook will make an outline of the major points to be developed; in the final printed copy this outline has become the major headings starting each section. Major and minor points are differentiated by the use of typographic devices, *e.g.*, centered and indented headings; as further help, these headings often are numbered. Some headings provide the gist of the discussion that follows; others merely announce the topic but do not give the answer. For instance, the heading "Learning and Intelligence" indicates that these two topics will be discussed but does not say what the nature of the relationship is. Although headings that state the main thesis are more helpful as guides to the material following them, a mere indication of the topic can help the reader in looking for the answer.

Other cues are used to indicate important points. Paragraphs usually have topic or summary sentences at the beginning or end that state the gist of the idea under discussion. Important statements of definitions are often put in italics or boldface type. Watch for numbers as in "three kinds" or "four causes" followed by sentences or phrases set off by (1), (2), (3), or (a), (b), (c), (d). Sometimes sentences begin with "First, Second, and Finally"; these are cues to important subpoints in an outline. Authors frequently use a listing device to indicate briefly what is to be discussed in the next sections or as a summary to show what has been discussed. Finally, the reader should pay special attention to charts, diagrams, and maps; almost invariably the author uses them to present his most important ideas visually.

It would be worthwhile to analyze several books to determine how these cues are used; some authors will prove to be more expert than others in using them. Sensitivity to these cues will do much to speed up reading and improve comprehension. In fact, it is through the use of such cues that phenomenally fast readers, the so-called page-at-a-glance readers, are able to quickly understand and retain what they read; that is, by merely spotting these important cues they can guess what will be said in between. However, such skimming skill or, even more important, efficient study skill is not to be obtained through mere knowledge of these cues; there must be practice in their rapid recognition and use.

2. CLASSROOM CUES

A teacher's time in class is usually so limited that whatever he says should be important. Students may feel that this is not true of some lecturers, but even these professors intend to cover certain important points and may have simply wandered, or it may be that the students cannot see the forest because they have been too engrossed with the details of the trees.

A teacher usually will try to cover about half-a-dozen points during a class period. They may be in any combination from a few major points with several important subpoints to a series of equal ideas. The important skill is analysis of each teacher's lectures to determine if his lecture points are also emphasized in the textbook. If they are also emphasized in the textbook, the student is doubly forewarned; these topics should be studied thoroughly, in both lecture notes and textbook. If the lectures do not treat the same items as does the book, it means that important supplemental points are being added that need to be known in addition to those in the textbook. Suggestions on how to take lecture notes will be discussed in Chapter 7.

Finally, some cues with regard to the types of future quiz questions can be obtained by analyzing the questions that the teacher uses in class discussion. One can determine in general if the emphasis runs to definitions, lists, applications, problems, or interpretations, and then study accordingly.

3. CUES FROM PREVIOUS EXAMINATIONS

When a corrected exam is handed back, most students fail to recognize it as an important tool in studying. Many look little further than at their test scores. Those who do look over the exam usually concentrate on those parts on which they have done well, or argue (silently or aloud) with the instructor over items missed. They do not realize that an instructor's second quiz usually follows the same pattern as his first. Looking over the first test, one can see what types of questions are asked. Whether they are primarily true-false, completion, or essay questions is not important. It is important to note whether definitions, problems, judgment questions, or lists are emphasized. Do the questions come primarily from the textbook, laboratory book, or class lectures? Can you find where the topics for some of the questions appear in the text? Do they coincide with the headings? From such an analysis, one can often point up one's study technique for the next examination and can then be more effective with no more effort.

In brief, three sources of cues—textbook, lecture, and previous quizzes—provide the skilled student with means for promoting greater reading and listening efficiency and for pointing up his attempts to review for examinations. To sensitize you to the use of cues, practice exercises are given on page 25.

B. Experiments to Discover New Methods

A second method for constructing higher-level study skills is to analyze experiments in educational psychology to find principles that might be used in devising new learning methods. These experiments fall into two general categories: (1) techniques of selecting and comprehending what is important, and (2) ways to retard forgetting. The discussion will be organized accordingly.

1. SELECTING AND COMPREHENDING WHAT IS IMPORTANT

Value of quick preview.   Several studies indicate that a quick preview of the headings or a look at the summary is of help in reading a chapter. Thus, in one experiment 118 college sophomores were put in two equal groups. One group was shown how to skim over headings and summaries; the other was not. When the two groups were then given a selection to read, the trained group read 24 percent faster and as accurately as the students who read in their usual way (233). Such a quick overview orients the reader and allows him to comprehend, at least partially, what is to come. With this preview he can then comprehend the selection more rapidly.

Value of previous questions.   Of probably greater importance, however, is the discovery of techniques that improve the quality, as well as the rate, of comprehension. One idea tried by several experimenters has been to give questions to the readers before or as they read in order to give them a basis for selecting and organizing the ideas presented (258). One experimenter divided 170 college students into two equal groups and had them read materials concerning science and the history of English literature (171). One group was given a list of 20 questions before reading; the other group was not. Comprehension was tested immediately after reading and again two weeks later on a 40-item test (the original 20 questions plus 20 others). As might be expected, the group that had been given a list of questions before reading did better on these questions, but also they did as well as the other group on the new questions. They were superior on the total tests, especially on the one given two weeks later. (This is shown graphically in Figure 4. Each bar represents a different selection for which results were obtained. All differences favor the method of using questions, and a critical ratio of four is statistically significant.) Other studies have obtained similar results (65, 126, 245, 270).

When is the best time to introduce these questions, *i.e.*, before, during, or after reading (264, 277, 405)? An interesting experiment sheds light on this problem (399). In this study 1456 high school students, divided into groups of equal ability, were given a selection about Florence, Italy, to study for 25 minutes. The selection

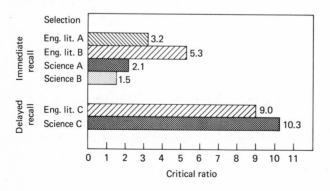

Figure 4. Reading, guided by questions, shows greater efficiency for both immediate and delayed recall than careful reading and re-reading without use of questions. (Adapted from 171.)

read by each group, however, varied to this extent: For one group questions concerning facts and generalizations in the article were presented at the beginning of the article; for another group these questions were presented at the end of the article; for a third group each question appeared at the beginning of the section in which it was answered; for a fourth group each question was placed at the end of the section in which it was answered; and for a fifth group no questions were given during the reading of the article. The test, which all the pupils took after reading the article, contained the questions already asked and other comparable questions. Of these patterns, the two most effective were: all the questions given at the beginning of the article; and each question placed at the beginning of the section in which it was answered.

Other experiments (126, 127, 128, 315, 317), on the other hand, show that presenting the questions *after* the section in which it is answered is particularly effective. A careful analysis of these several experiments shows not only that each location is helpful but that each location calls for different types of questions (20, 423). Thus, at the beginning of a chapter a brief summary or a few organizing questions are most helpful in order to orient the reader so that he can fit the facts he will be reading about into a meaningful picture. The use of a question at the beginning of a section promotes a questioning attitude and a core idea around which to organize the material that follows. After reading a section having a specific question on which to recite or about which to write a brief note helps check if there has been adequate comprehension and helps fix the idea in mind. Finally, at the end of a lesson, answering a series of questions or doing a general review helps organize the total lesson. As will be seen later, these several types of timing and questioning will be combined into one effective study method.

The study by Frase (126) indicated some additional aspects of question asking that are helpful here. He found that if the reader were provided with "knowledge of results" after answering a section question, he did much better than if he saw the question and merely thought about an answer. In brief, the reader needs to work actively at answering the question and then at looking back at the section to check an answer. This answering and looking back more adequately fixes the material in his mind.

What source can the student use to find such helpful questions? Teachers occasionally provide students with lists of questions to direct their study, or questions may be stated at the end of a chapter or in a laboratory manual. Such lists, if given in a way to make the reader want to find the correct answers, are useful in providing an overview. Where can the reader obtain the all-important question he needs as he starts to read each section of the textbook? One excellent source has already been discussed: that is, the cues that authors place in their writings to indicate the main theses under discussion, the most obvious of which are boldface headings and italicized phrases. It is a simple trick to turn each of these into a question as the reader comes to it; he then reads on, seeking the major points that answer the query.

As noted earlier, many readers pay little attention to headings and other cues, so a twofold problem exists: (1) printing books so that the cues are optimally indicated, and (2) training students to use these cues in order to read with an inquiring attitude. With regard to the first problem, it has been found important to keep this cueing simple, *e.g.*, italicized key concepts and headings written as actual questions (161, 199, 248). Studies of attempts to get students to use these questioning approaches show that the students have difficulty in retaining this questioning attitude during an entire lesson but that there are significant differences in the achievements of those who state and hold these purposes well and those who have difficulty in stating and holding this questioning set (158, 378). Quite obviously practice is needed to make one skillful in reading in this manner.

A related problem in learning is to determine the most efficient size of a unit of reading material that a given reader can handle in a meaningful way. Frase (126) compared the effect on comprehension of placing questions every 10 lines of print, every 20 lines, and every 40 lines. He found that placement every 20 lines was the most effective of these three rather arbitrary divisions. However, students vary in the size of the unit of reading material that they can assimilate at one time. When material is familiar one can more easily handle long sections than when it is unfamiliar or difficult. Some students, in addition, are not as well trained as others in grasping large ideas. Each reader has a problem, then, of finding how far he can read before he must pause and reorient himself. If one continues reading straight along, the ideas tend to crowd each other out and cause confusion. A stop at the end of a large unit of thought gives a check on comprehension and is a help in fixing it in one's memory.

It is obvious that these "stopping pla es" should coincide, if possible, with the breaks in thought of the author, *i.e.*, at the end of headed sections. Even though more material can be read, it is a good idea to stop at the end of a headed section to see if the question devised from the heading can be answered. If such headed sections extend over several pages and this amount seems too much for the reader, then he should use paragraphing and other cues to find the best places for brief stops in order to summarize ideas and to reorient himself to the coming material. A student can train himself to handle larger and larger units with resulting increased effectiveness in his work.

Value of outlining and related techniques.   The emphasis above has been on understanding the major ideas that the author presents and on seeing the relationships among these ideas. Various experimenters have tried to devise techniques that would help the reader clarify and verbalize his insights and that would give a visual picture of the ideas and their relationships. Of these techniques, outlining, underlining, and writing brief summaries are the most frequently suggested.

Many students have definite opinions about the value of these techniques. Although it is true that good students more often tend to keep notes on their readings than poor students, many good students do not do so. Practically all students agree that taking notes is a lot of work; they often say that they scarcely have time to read the lesson and certainly would not have time to read *and* take notes. Many students, having given note-taking a trial, report that it slows them down and does not seem to help; in fact, some feel that the extra time and activity make the lesson harder to assimilate.

These observations have been verified by experiments in which students' effectiveness with various of these techniques, tried more or less for the first time, was compared with simply reading and rereading (360). In one experiment 242 college students tried the techniques of underlining, outlining, writing brief summaries, and simply reading and rereading different selections equated for difficulty (16). Little difference was found in the effectiveness of these techniques. Analysis of students' behavior in this and other experiments (419) showed that the students did not know how to use these higher-skill techniques very well and became so involved in indiscriminate note-taking and composition efforts that their reading comprehension was actually hindered. Having tried these techniques once or twice, many students decide to rely on the one technique with which they are familiar—usually reading and rereading. These students are like the bashful boy who complains of great difficulty in talking to girls; after hearing arguments that it is easier to talk to a girl while dancing, he decides to try it on his next date, although he is not a good dancer. Afterwards, when asked how it was, he replies, "Gosh! I was so busy placing my feet that I couldn't talk at all."

It is obvious, then, that any technique used, if it is to be effective, must be so automatic and simple as to be subordinate to the task of reading. Rather than interfere with reading, it should help and not demand too much extra effort. Many students consider underlining to be the easiest supplementary system to use. However, underlining has enough disadvantages—tendency to underline too much, difficulty in revealing relationships, and so on—that the best approach is a modified form of note-taking known as "working notes." It is quite different from the note-taking with which most students are familiar. To save the note-taker's time in writing and in later reading, short headline phrases rather than complete sentences are used. To promote easy visualization of the main ideas in the lesson and, again, to save time, only the main ideas and main subpoints are jotted down. The notes on a chapter will cover a half-page or, at most, a page, and the indentation of subpoints allows the major points to stand out. Thus, working notes become a terse outline. To cut out clerical, slavish copying of the material read into a notebook, the student jots down notes from memory after reading a meaningful unit, such as a headed section. A sample of such notes is presented later.

Note-taking may not be particularly effective the first time it is tried; the newness of any technique tends to upset previous reading habits. With practice, however, a student can develop a learning skill that is far more efficient than the usual student method. The need for practice in the higher-level skills and the possibilities of gain with it are shown graphically in Figure 5. The chart shows that the first time three groups of students used outlining as a technique on study units in history it was not very effective. However, after a month's practice, each group found the technique to be highly beneficial (comparison is to the efficiency of equated control groups who were not shown how to outline) (25).

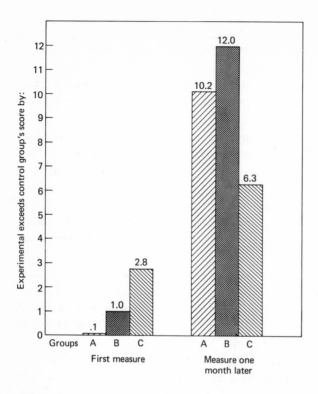

Figure 5. Gain in quiz grades when outlining is used as a study technique for the first time and after a month's practice; comparison is made to equated groups not taught the outlining technique. (Adapted from 25.)

Evidence of possible increased efficiency with extended practice and of the extension of efficiency to other courses is shown by still another experiment (320). Several hundred high school students received intensive training (daily lessons for six weeks) in outlining typical study materials. Emphasis was placed on the thinking side of outlining. At the end of the experiment it was found that the trained group was better than a matched control group (not given any training in outlining) in ability to comprehand what they read and in performance on study materials in other courses.

Therefore, in selecting and comprehending what is important, the student will find it helpful to make a preview of the headings and final summary before starting to read, to ask a question based on the heading as he starts to read each headed section, and to write brief summary phrases after reading each section in order to check his comprehension and to express visually the relationship among the ideas. Further, it has been shown that any method of outlining must be brief and easy to do and must be practiced before its benefits can be obtained.

Number of words in this section: 4651

Time when section was completed: _____

Work rate per minute: _____

Answer the quiz.on page 231.

**List your work rate, comprehension accuracy, and
note-quality rating on page 40.**

Practice Exercises

For practice in recognizing and using cues, making quick surveys, and writing more efficient notes, you are asked to do the following things:

1. Go back over this chapter and mark the cues that were used, *e.g.,* headings, numbers or letters, key words such as "First" and "Finally," summary sentences, etc.

2. Go back over Chapter 1 and mark the cues that were used to indicate what was important. Note their degree of importance.

3. Select a chapter in another textbook and mark the cues that the author used to indicate what was important. Does this author give good cues? Look for cues in other textbooks. If you have difficulty in finding such cues, ask your instructor for help.

4. After you finish reading this chapter, go through and mark the cues that were used to point out important points. Did an awareness of these cues help you in reading?

5. Jot down the headings used so far in this chapter. Be sure to watch the typographical nature of each heading, *e.g.,* centered or indented and kind of type, so that the relative importance of each heading is noted correctly in your outline. Indent quite a bit so the organization of headings can be seen clearly.

6. Does this outline of headings cover all the important points as you remember them? How does this outline compare with the notes you made while reading the chapter? What are the advantages and disadvantages of this outline of headings as compared to your notes as a summary of the chapter? (For instance, the outline of headings is probably much shorter and the phrasing is much briefer as compared to your notes, but some of the headings only state the topic of the section and not the final conclusion reached.)

7. Go through your notes, editing out the excess words. Try to reduce each line to a word or phrase that states the point made, *e.g.,* "Quick preview helps rate." If your notes are long, omit lines covering small detail, most of which you you could guess if you know what topics were being discussed.

8. Have your instructor check over other notes and make suggestions on how to go about note-taking more efficiently.

9. Practice making quick surveys of headings and summaries in assignments (take less than one minute for it). With this survey can you briefly state what main points will be discussed in the chapter? Does this survey make studying the lesson quicker and easier?

Time started to read _____.

2. WAYS TO RETARD FORGETTING

As every student is well aware, forgetting one's lessons takes place too rapidly. Students occasionally reply when queried in class, "I knew it yesterday, but it's gone now." This rapid deterioration of learning was graphically shown in Figure 3; two weeks after reading a lesson a student usually remembers only about 20 percent of what he knew immediately after studying the lesson.

"Studying is a vicious circle—the more I learn, the more I forget!"

Figure 6. "Tizzy" by Kate Osann, reprinted by permission of Newspaper Enterprise Association, © 1960 by NEA Service, Inc.

The student's problem in studying is twofold: learning what should be known, and then fixing it in one's memory so it will be there when wanted. A student may develop facility at picking out important points so he can do well on an immediate quiz (this is one reason why many students cram before exams), but this facility does not necessarily insure that he will remember those points. There is need to investigate the causes of forgetting and to develop techniques that will slow it down (389).

Nature of forgetting. Contrary to popular opinion, forgetting is not simply a fading away of once-known impressions. For instance, an instructor in making a reading assignment may want the student to do several things, *e.g.*, get the general meaning, know the important facts, relate the message to other known material, even memorize an important definition or formula. These are forgotten at quite different rates; generalizations are remembered more easily than specifics (241, 256). For any particular type of learning certain dynamic patterns occur in the process of forgetting that permit the scientist to develop particular techniques to retard forgetting. Studies show that there may be a simplification of material into more meaningful organization, and a sharpening and normalization of points made (9, 21, 99, 114, 417). Thus everything is not forgotten at the same rate, nor in the same way. One study shows that eight hours after reading a story 86 percent of the ideas essential to the plot can be reproduced but only 23 percent of the nonessential ideas can be reproduced. Another study shows that persons tend to forget the content of an article on a controversial subject more rapidly when they disagree with its point of view than when they agree (61, 219). Darwin said he found it necessary to jot down immediately any data that disagreed with his theory of evolution but that evidence that supported his theory was much easier to remember. Still other studies show that memories gradually change to fit previous knowledge and thought patterns. For example, the reddish hair of a long-absent friend tends to become redder and redder in memory because it is always thought of as "red." The bad acts of a "good" king are harder to remember (unless they are so atrocious as to stand out) than the bad acts of a "bad" king. The implication of all this is that the student should try to get a thorough understanding of the lesson, since this will help him retain the essential ideas. Further, he should study carefully those items that tend to disagree with the general theme of a unit.

Secondly, not all students forget at the same rate. The student who remembers the most immediately after reading may not remember the most after two weeks; nor will several people who receive the same score immediately after reading score the same two weeks later (332, 429).

A study of those people who tend to remember the most indicates that the prime factor in their superiority is not inherent but, rather, is the result of learning certain skills and attitudes. The four primary methods of attacking the process of forgetting, to be discussed in the sections that follow, are: (1) interest, (2) selecting major points, (3) recitation, and (4) distributed learning.

1. Interest and intent to remember.   Every student intends to remember what he studies—at least, until the next quiz is over—but students vary in the degree to which they mentally clarify the specific things they intend to remember and in the strength of this intent. Some students have little more than a vague urge to remember what they are reading, but habits of reading for the moment's comprehension, as in fiction reading, really determine their behavior. Other students carefully select the points they feel they will need to know and definitely attempt to fix them in mind. The difference in efficiency is illustrated by a simple little classroom experiment. The teacher in one class asked the students to copy down 20 words in their notes, but no indication was given that they would later be expected to reproduce these words. The teacher in another class asked the students to copy down these same 20 words, but they were told that a test on these words could be expected. On an immediate test the warned group did 30 percent better, and on a delayed test one week later the warned group did 50 percent better.

A student's interest in a subject, in addition to his choice of facts to be remembered and carrying out of activities that will strengthen memory, seems also to foster memory (34, 411). For example, one more clearly remembers incidents from high school dramatic and athletic events than from most of one's classes (191). Material that is of interest is more apt to be meaningful, and therefore, the student is more apt to remember it. Because this fact is well known, teachers attempt to make their material interesting to students; the student in turn should make every attempt to make the material meaningful and, therefore, interesting to himself. If he cannot see its value, the student should ask the instructor to explain its possible relationships to his needs.

2. Selection of major points and key phrases.   One study in England attempted to find out why some students comprehend and remember better than other students (389). It was found that the better students organized the main ideas of the selection they were reading into a short outline and noted the key phrases used to state these ideas. This plan gave a general understanding of the lesson, around which to bring together the rest of the ideas, and a basis for later reminding themselves what the lesson was about. On the other hand, in the same study it was found that poorer students tried to remember "everything" more or less as a jumble of facts with the result that they got confused and forgot a great deal of material. In brief, organizing an outline of major points makes the whole lesson more meaningful and interesting and orients one's memory sufficiently so that a basis is provided for reminding one of what the other points are. Also, research shows that effective learners form organizational clusters to help them in memorizing such things as lists or arbitrary associations (86, 387).

3. Recitation. One of the most effective devices to retard forgetting is a very simple one, yet few students make use of it and when they do, scarcely ever do so at the best time. An axiom in preparing oneself for a task is to practice it the way it will later have to be done. Since students have to show their learning through recitation in class or on tests, the student should practice reciting beforehand. Students often mistakenly believe that, having understood something as they read through a lesson, they do know, and therefore will retain it. (Remember the example cited earlier of the list of 10 numbers that were easily comprehended as individual numbers but were learned with difficulty as a unit.) Such self-recitation insures that the material is understood, acts to fix it in memory, and reduces reactive inhibition in learning (276, 398). A study of people who were good at remembering in a difficult situation, *i.e.*, recalling what has been said in a long listing which was stopped without warning, showed that those who were effective had hit upon a strategy of deliberate recall while listening (287).

The technique of the expert at remembering names is a good illustration here. Have you ever watched such a person? The first thing he does on being introduced to someone is to repeat the introduced person's name aloud immediately; he wants to be sure he has it straight. Other persons are usually engrossed in their own thoughts when introduced because the stranger obviously means nothing to them at the time, or if they are paying attention, they may feel sure they will not remember it anyway. There is no particular intention to remember. And, to make matters worse, the introducer is often so unsure of the name that he mumbles it so that a person does not quite hear it in the first place. Let us return to the expert again. He not only says the name immediately, he also may try spelling it out to be sure he has it straight; during the course of the conversation he may also use the new name several times. In other words, he learns and uses the new name until it is fixed in his mind.

Strong evidence of the value of self-recitation and further clarification as to the best time for its use is given by a study of several thousand high school students in Iowa. Reference to part of this study was made earlier in order to show how rapidly students tend to forget a single reading of an article. (See Figure 3 on page 17.) In this experiment, the groups took an initial test at different intervals after the reading and then took it for the later tests. The results of such testing and review are indicated by the broken lines in Figure 3. The group that took a review test immediately after reading remembered 83 percent on a second test seven days later; another group that did not take its review test until one day after reading remembered only 46 percent on a second test two weeks later. Both of these groups, however, did better than a group that had no intervening review—that group remembered only 20 percent after two weeks (353). Two things stand out: (1) The recitation test acted to retard forgetting, and (2) the earlier it came, the better the group did. As the experimenter said, "More is forgotten in one day when retention is unaided than is forgotten in 63 days when retention is aided by recall." Such a gain is far beyond what rereading will produce and yet such recalling takes less time.

The best time to use recitation to retard forgetting, therefore, is immediately after reading a lesson. Where in the lesson should this self-recitation take place, *i.e.*, should it be done after the lesson is read or after each headed section within the lesson? If the student waits until the end of the lesson before jotting down an outline from memory, he will find that he has too hazy a notion of the details. On the other hand, the student should not stop to recite each time he finds an important point. It seems best to read through a meaningful unit, such as a headed section, and then try self-recitation. This forces the reader to organize his thinking in terms of main ideas and does not interrupt study so often as to break the train of thought.

What form should this self-recitation take? Many of the characteristics found necessary for an effective technique in organizing comprehension are also pertinent here. Any such technique should be simple and automatic; it should be an aid and not a distraction to thinking. The easier a recitation technique is and the less time it takes, the better. However, just promising to think about an answer rather than actually reciting each time is not as effective because it can be so easily skipped (76, 205). Recitation techniques of complete outlining, underlining, writing summaries, jotting down summary phrases, and discussion have been tried, and the system of reading a headed section and then jotting from memory a key phrase or so in the reader's own words has been found the most effective (16). If the reader feels unsure as he writes these summary phrases from memory, he can check back over the reading material. As he progresses through the chapter he will find that these cue phrases are arranged in outline form in order to present the ideas of the total lesson in an easily visualized form. Underlining is not particularly effective as a recitation technique because the reader merely checks back over the material and recognizes important points; he is not forced to check his understanding of the section.

It is comforting to note that the technique that has been found to promote comprehension (changing headings into questions that are then looked for in the section and recited on) can also be used to retard forgetting. One general technique serves several ends: The heading reworded as a question tends to promote reading for important meanings. After a section is read, this same heading-question can be used as the basis for self-recitation to check whether the answer is known. The self-recitation tends to fix the knowledge in one's memory (151, 160). Also, these heading-questions are useful in predicting and answering for later review. This varied value of a single technique is used to advantage in a later section, which presents an over-all technique (SQ3R) for going about textbook studying.

Two other types of self-recitation are also useful but demand the assistance of another individual. Whenever the teacher or author provides a list of questions covering the main points of an assignment, these can be used for self-recitation. If quizzes were used as learning aids rather than as end measures for purposes of grading, they could be useful in checking comprehension and in review. Discussion is another effective device because it is so easily done and emphasizes understanding rather than memorizing. It is usually difficult to find another student taking the same course at convenient times for study, and the urge to talk about things unrelated to the lesson may be so powerful that it prevents an efficient use of study discussion.

4. Distributed learning. A relatively simple way to increase learning and to improve retention is to distribute the learning over a number of periods instead of trying to master the entire task at one longer but equivalent time. In one experiment two groups of adults were called upon to read passages of a technical nature five times: one group, five times consecutively in one sitting; the other group, once each day for five days. A test given immediately after the fifth reading showed a superiority in retention of only 4 percent for the group who did all its reading in one day (231). This experiment suggests a defect of cramming: There is reasonably good immediate recall but rapid subsequent forgetting.

The distribution of study sessions will vary according to the function the study is to serve: (1) obtaining clear comprehension or quick learning, or (2) renewing learning through review. Let it suffice to say here, since a thorough discussion of reviewing for examinations will be presented later, that the rate of forgetting and the value of review near examination time are prime factors in determining the distribution of review sessions. When one attempts for the first time to understand a difficult problem or learn a task demanding exact reproduction, as with a poem or foreign vocabulary, a different distribution of learning sessions is needed. In the latter case, time enough should be taken on the first reading to get a meaningful view of the whole task. Evidence already discussed indicates that, rather than rereading the lesson, an immediate effort at self-recitation is very worthwhile. How long should the student then wait for the next session? If he waits too long he will forget so much that studying again will seem like a new task. If the next session is too soon the factors of fatigue and boredom may be operative. One experiment sheds some light on this problem. Different equated groups tried reading a lesson four times, with the reading sessions distributed as follows: four times in one session; once a session, each three hours apart; once a session, each one day apart; and once a session, each three days apart. As shown in Figure 7, the four study

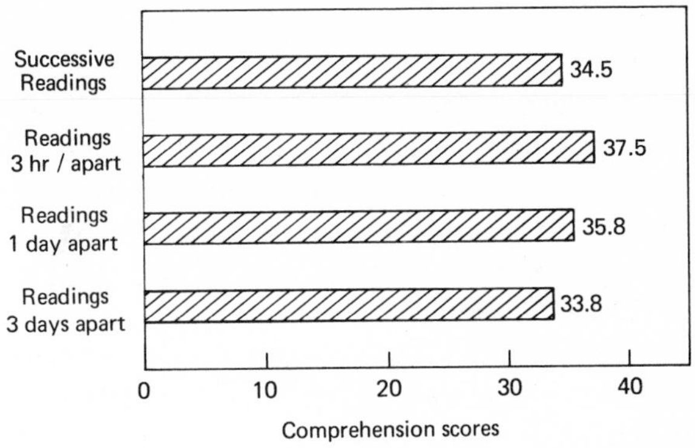

Figure 7. Comprehension scores made by equated groups who read a selection four times but with different spacings between the readings. (Based on data from 118.)

sessions three hours apart proved to be the best of the four plans (118). In general, then, it would seem wise for a student with a difficult problem to give it a thorough try, then return to it later.

In planning distributed learning periods, some consideration should be given to what is done immediately after each period of study. A similar task may interfere with the previous learning, especially if it is one demanding rather exact reproduction; thus, in memorizing a poem, there will be more rapid forgetting if it is followed immediately by study of another poem than if some dissimilar activity follows (243). The usual 10 minutes between classes not only provides time for travel but also lets what is learned become "set" before the student has to start on new material. The student, when studying in the evening, may well reward himself with a brief respite after finishing a lesson and before starting a new one. A rest at this time will make a break in the middle of the new lesson less likely.

It has been shown that forgetting can be retarded if a student becomes interested in the material he is reading, selects the major points, intends to remember them, and distributes his study time. Of further help, and probably most important, is the use of a self-recitation technique after reading each headed section, the preferred form for such self-recitation being "working notes." The experimental findings of this and of the preceding section on selecting and comprehending what is important provide a basis for devising a new, total method of studying that is highly efficient. This method is the subject of the next section.

C. Development of SQ3R Method

Many books have been written on special skills useful in reading books. Some have emphasized increased speed of reading; others, techniques for getting the most stimulation from an author's ideas. Students, however, want a skill that will be particularly effective when reading school textbooks.

A new technique must be devised, since the methods of good students are too often inefficient and no one of the experiments previously discussed has found the perfect method. The findings of these experiments, however, did contribute a scientific foundation from which a higher-level study skill could be devised. They showed that a quick survey of headings and summaries before starting to read gave an orientation that speeded up reading and aided retention. They showed that asking a question before starting each section also helped reading. They showed that the very rapid forgetting that is so typical after reading can be markedly slowed by the simple expedient of forcing oneself to recite from memory after reading. Other experiments showed when the best timing of this self-recitation would be during the study period. Various studies emphasized the importance of understanding the larger meanings in the selection and of seeing their pattern of relationship. Outlining, relating the material to one's interests, and a brief review at the end of a reading session were shown to help with this understanding. Still other experiments showed the value of distribution of effort in studying.

The creation of a study skill that uses these findings, that satisfies the demands of school study, and that pleases the student with its efficiency is a challenge to the reading specialist. The student wants any suggested method to help him (1) select what he is expected to know, (2) comprehend these ideas rapidly, (3) fix them in memory, and later (4) review efficiently for examinations. The method must be more efficient and less time consuming than rereading lessons; and it should not be difficult to learn.

For years this writer has had students try out various methods that such experiments have suggested; such trials have led to further refinements and suggestions. One method has finally been devised that fits the criteria above. Further research may show other possible refinements, but it is felt that this now represents a higher-level skill of great effectiveness for schoolwork. The material that follows is devoted to a description of this study technique and to exercises directed toward developing such skill.

STEPS IN THE SQ3R METHOD

The title for this new higher-level study skill is abbreviated to make it easier to remember and to make reference to it more simple. The abbreviation SQ3R stands for the steps that the student follows in using the method. A description of each of these steps is given below.

Survey 1. Glance over the headings in the chapter to see the few big points that will be developed. Also read the final summary paragraph if the chapter has one. This survey should not take more than a minute and will show the three to six core ideas around which the discussion will cluster. This orientation will help you organize the ideas as you read them later.

Question 2. Now begin to work. Turn the first heading into a question. This will arouse your curiosity and thereby increase comprehension. It will bring to mind information already known, thus helping you to understand that section more quickly. The question also will make important points stand out at the same time that explanatory detail is recognized as such. Turning a heading into a question can be done at the instant of reading the heading, but it demands a conscious effort on your part.

Read 3. Read to answer that question, *i.e.*, to the end of the first headed section. This is not a passive plodding along each line, but an active search for the answer.

Recite 4. Having read the first section, look away from the book and try briefly to recite the answer to your question. Use your own words and cite an example. If you can do this you know what is in the book; if you cannot, glance over the section again. An excellent way to do this reciting from memory is to jot down brief cue phrases in outline form on a sheet of paper.

Now repeat steps 2, 3, and 4 with each successive headed section: that is, turn the next heading into a question, read to answer that question, and recite the answer by jotting down cue phrases in your outline. Read in this way until the entire lesson is completed.

Review 5. When the lesson has been read through in this way, look over your notes to get a bird's-eye view of the points and their relationship and check your memory as to the content by reciting the major subpoints under each heading. This checking of memory can be done by covering up the notes and trying to recall the main points. Then expose each major point and try to recall the subpoints listed under it.

These five steps of the SQ3R method—survey, question, read, recite, and review—when polished into a smooth and efficient method should result in faster reading, picking out the important points, and fixing them in memory. The student will find one other worthwhile outcome: Quiz questions will seem familiar because the headings turned into questions are usually the points emphasized in quizzes. By predicting actual quiz questions and looking up the answers beforehand the student feels that he is effectively studying what is considered important in a course.

EFFECTIVENESS OF THE SQ3R METHOD

Evidence of the success of this method has been obtained from several studies. In one experiment several sections of a how-to-study class measured their reading ability (reading rate and comprehension accuracy) on a test that dealt with the history of Canada; they were then given practice in the use of the SQ3R method for several days, after which they took another comparable reading test. Before training, the average rate of reading for the sections was at the 34th percentile and after training it was at the 56th percentile; before training the average accuracy of comprehension was at the 43rd percentile; after training it was at the 53rd percentile. In another experiment an attempt was made to measure the effectiveness of this method for examination preparation. Two quizzes of equal difficulty were prepared; for the first quiz the students were permitted to study in their own way, but for the second quiz they were shown how to predict questions. The average number of errors on the first quiz was 15, but on the second quiz the average was only 6. One of the most convincing arguments for the method has been the comments of students who have tried the method and found that it works. Students have walked into class and said, "I predicted 15 of the 20 questions he asked" or "Boy, oh boy, I've been getting Ds in chemistry but I got a B yesterday" or "It looked as if he had picked the quiz questions from my list."

FURTHER DETAILS OF THE METHOD

A description that is an over-all picture of the method has been given. Experience in teaching its use, however, shows that certain typical errors may occur, usually because old study methods interfere (427). An indication of certain critical points, so the student can be particularly careful concerning them, is helpful in learning a skill. These cautions are arranged according to the steps in the method:

1. Survey. A survey of headings in a lesson should take only a minute. Some students are so in the habit of reading on once they start that, until they have learned how, they need to make a conscious effort to look just at the headings and then to estimate what the lesson is about. It is worthwhile to practice this skill. Take some reading material on topics with which you are familiar, e.g., newspapers, digest magazines, previously read textbooks, and so on. Glance at the headings in an article or a chapter and then make guesses as to what the material will actually say. Check to see how well you have done.

2 and 3. Reading to answer questions. Changing a heading into a question should be a conscious effort to orient yourself actively toward the material to be read. You definitely should have in mind what you want to learn as you read each section and not read it passively line by line. Habits accumulated from reading fiction often make textbook reading difficult, for it has been found that most people read fiction in order to forget their troubles and not to remember what is in the book. Such an attitude of comprehending for the moment, when carried over into textbook reading, gives rise to a delusion that since the ideas are comprehended as they are read, they will, of course, be remembered and unconsciously organized as answers to questions. This is far from the truth. Reading a textbook is work; you must know what you are looking for, look for it, and then organize your thinking concerning the topic you have been reading about.

4. Reciting. The tendency in reading is to keep going, but you should stop at the end of each headed section to see if you can answer the question asked at the start of the section. As indicated before, this procedure tends to act as a check on whether you have comprehended the material, and the recitation fixes the ideas in your memory. Furthermore, this insistence on answering the question makes it easier to force yourself to read with an active, inquiring attitude.

Self-recitation may consist of mentally reviewing the answer or of writing it out. The latter is more effective, since it forces the reader actually to verbalize the answer, whereas a mental review often may fool a reader into believing that a vague feeling of comprehension represents mastery. Furthermore, the more sensory channels are used in learning, the more effective they are; for example, in writing notes one receives visual and kinesthetic (muscle) cues as well as verbal imagery in thinking about the material.

It is very important that this note-taking require little time and energy; the notes should be exceedingly brief. It is at this stage, in fact, that many students have much difficulty with the SQ3R method. Some think they should use old habits of lengthy note-taking, in which all details are copied from the book, usually as complete sentences. This technique so disrupts the progress of reading that the train of thought is lost. Other students, when they see something important, are in the habit of stopping to copy it into their notes—with one finger marking each phrase as they look back and forth between book and notes. It truthfully can be said that many students copy a sentence into their notes without ever having read it for meaning.

The student will have to practice taking the type of "working notes," as they are called, recommended here. First, no notes should be written until the whole headed section is completely read. Second, the notes should be jotted down from memory and not from the book. And third, the notes should be taken in the student's own words and should be brief, i.e., little more than a word or phrase. Just as a public speaker's notes usually consist of a list of topics as reminders of what to talk about, so the student's notes should include only cue words and phrases to demonstrate to his own satisfaction that he knows what points are included. The student, knowing a topic, can then easily supply an explanation of it. Such brief wording also keeps the notes in compact form so that they can be easily visualized later in review.

The following sample of working notes based on the preceding section shows how indentation makes points stand out and how brief wording makes visualization of the subpoints easier. The brief wording will not convey full meaning to a stranger—he should read the article—but to the student who made the notes, the cue phrases are sufficient reminders about what is in the article.

Notes on Previous Sections

A. Discovering new study methods
    1. To select what is important
        a. Quick preview helps rate
        b. Previous questions help
            1. When?
                (a) Before whole lesson
                (b) Before each section
            2. Headings give questions
        c. Outlining
            1. Little value first trial
            2. Work notes help if trained

2. To retard forgetting
    a. Not a wearing away
    b. Helped by
        1. Interest and intent to remember
        2. Selecting major points
        3. Recitation
            (a) Remember 80 vs. 20% after 2 weeks
            (b) Immediate recitation better
            (c) Best: brief note from memory after a section
        4. Distributed study

It is difficult to maintain an attitude of active attack on any type of work over a long period of time. In industry it has been found more efficient to alternate periods of working at different activities; the change of activity is less boring and one can start each new period with zest. In studying, an alternation of reading and note-taking makes it easier for the student to keep studying his lessons and to maintain an attitude of active searching for ideas. It is easier to keep reading until a headed section is finished than it is to complete the whole lesson. Therefore, breaks in attention are apt to come at logical places in the reading material and so do not disrupt the student's thinking too much. This alternation of tasks, in fact, helps make concentration much easier in studying lessons.

5. Review. Review immediately after reading should be brief; probably not more than five minutes will be needed. This is certainly much faster than rereading the lesson. The total outline should be looked over to get an over-all, easily visualized picture, but the review should not be limited to this. As indicated earlier, self-recitation should be used to make sure that the material is fixed better in your memory. A good way to do this is to cover the notes, recite on the main points, and then check to see if you are correct. Then, cover up the notes again, recite on the subpoints under the first main point, and again check for accuracy. This system should be repeated with each major point. This method will help you to see the organization that exists between the various ideas, will help to indicate what is not yet mastered, and will help to fix known ideas more clearly in mind so they are forgotten more slowly.

Later reviews are also worthwhile because of the forgetting that takes place. The factors influencing the efficiency of these delayed reviews will be discussed in the next chapter.

Number of words in this section: 5200

Time when section was completed: _____

Work rate per minute: _____

Answer the quiz on page 232.

List your work rate, comprehension accuracy, and note-quality rating on page 40.

Practice Exercises

In spite of all the "do's" and "don'ts," the SQ3R method probably sounds simple. However, just as in learning any skill, learning this one will take much practice to make it highly effective and as habitual as your present methods. Also, as with any new skill, this one may seem awkward and ineffective when it is first tried, so a series of practice exercises has been set up to give you training in the use of this method.

This textbook and other laboratory materials will be used at first because they are constructed so as to show what is wanted, and your errors in method can quickly be checked. As soon as possible, however, practice should be carried out in your actual school courses.

In learning a skill such as the SQ3R method, instruction must be given in the separate steps before practice can be done using the whole skill. In the first half of this chapter some time was spent in learning to spot typographical cues quickly and in learning to reduce the amount written in taking notes. Attention will now be given to some of the other aspects of the SQ3R method.

1. Practice changing headings into questions. This step is not particularly difficult; it consists primarily of developing a habit of raising a question as one starts to read a headed section. Usually students merely consider headings (or just skip over) as more or less nonmeaningful phrases; what is necessary is to actively turn each heading into a question and start to read each section with a real question in mind. This questioning should be done in a moment; do not spend time and effort in trying to word it well. Basically, the skill is an ability to make an attitude-shift at the start of each section and ask yourself, "Well, now, why am I going into this?"

2. Some effort was spent earlier in learning to cut down excess words in one's notes and in learning to indent. Now we need to be more systematic in presenting what is meant by "working notes" and in explaining the rating system that will be used in evaluating your development of note-taking skill.

Working notes consist of a series of positive phrases stating the main points made and arranged in indented form so that relationships among ideas are clearly shown. Typographical cues indicate most of these items; omit subordinate detail that can be guessed from common knowledge. Notes should be written *after* reading a whole section and from memory in your *own* words; this insures selection of the main idea and full comprehension, and helps fix the idea in your memory.

Compare your notes for the designated parts of this chapter with the sample included on pages 35–36. Differences in wording are not too important, but note whether your phrasings are as brief and the organization or indentation as obvious as those in the sample. In general, are your notes as limited to the major points as those in the sample?

Students commonly make the following errors in using working notes. This list may help in eliminating possible errors in your own notes.

Although this list of typical errors and the sample notes presented earlier help point out ways to improve your notes, the assistance of an instructor is needed to point out additional items and to evaluate the general quality level of your notes. Therefore, your instructor occasionally will rate your notes on a 100-point scale. In the list on page 38, general format, organization, and phrasing have

Common Errors in Taking Notes

Error	Reason
General format (30 points)	
Handwriting illegible	Hard to read in reviewing
Notebook too small	Hard to indent and show organization
Too many notebooks; course notes mixed; loose pages	Hard to keep track of; may lose
Too detailed	Waste time in taking and in reading
Organization or form (35 points)	
Poor labeling at top	Hard to use quickly
Just listing; inadequate indentation; equivalent points not equal distance from paper edge	Hard to see organization; a text is more than a "telephone book" of facts
No numbering or emphasis marks	Hard to see organization
Subtopics not related to head	Poor comprehension
Phrasing (35 points)	
Wordiness	Wastes time in taking and reading
Meaning not conveyed	No value in "cold" review
Some main ideas missed	Poor comprehension
Cue word buried in phrase	If possible, put cue word first for easy spotting
Not in own words	Book phrasing good at times, but own words insure comprehension, communicate better to you, and are usually briefer
Writing before finishing section	Tend to copy, write too much

been assigned 30, 35, and 35 points, respectively; this distribution of points will be used in evaluating your notes. Any rating received should be listed on page 40 so that progress in your note-taking can be seen.

3. One of the most difficult aspects of the SQ3R method is developing the ability to wait until the end of a section before writing any notes. Most students are afraid that they will forget a point if they do not write it down immediately, and they tend to use the words of the book, since they feel, "This must be the best way to say it." However, this practice usually results in the students' clerically copying with little comprehension, and too many points are written down, because what initially looks important may turn out to be unimportant or refuted by the end of the section. Therefore, intensive practice is needed in continuing to read to the end of headed sections and in then writing brief summary phrases from memory in your own words. Initial practice may have to be on short easy selections in some of your texts or on brief articles like those in the *Readers' Digest;* eventually, however, you must work up skill so that longer sections can be handled. As noted earlier, some texts may have such extremely long sections that you will have to learn to make breaks at meaningful subsections.

4. The last step in the SQ3R method, "reviewing," consists of two stages: (a) a quick checking over of your notes to get organization cleared up and marked, and (b) an active process of reciting on sections of your notes. Many students try to stare at their notes, hoping that a deep impression will be made, but it is much better to practice what will have to be recited or examined—recall from memory. If you have trouble recalling a point, you can peek at your notes and try again. This review step at the end of reading a lesson should not take more than five

minutes; when the material is fresh in your mind this type of recitation goes rapidly. Practice this method of reviewing your lessons and note how much better your memory of this material is the next day.

5. This completes a review of the steps in the SQ3R method. Now attention must be given to practicing the SQ3R method as a whole. Practice will be received partly on material in clas, but the method should also be used in your other courses. Ask your instructor about particular difficulties that you discover in applying the SQ3R method to these courses. Make occasional measures of your note-quality and comprehension.

Scores of work rate, note-quality, and comprehension accuracy obtained from class practice and outside study should be summarized on the chart for Results of SQ3R Practice on page 40. Although scores may fluctuate from time to time depending on the difficulty of material and examinations, a trend upward in scores will be indicative of improvement. Although initial "work-rate" scores may be rather low, you should try to get a work rate above 150 words per minute as a minimum; below this rate, your progress is so slow that you will have difficulty getting through your lessons.

Gains in work rate tend to be rather large at first but are more difficult to obtain later on; also, new skills have to be practiced at length before they become habitual and stay at their attained level.

Results of SQ3R Practice

Date	Selection	Work rate per minute	Comprehension accuracy	Note-quality rating

CHAPTER 3

Other applications of
the SQ3R method of study

Chapter 2 presented the SQ3R method of study as a way of handling the usual textbook assignment and cited experimental evidence to indicate the advantages of this method over typical student's hit-or-miss methods. Two possible variations of the SQ3R method now need to be discussed: (1) Some students prefer to modify their present study method rather than substitute a new, specially designed one, so such an approach, particularly the use of underlining, needs to be discussed, and (2) since many assignments are not written or studied in the usual textbook style, *e.g.*, collateral readings, literature, charts, tables, maps, and so on, necessary modifications of the SQ3R method for handling these types of material need to be discussed.

The Use of Underlining in Textbooks

Although research in skill instruction indicates that learning a new skill as a whole is better than patching up a self-taught method, many people dislike giving up a comfortable method and the insecurity engendered in substituting a brand new and, at first, inefficient approach. The first time students use the SQ3R method they sometimes get poorer results than with their own method; practice is needed until the new skill is polished and a habit (268, 270, 419). Other research indicates that certain personality types gain more from a how-to-study course than others and that certian types are more able to substitute a new method, whereas others prefer to modify their present method (130, 138, 139). Because many approaches to study can be effective, it is important to present several variations so each student can learn a better approach that he feels is worthwhile and with which he is comfortable.

More students underline in their textbooks than take notes because it seems easier to do and, as they say, "Everything is then in one book" (80). Some attention to showing how the SQ3R method can be modified in order to use underlining will now be given.

One reason underlining causes difficulty, paradoxically, is that it is so easy to do. Students underline every seemingly important sentence as they read along, and if it is said better later on, they underline that sentence also. If a different point later turns out to be really the central idea, it is underlined, but the momentum of reading makes it too difficult to go back and erase the other lines. As a result, an underlined page is usually heavily marked with important, repeated, and conflicting points indicated. Furthermore, underlining the long sentences that authors use to state clearly what they mean will later cause much more reading than the brief phrases used in notes.

In review these many markings cause extra work; the conflicting underlinings confuse, and since underlining in this manner usually results in only one kind of symbol being used, it is difficult to see organization when reviewing. One has to read *all* of the underlinings and then puzzle out what the main points really are.

Some help on how to improve underlining is provided by research on how to print training materials to facilitate learning (161, 199). It was found in comparing different kinds of "cueing" in printing books that a simple marking of the important key phrase in a paragraph or section was far better than underlining complete sentences or underlining many sentences. Readers give more attention to the fewer items, and the short phrase is more quickly perceived, better remembered, and more useful in quick review afterwards.

Another difficulty occurs when students, without quite realizing what they are doing, get into the habit of reading merely to mark important sentences rather than of reading to comprehend *and remember* the major points stated. Students falling into this trap have been known to underline an italicized sentence as soon as they see it and then continue reading beyond it without ever having read the actual italicized sentence. In brief, underlining as usually done does not force the reader to think about the over-all structure of what he is reading. He reads and underlines, much as a stenographer marks down dictation, without giving much thought to what the message is.

It will be recalled that in making working notes the reader waits until the end of a headed section before writing down a brief phrase covering the important point made. This forces him to think about what what he has read; phrasing in his own words checks his comprehension, and writing it down fixes it in his memory. *Expert* underlining can also do most of this: By waiting until the end of a headed section before going back to underline anything, the reader will insure that only the main idea, in its best statement, will be marked. Although a little rereading is required for this sort of underlining, it will cut down a great deal on what has to be read later in reviewing. To check his comprehension, the reader can think about the point and be careful to underline only what is needed to indicate the main point. The random appearance of most underlining can also be improved if, while this delayed underlining is being done, or even afterwards, an attempt is made to "outline" right in the book, *i.e.*, to number and letter the phrases underlined according to their importance or double-underline or star the most important points, or both. In reviewing later, the student can quickly tell what are the important points and how many subpoints there are under each main point. Though it is easier to see this organization in notes, such organized underlinings can be quite helpful. Several systems of numbering or marking are possible, and it is important that a student develop one system with several steps in it and stick to it. In this way, in reviewing he knows immediately how important an idea is from the symbol he has used.

Underlining, then, can be used as an effective study method if the reader (1) waits until the end of a headed section before marking, (2) thinks about what the important point is, (3) underlines only the key phrase or phrases, and (4) uses a numbering or marking system that shows relationships among the points marked. Using the SQ3R method of study (using underlining) one would proceed as follows:

1. Survey the headings and summaries quickly to get a notion of what major points will be covered.
2. Turn each heading into a question as you start to read that section.
3. Read the section to answer the question.
4. Recite your answer to the question first by thinking about what is important and then by finding the phrase or phrases that briefly state this point. Be careful not to underline more than a cue phrase, and use a marking system that shows the degree of importance of each point.
5. After reading the entire lesson in this manner, review your "outline" of underlinings to get a picture of what the chapter has been about, and recite again to fix these ideas in your mind.

The important difference between this method of underlining and the usual method of underlining is that this one is an active, thinking process rather than a mechanical marking. You will also note that, except for step 4, this method is quite similar to the SQ3R method discussed in the preceding chapter. Step 4 has been modified, not only to make use of underlining, but also to insure that it is done after thought, with a minimum of marking, and with organization indicated for use in later review.

Studying Collateral Readings

The discussion of the SQ3R method so far has emphasized its relevance to studying the type of textbook usually used in most courses, *e.g.*, social science, biological science, physical science, business organization, agriculture, home economics, military science, fine arts, and so on. Ideas in these texts are presented in an organized outline sequence, and this organization is further pointed up by headings and summaries. On the other hand, students occasionally have collateral readings in these courses and wonder how best to go about studying them. These collateral books or articles may be written in the same style as the text, but the questions asked about them may not be directly related to specific headed sections; or the collateral reading may be written quite differently, *e.g.*, in the style of an essay or a historical novel, and the questions asked may seldom deal with specific sections. Again, students wonder how best to go about studying these books or articles. If a student reads these collateral readings as he does textbooks, he may find that his method is much too slow and actually does not prepare him very well for examinations. He wants a faster and more effective method of study.

DISCOVERING THE MAIN PURPOSES IN COLLATERAL ASSIGNMENTS

The first step in developing a method for reading collateral materials is to think about why they are assigned. The basic textbook assignments present the various points to be covered in the course, but the instructor likes to use collateral readings to give fuller meaning to certain major points. For instance, in history a novel may be used to show what life was like at the time of the French Revolution; in science an autobiography may be used to show how a famous scientist's interests developed and to tell something of the story behind a particular discovery. Sometimes a book other than the text may be used to provide a fuller explanation of some point that the instructor thinks is not fully covered in the text.

Obviously, in such readings the instructor does not expect his students to remember all of the points made; only major points are wanted. Although some instructors may ask occasional "detail" questions to see if the students have really read the assignment, even these will tend to refer to major episodes or ideas. The reader, then, needs a way to determine what major topics will be covered in the reading so that he can predict questions that will be asked. To discover the organization and major topics of a book he should look first at the preface, the chapter headings and, if included, the summary chapter. Next, he should consider how the subject of the collateral reading is treated in the basic text and in the lecture; this treatment gives a basis for evaluating what is in the collateral reading. As an example, if an instructor says that the collateral reading gives a contrasting viewpoint to that in the text, it would be important first for the reader to consider what the thesis of the text is and then to keep this in mind as he looks for similarities and differences in the collateral reading.

MODIFICATION OF THE SQ3R METHOD FOR COLLATERAL READING

In using the SQ3R method for reading collateral assignments the *survey* step consists of thinking why the book has been assigned and of looking over the preface and chapter headings for an over-all orientation. In the *question* stage, instead of taking one question at a time as he reads, the student has to keep these several questions in mind as he reads. The student should jot down these items to look at from time to time to help keep them in his mind. Furthermore, if these questions are widely spaced on a sheet of paper, he can jot down major ideas that seem to pertain to the questions as he finishes particular sections or chapters. As indicated above, the *reading* step is carried out by reading along to answer the various questions listed. Since the major ideas are of most interest, and since we are trying to increase speed, the unit of reading before stopping for recitation may be larger than a headed section. The ends of long sections or of chapters generally represent good places to stop for evaluation. The *recitation* step then consists of recalling the material that seems relevant to each of the questions listed. Since he will have read more than the usual amount of material before stopping to recite, the reader may occasionally need to glance back to get a particular point correctly in mind and jot it down. This glancing back, however, should not take very long. Finally, the *review* step consists of looking over the notes when finished reading the book to be sure that the answer to each question is clear (edit as necessary) and then of spending some time reciting the answers to each question without looking at the notes.

Sometimes in assigning collateral readings the instructor presents a list of books and lets the students choose the ones they want to read. He frequently does this so each student can read further something of particular interest to himself. In such an instance the instructor is more likely to ask for a book report than to give a quiz on each book. The same principles of reading apply in this case, however, if the student wants to be effective in completing his reading and in making his report. He should think about why he wants to read the particular book and what the instructor wants him to get from it; he should also *survey* the preface and chapter headings to get a notion concerning the content of the book. The usual following steps of *question, read, recite,* and *review* can then be used in reading the book.

Studying English Literature

Students usually have difficulties of two types as they read assignments in literature courses. Some try to read assigned novels as if they were reading for pleasure. At quiz time these students will have difficulty remembering what is in the book because they have been reading in such a casual manner that unconsciously they have no intention of remembering what happens and no desire to analyze why the book is, or is not, an effective presentation. If students do try to read to remember, they frequently read literary assignments much as they would a textbook: to be able to recall details of what happened—who went where, who married whom, and so on. Also, students will be bothered to find, first, that there are no headings to give direction to his reading and, second, that few quiz questions cover these details. As a result, students often feel stumped in reading assignments in literature courses.

It is important to see how requirements for reading novels, essays, poems, and dramas in courses in English literature differ from requirements for reading the usual textbook (67, 371). First we will look at some differences between literature and the usual textbook and also consider why one essay, for instance, is considered a "classic," and another is not. Second, we will consider how the purposes in reading English literature differ from those in reading the usual textbook. These points will then provide a basis for suggesting how reading efforts should be directed in English literature courses.

HOW ENGLISH LITERATURE DIFFERS FROM TEXTBOOK WRITING

The writings that make up the great body of English literature—essays, poems, novels, plays—differ greatly from the writing to be found in most textbooks. Some of the structural differences are obvious to even the casual reader. A sonnet, to take an example of a strict form, could never be mistaken for a textbook; for one thing, it has only 14 lines. Similarly, a dramatic work, consisting entirely of dialogue, except for brief stage directions, is obviously different from a textbook in its structure.

What are the differences between an essay and a textbook? Both textbook and essay are works of prose, with the authors' thoughts set up logically in paragraphs and leading to a conclusion or set of conclusions. Textbooks are usually of considerable length and are divided by topic into chapters—but so are some essays, e.g., John Stuart Mill's "On Liberty." There are, to be sure, structural differences between textbooks and essays, but the primary difference is in the *quality* of the writing. Textbooks are written in a strictly informative manner, for the purpose of giving instruction. Factual material is set forth in straightforward sentences, and headings point up the author's important topics. A successful essay, on the other hand, must be written with clarity and felicity of style; its topic is often of secondary importance. Some model essays are well named belles lettres, for they are examples of beautiful writing.

The following comparison has been made between the manner in which Lincoln wrote his Gettysburg Address and the manner in which a professor might have written it:

> Four score and seven years ago our fathers brought forth on this continent a new nation, conceived in liberty, and dedicated to the proposition that all men are created equal.
> Now we are engaged in a great civil war, testing whether that nation, or any nation so conceived and so dedicated, can long endure. . . .

> Eight and seven-tenths decades ago the pioneer workers in this continental area implemented a new group based on an ideology of free boundaries and initial conditions of equality. We are now actively engaged in an over-all evaluation of conflicting factors in order to determine whether or not the life expectancy of this group or any group operating under the stated conditions is significant. . . .[1]

In what ways does the Gettysburg Address, as Lincoln wrote it, differ from its rewording by a less talented writer? Your English teacher will be emphasizing differences and illustrating them in his assigned readings. He will expect you to be

[1] American Technical Society, *Technical Training*, Nov., 1951, p. 6, used with permission.

able to perceive the techniques of good writing found in your readings. Some of these differences are as follows: The really effective writer of essays carefully chooses his words and composes his sentences and paragraphs so as to state clearly and precisely what he means. Furthermore, the author so arranges his sequence of ideas that the reader is swept along easily to the desired conclusion of the essay. The essayist uses figures of speech to make relationships clear, by skillful exaggeration he may emphasize a point. Prose rhythm, as in a series of parallel constructions, may be used to add to the effectiveness of his work. In brief, literary essays show how highly effective good writing can be through choice of words, structure of sentences and paragraphs, movement or flow of ideas, and the use of such techniques as metaphor, irony, and rhythm.

Literary essays also differ from textbook writing in that some or even major emphasis may be given to presenting the emotional, aesthetic, subjective aspect of the topic, in addition to, or even in place of, describing its concrete or factual nature. Thus, John Stuart Mill wrote his famous essay with a passionate and openly stated bias. Some essays may serve both functions—communication of facts and ideas as well as presentation of the author's subjective attitude toward a topic—and some may quite simply be expository, but written with great skill and command of style.

PURPOSES IN READING ENGLISH LITERATURE

These differences in manner of writing indicate one of the reasons why the student reads good literature in English courses—to learn how to appreciate good writing. Thus, in English examinations you can expect questions concerning techniques used in such excellent writing. The instructor will also expect your own writing to contain some of those techniques. You can also expect the English instructor to be interested in your becoming familiar with the content of famous literary selections so that when reference is made to them you will know what the allusion is.

Further, the English instructor is interested in your obtaining certain vicarious and emotional experiences through his assigned readings that might not be attainable in normal everyday occurrences. These experiences, such as meeting a famous person, can be interesting and worthwhile; but each person is affected quite differently. Some of the instructor's questions, therefore, will be designed to bring out this unique effect on you; that is, he wants to know how you liked the selection, what it meant to you, and why. The good instructor of English literature is interested in helping students develop skill in selecting and appreciating such emotional outlets. Each person needs some means of expressing himself emotionally and various forms of literature can provide this experience. Furthermore, through reading such literature a student can attain higher levels of satisfaction by learning discrimination in selection and by developing skill in responding to these selections. Also related here is the interest of the English instructor in having his students become familiar with particular phrasings or quotations, since these can at times be of use in communicating to others one's emotional, aesthetic, or subjective feelings.

Finally, the English instructor is interested in the student's learning to determine not only what the writer has said but also his intent in writing what he has written. This may vary from an analysis of intent behind propaganda to determination of a fiction writer's motivation in writing a particular story.

In brief, then, the differences between reading assignments in English literature and your other reading assignments determine the purposes for which the English instructor wants you to read. He wants to know: (1) what techniques the author has used to make his writing particularly effective in attaining his goals; (2) what subjective or emotional purposes this piece of writing has; (3) what outstanding episodes or quotations in the selection should be learned because they are often referred to by well-educated people; (4) what you think of this piece of writing, what effect it has had on you; (5) how you have learned to select and appreciate better forms of aesthetic or emotional expression; (6) what the writer's intent is in producing this particular selection. Although a particular assignment may not be used for all of these purposes, the teacher's instructions and a little thought will indicate which ones are pertinent. Using these orientations should make English assignments much easier and more productive.

Studying Graphs, Tables, Diagrams, and Maps

Almost every textbook contains graphs, tables, diagrams, or maps, and authors of modern textbooks are making ever increasing use of these visual aids. At one time an occasional picture was used to make a book look more attractive and many students became accustomed to skipping these pages of illustrations as so much less to read. Now all types of visual devices form an auxiliary and highly effective means of presenting important ideas; occasionally they represent the basic means of presentation, and the prose text merely is used to explain or supplement the illustration. Although many ideas can be presented very effectively through visual devices, such illustrative material costs more to print than straight text, so it is usually used only for important topics and for those best presented in a visual manner. In brief, every graph, table, diagram, and map is important, so be sure you know how to read and study these materials.

LEARNING TO FIND THE MAIN IDEA IN GRAPHIC MATERIAL

Skill in reading and studying graphs, tables, diagrams, and maps has two aspects. First, you should possess the ability to read them, *e.g.*, you should be able to answer a question about a graph you are looking at. This basic reading skill is discussed more fully in Chapter 10, and tests are provided to test your ability to read graphic material. The second aspect, and the one to be discussed here, deals with determining what is important in the presentation once you have learned how to read it. A table, graph, or map contains a great deal of detail, but one does not need to know and remember most of it. As in prose, there are cues for helping a reader determine what is important and how to speed up his analysis of the material.

As an author uses paragraphing or sectioning in writing prose, he usually uses a particular graph or table to present one major idea. Sometimes a few secondary ideas are also included as important, but basically the student's problem is to find out what the main points are in the welter of detail that is presented.[2]

Several cues are available to determine what is important: (1) The legend accompanying the graph or table usually states what main idea is being presented, e.g., "The relation of teachers' salaries to the tax rate." The reader then knows that he is to find out whether or not there *is* any relationship and, if so, whether it is a positive or negative relationship. However, it would not be important to remember the relation of one particular salary level to a particular tax rate.

(2) The written text near the graph or table provides a second source for finding out what is important. Here the author frequently summarizes the main point or two that the graph or table shows. Although it might seem that one could read the text and not bother with the graph or table, these latter devices make the point much more meaningful, and the shape of the curve in a graph may be easier to remember than the words of the text.

(3) The third way of spotting what is important in a table, map, or graph is really the most important and, if skill is developed in it, the other two devices may not be necessary. This is the ability to look at a graph or table and note the major trend; that is, does the line in the graph go up or down or remain level? If there are two or more lines, do they go in the same general direction or in different directions? The author in preparing his graph or table usually eliminates extraneous material to emphasize his main point and may even draw his graph in such a way as to exaggerate the trend he is trying to bring out. The reader's skill is in his ability to glance at a table or graph and note this trend. Later on, some practice will be given in spotting these major trends.

The application of the SQ3R method to reading graphic materials would then be as follows: The initial survey of the lesson gives you a notion of what major points are going to be developed in the chapter and also in the graphs. When you find a graph or table turn its legend into a question. Then, look at (read) the graph or table to answer your question. The next and very important step is to recite the answer to your question; this is best done by jotting down a phrase or so in your notes indicating what the major point or points are in your answer. After completing the chapter, you should go back over all of your notes and review.

ADAPTING THE SQ3R METHOD TO SCIENTIFIC DIAGRAMS

In courses such as zoology, botany, and physiology some diagrams are used in a somewhat different manner. The diagram of a plant or animal, for instance, is presented in pictorial form because this is the easiest way to see what the plant or animal looks like. In fact, this form of presentation becomes so important that much of the factual material of the course may be presented diagrammatically.

---

[2] Occasionally a table (of square roots, for instance) may be used simply to list a great deal of data that a reader uses only when he has a particular question in mind, e.g., the square root of 256. Such tables, however, are usually found in the appendix of the book and are not the type referred to here.

Thus, rather than to present one main fact or idea, the diagram may be used to designate various parts of the animal or plant. The difference between studying this type of illustrative material and those in other courses is that the instructor wants you to study the diagrams in more detail and be able to recognize and label important parts.

The method of study here is still a variation of the SQ3R method, but let us see what differences are suggested in certain steps. The initial survey of the lesson indicates what the chapter is to be about. The heading of a section and the legend of the diagram indicate what question should be asked. However, in looking at (reading) the diagram, a glance will not suffice; some intensive study is necessary. Instead of just staring at the picture, it is much better to take an active approach to your study. Look over the picture or diagram to see what it is about and then try direct recitation for the recall step. Do this by pushing the book aside and trying to sketch the diagram from memory, putting in the important labels. This type of recall will show you what you have learned, and it will also help fix it in your mind. Then, recheck the diagram in the book and make a second attempt at recall, paying special attention to the parts you forgot on your first try. Remember that in courses such as zoology, botany, and anatomy this step of recall through drawing and labeling from memory becomes very important. It has been found in some experiments in learning music, diagrams, nonsense syllables, and so on, that this stage of active recalling may take efficiently over half of your learning time. When you have learned a diagram well enough, you can then go on with the rest of the lesson until it is completed. Finally, in the review stage it is a good idea again to try redrawing and relabeling the diagram from memory. This procedure will help fix it in your mind so that you will forget less until the time you need this information.

Summary

In this chapter we have talked about several modifications of the SQ3R method of study for use with (1) underlining, (2) collateral assignments, (3) English literature, and (4) graphs, tables, maps, and diagrams. In each instance the basic five steps of the SQ3R method were carried out, but slight modifications were suggested to fit the type of material or the different purposes of each instructor. In each case extended practice will be necessary if you want to become proficient in using the SQ3R method with these types of material. Practice exercises are given below.

Number of words in this chapter: 5447

Time when chapter was completed: _____

Work rate per minute:_____

Answer the quiz on page 233.

**List your work rate, comprehension accuracy, and
    note-quality rating on page 40.**

Practice Exercises

UNDERLINING

1. Work out a three-level system that can be efficiently used in underlining in your textbooks. The system should quickly make evident whether a point underlined is major or minor, and in later use of the text should show almost an outline right in your book. This system might employ single and double underlinings, it might include use of symbols such as "A," "B," and "1," "2," or other devices. Check this proposed system with your instructor to see if some further refinements can be added, then, learn the method and use it until its use becomes habitual.

2. Do some underlining in this text and be sure that you underline *after* reading a section. Furthermore, after you have read and underlined an assignment, check over your underlinings during the review stage to be sure that the degree of emphasis of each underlined point is clearly and correctly marked.

3. Underline some assignments in other classes and check with the instructor of the class to see if you have been selecting major points and have been marking their emphasis correctly.

4. If you find that you are able to postpone underlining until *after* reading a section and that you can carry out the underlining as active recall rather than just as a clerical marking, then you may wish to develop this as your mode of using the SQ3R method. However, if you find that you tend to slip back into checking points as you read, or if you find that a particular text does not contain good brief phrases stating the points, then you will do better to develop a note-taking approach for use with the SQ3R method.

COLLATERAL READING

1. Check some examination questions covering collateral readings in other courses to see what types of questions are asked.

2. Practice preparing questions for samples of possible collateral readings in your how-to-study class. Develop an effective way to jot down notes from such readings. That is, since you cannot jot down complete notes at the end of each headed section, a way must be devised to mark down notes under your different questions as you complete each section until at the end of reading the collateral assignment you have a complete set of notes organized under each question.

3. Practice reading sample collateral texts to answer questions that you think might be asked. Work to improve your efficiency in selecting these questions and in reading to find their answers.

ENGLISH LITERATURE

1. Find typical questions asked in English examinations. Make a list of the typical kinds of questions asked for literary assignments.

2. Practice making questions for literary assignments. Also, devise a method of jotting down notes under your various questions as you complete each chapter. After you complete your assignment, learn to look over these notes to organize them.

3. Practice reading and answering questions for some literary assignments. Check your method and notes with your how-to-study instructor and with your English literature instructor.

GRAPHS, TABLES, MAPS, AND DIAGRAMS

1. Complete the tests in Appendix II (pp. 253–263) to be sure that you are able to read graphic materials correctly.

2. Check some of the graphs and tables in this text and in other materials supplied in class to see if you can quickly spot what one or two main points are developed in each example.

3. Look at tables and charts in other textbooks and practice looking for the main point developed by each sample. Check these with your instructor if you have any questions. Practice answering the questions that you raise.

4. Check quizzes where possible to see what types of questions are asked about tables and charts in your assignments.

CHAPTER 4

Effective examination skills

A chapter on examinations follows rather naturally two chapters on how to study textbooks. Since students usually differentiate between studying a lesson for the first time to understand it and reviewing it later for an examination, the skills needed for each of these tasks are presented in separate chapters. The skills dealing with examinations are of three general types: (1) preparing for examinations, (2) taking examinations, and (3) making use of returned examinations. Each of these areas will be discussed in turn.

Before doing so, however, reference might be made to a study of factors affecting test performance as seen by students who described how an A grade and how a D grade in the same course could be explained (131). The 1207 explanations given by the 276 college students were classified into three categories: (1) student's own efforts, (2) instructor's efforts, and (3) external factors. The A students attributed their success to their own efforts much more than did the D students; on the other hand, the D students attributed their results to external factors three times more often than did the A students. To summarize, people attribute any success to their own efforts, but blame external factors rather than themselves for difficulties; no doubt *some* difficulties on examinations must be a result of a student's own deficiencies.

A. Preparing for Examinations

Knowing that an examination will come sometime after he has read a lesson, a student should want to set up a review schedule that, with the least effort, will be the most efficient for the examination. Research studies give some information concerning the best timing for these reviews, as well as the most effective types of review.

TIMING OF REVIEWS

Since forgetting takes place so rapidly after learning, it is evident that reviews should come early when review will be easy and most effective. The time-honored custom of cramming also has the value of returning memory to something of its original freshness just before the examination (343). Research studies show that both of these methods—early and late review—are more effective than review "in between" (282). The student's problem is to distribute his review so that no single review takes much time and so that studying before an examination does not become a hectic and fatiguing effort.

The best way of going about immediate reviewing after reading a lesson has been discussed in the preceding chapters. It was evident in Figure 3 that the immediate self-recitation and review that are a part of the SQ3R method are of great help in keeping memory at a high level. Another method frequently used is rereading the lesson. Reading and rereading during the same study period has been shown to not be very helpful, but doing this rereading several hours later is more effective.

Certain principles are also of value in determining the distribution of review time as the student approaches an examination. The very size of the task of reviewing for a midterm or final examination tends to lead to procrastination. The lengthy cramming session that finally occurs just before the examination greatly fatigues the student so that he cannot be as alert the next day during the test (343). During a given study period there is a tendency to study the next day's lesson before starting to review; as a result, there is rarely time for review. The following principles have been found to help with these difficulties: (1) Several review times, rather than one lengthy session, should be scheduled; (2) a review time should be scheduled separately from study time; (3) a definite segment of the lesson should be assigned to each review time so the task looks possible to complete and does not lead to procrastination; (4) finally, a student probably should not review for more than an hour or two the night before an examination.

Between immediate review and review just before the examination there is need for some intermediate review to keep the material fresh in the student's memory. Because, as indicated in Chapter 2, memories tend to become reorganized in a dynamic way with the passage of time, such intermediate review tends to keep ideas associated with the actual facts read. An occasional looking over of one's notes, with rereading on obscure points, will do much to reduce forgetting and will tie in previous material with what is being studied.

METHODS OF REVIEW

Just as there are the most efficient methods for studying a lesson for the first time, so there are the most efficient methods for reviewing a lesson. Furthermore, it has been found that the closeness of the review to the original time of study determines which method of review will be most effective. In the SQ3R method it has been shown that immediate self-recitation is much more efficient than rereading soon after the initial reading; on the other hand, if review does not occur for some time after reading, so much may be forgotten that self-recitation cannot be fully effective. This is demonstrated in an experiment in which large equated groups read a selection and were tested on it 42 days later; in the meantime the various groups used different methods of review, *i.e.*, taking tests or rereading, spaced at different intervals. The results, summarized in Figure 8, show that checking comprehension with a test is more efficient than rereading as a method of review soon after studying a lesson, but that rereading is more efficient some two or more weeks later (344).

Predicting examination questions. An active, organizational attack on material is more effective than a passive approach in both reading and review. In review there should be a prediction of quiz questions with an active searching for, and organization of, the answers (250). Although many students may believe that "there is no predicting what an instructor will ask," in actual fact the topics of questions can usually be readily spotted from various course cues. In review a student should use his notes or textbook headings as cues to probable questions. He should *not* work hard to formulate questions in precise test form, *e.g.*, multiple choice or true-false; rather, he should ask himself a simple essay question, such as "What is question prediction?" in looking at the heading above. Whenever an answer is recalled immediately, a student can pass on quickly to the next question. Whenever recalling an answer is difficult, the student can skim and reread until the answer is found. One experiment shows that if question-asking is done *without checking the accuracy of the responses*, there is much higher selection of plausible wrong responses on a later test than if there were a comprehension accuracy check (192).

Such review through question-answering provides a feeling of completeness when the job is done that does not usually follow attempts to reread a whole book. Students who undertake to reread six weeks' or a term's work usually find the task so enormous that they resort to skipping areas or material and merely glance at pages here and there. The increasing accuracy with which a student finds himself studying the right questions also gives him a feeling of energy well spent in review. Rather than an attitude of "There is no telling what he will ask" or "One has to know everything," the student predicting questions feels definitely oriented with a realization that "These twenty things almost certainly will be asked."

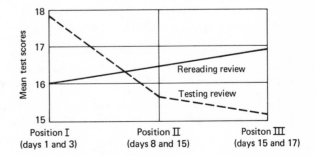

Figure 8. Relative effectiveness of two kinds of review at three different intervals after initial learning. (Adapted from 344.)

Too much cannot be said about the value of notes for review. Rather than being overwhelmed with a hundred or more pages to reread, the student with three to five pages of notes easily obtains an outline picture of this material. Indentations in the notes make major points stand out and make relationships among them easily seen.

Effect of type of examination on review method.   Most students believe, or at least used to, that one should use a different method of study for an essay than one uses for an objective examination (85, 257). They often believe that the objective examination is easier, since one has only to recognize rather than recall topics from the lesson; therefore, the need to study is not so great. There is also a feeling that one should study details rather than organization of ideas when preparing for an objective examination. Actually, it is equally difficult to receive a good grade on either type of examination, and a method of study that emphasizes an understanding of the main ideas and their relationships should be used for both (84). It is true that scores tend to be higher on true-false examinations than on essay examinations, because it is easier to recognize answers than to recall them and because the former type provides an opportunity for guessing; however, since all students have these same advantages, a given student will find himself in the same relative position to the other students. And although objective questions may seem to deal with "small points," actual comparison of the topics of these questions with headings in the text will show a great similarity.

PREPARATION FOR FINAL EXAMINATIONS

The principles that apply to preparation for quizzes also apply to preparation for final examinations. However, because the latter so often cover the whole course and count for so much on final grades, this special section on final examinations is included. You may feel that final examinations are a long way away and need not be considered yet. For the present, then, you may read this section as a summary of the foregoing material. Near the end of the school term you should return to it for more careful study.

Since final examinations are given infrequently, students do not have much chance to develop specialized study skills for them. On the contrary, many students, under the pressure and anxiety of preparing for this major hurdle, frequently regress from their habitual study habits to even more primitive techniques—some bordering on the use of fetishes. For example, the campus newspaper at Ohio State University once conducted a poll among students concerning the question, "Do you have any special study habits during finals week?"[1] Typical responses were:

When the quarter begins I cut the thumbnail on my right hand real short and then don't cut it until I get my grades at the end of the Quarter. It gets pretty long. Last quarter it broke off, but it didn't matter because I got a 4-point anyway.

I usually go to bed pretty early and try to get all my studying done during the day. Sometimes I say "to heck with it" and go to the movies.

[1] *The Ohio State Lantern*, Feb. 27, 1956, p. 7.

I never go to the library to study because it's too uncomfortable. I like to stretch out on my bed, with things to eat.

I never sleep during finals week. I get three hours of sleep at the maximum—three because you need the rest of the time to study. My finals always pull me through.

This quarter I might even go home during the middle of finals week. Last quarter I got more sleep during finals week than I got all quarter.

It is obvious from these differing comments that students do not have clear ideas about the best methods of study for finals.

Review for a given course should be divided into blocks of material assigned to three or four spaced sessions; the last session before the examination may be well spent in looking over notes for the whole course. No review session should be very long; the task of recalling and organizing many ideas is so fatiguing that efficiency decreases rapidly after an hour, or one-and-a-half hours, of review.

The 10-day period before and during final examinations should be one in which you live normally. The extra review time may cut down somewhat on your recreation, but you should be careful to maintain usual habits of eating, exercise, and sleeping. Examinations demand a "clear head," which staying up half the night will not produce. Do not worry about examinations. The night before an examination is too late to learn much in preparation; review the material thoroughly and then relax.

The practice exercise on pages 70–71 contains a blank time schedule for the period before and during final exams. Filling in this chart near the end of the school term should help you to budget your review time for maximum efficiency.

Review selectively. Review the important points, especially those you have trouble recalling. A good way to do this is to take the main headings in your notes or in the text and see if you can recite the main ideas from memory. Look up those items with which you have trouble and try reciting again; or, as previously suggested, guess what questions will be asked on each chapter and recite the main points from memory. The headings in the textbook, your class notes, and previous quizzes are all useful in this prediction of questions.

Mere rereading is time consuming and not very efficient. Reread sections only if, after looking at their headings, you have trouble remembering what they are about. Thus, you will tend to review in a different way than when you first studied the lesson. Ask questions, prepare examples for each topic, diagram relationships, and discuss the points with a friend. At the University of Copenhagen in Denmark, college students study mathematics all year and then take an examination at the end of the year, which determines whether or not they pass. A comparative analysis of the study methods used by those who passed and those who failed showed that those who passed differed most in that they used active recitation in their review (288).

During the school term you should try question-prediction many times and find it effective. It should also help with your final examinations. If, as sometimes occurs, the final examination is simply a quiz on the last part of the course, then the nature of such quizzes and of the cues that indicate what is important in studying for them should be well known by this time. If the final examination covers the entire course, then earlier question-predictions are still useful, because what was important then is still important for the final examination. Such final examinations tend to differ from the usual midterm exams in that they cover primarily the major points and ask the student to show interrelations among the points developed in various chapters, e.g., "Compare the political developments in England, France, and Germany during the last half of the eighteenth century." Review, then, should be centered on major points emphasized in the text and in class, and an attempt should be made to relate the major points in the various chapters.

B. Taking Examinations

Did you ever thank a teacher for giving an examination? In theory one ought to be grateful for the hours an instructor spends in making and scoring a test so that you and he may know what you have learned and where further work is needed. Furthermore, research shows that students given frequent quizzes in a course do better on a final examination than do students who have not had frequent quizzes (124). Almost all students, however, look forward to taking tests with trepidation and find taking the test an ordeal. Rather than seeming to be a cooperative effort between instructor and student, examinations seem to many students to be a battle in which each tries to outwit the other. In any case, the role of tests in determining grades places so much pressure on students that they often become upset during an examination. All too often students forget, until after the examination, what they should say on some questions. On other questions, they may know the material but do not understand what information the questions are trying to bring out; sometimes they cannot understand why points are taken off their grades. Skills needed in taking exams, which will help with these problems, are discussed below.

EMOTIONAL EXCITEMENT DURING THE EXAMINATION

Not all tests are equally upsetting; nor are all students affected by them equally. In fact, for some students the anxiety caused by taking a test may have an exhilarating effect on insights and output that can be compared to the peak performance of athletes in important meets. In a series of studies (10, 103, 396) it has been shown that anxiety on tests is specific rather than representative of a general personal anxiety, and can be treated as such; further, tests of "facilitating anxiety" correlate positively with grades, but tests of "debilitating anxiety" correlate negatively with grades. Our task is to help find ways to overcome anxiety attacks that cause mental blocks but also to admit that certain types of tension in taking examinations are normal and often can be helpful.

Careful study (including analyses of pulse rate, respiration change, and change in skin resistance) of anxious students during difficult examinations (272) shows that the relationship between intellectual ability and achievement is much lower among anxious than among nonanxious students. Also, the evidences of stress occur in some anxious students before the examination and in others, particularly during the examination. Our task here is to explore some of the causes of this type of difficulty and to suggest ways of limiting its crippling effects.

If examination questions cover familiar material, the student hurries to write down what he knows. Unexpected questions, on the other hand, scare many students so that they immediately set up a block. In the preceding chapter it was shown that posing questions and then reading to answer them helps to organize learning so that it is remembered much better. If these study questions and the questions in the examination cover the same topics, the examination will seem easy. Therefore, one of the most effective ways of combating a tendency to "blow up" on examinations is to predict quiz questions and concentrate on answering them in your study. As indicated previously, this question-predicting can be developed into a highly effective skill. Even if you are unable to predict all the questions that will appear on a test, you will find this method of study valuable. It has been shown that studying in this way is as effective as, if not more than, the usual student attitude of "study every little thing, because there is no telling what will be asked on the exam."

Students sometimes feel frustrated because, as they say, they know so much but do not know how to begin to express it; or they get so engrossed in answering the early part of an examination that they have to hurry over or omit the last part. Habits of calmness and systematic attack on a test help here. A good instructor builds an examination that can be answered in the allotted time, although it is usually planned so that students have no time to dawdle.

The first step in starting an exam should be to glance over the test to get an idea of how long it is and to see whether or not certain parts carry more points for a correct answer, require more time, or are easier to answer. On the basis of such a thirty-second survey, you should then roughly budget your time for each essay question or for each page or section of an objective test. Remember that although questions are not equally easy, they may very well count the same in scoring; it is better to work on many easy items and omit a few difficult ones than vice versa.

Information from one study suggests that encouraging students to write comments about seemingly ambiguous questions relieves enough anxieties so that higher scores are made than when no comments are written (246). However, care has to be used by a student so that he will not become involved in writing comments and fall behind schedule. In brief, an occasional note will explain a point and free a student from worrying about the question as he goes on.

Students often get unnecessarily excited immediately before an examination. They hurriedly compare ideas as to what the answer is to some expected question and find themselves in disagreement. The ensuing frantic argument among partially informed and mistaken students produces a feeling of insecure preparations that may serve to upset all the students and hinder their ability to think. So, if you get to the examination early, keep calm with small talk. Other students try to keep calm by delaying their arrival in the examination room until the last minute, with the result that they often arrive late. This is upsetting and they may also miss opening instructions.

A final suggestion on attitude is simply: Do your best. Although every student would like to get every question correct, it must be remembered that the test has been made difficult enough to give a range of scores for grading. Think and write on one question at a time. Do not worry about questions further down the list until you get to them.

TECHNIQUES FOR TAKING ESSAY EXAMINATIONS

Each type of examination requires certain unique skills and has its special difficulties. One common error in writing answers to essay questions is to waste time by writing about topics that do not pertain to the subject matter of the question. Because of the press of time during an exam, the instructor has to limit what he asks for; he therefore directs the student *not* to write everything he knows about the topic. Sometimes, instead of asking for an answer in essay form, he may ask the student, for example, to "*list* the causes," or "*compare* the outcomes," and so on. Your first step in answering an essay question should be to note the key word in the question; its purpose is to tell you the limited area to cover or the quick form for answering, so that both you and the instructor (when he grades the exams) can save time. If a question asks for a "list," do not write an essay, that only will take up more of your time and the time of the grader who must read to determine which points you have covered. Other key words frequently used are "illustrate," "outline," "diagram," and "contrast." Only when the question asks you to "discuss" a topic will a rather lengthy coverage of that topic be expected.

After you have found the key word in a question, your second step should be to look for further limiting words, so that you will give only what is called for as your answer. Note in the examples of instructions given in the preceding paragraph that the teacher further limited what was to be covered in each question by referring to "causes" in one instance and to "outcomes" in the other. In the discussion of "causes" (of a war, for example) he would not expect you to cover the outcomes nor many of the incidents. In discussing "outcomes" he would not expect you to discuss causes, earlier incidents, and so forth, but merely what the later effects were. In brief, teachers realize that students do not have time to write all that they know about a topic; hence, they suggest that only a segment be covered so that other questions can also be answered. To give more than what is asked for will not add to your grade; it may make the teacher think you cannot read directions, and will take time away from answering other questions.

Any essay question that asks for more than a brief definition needs to have an organized answer. Most students start writing about the first idea that comes to mind after reading a question and then continue with whatever ideas come to mind next; as a result, some strange sequences of ideas are produced. The grader, who has a list of points that should be covered, finds it difficult to determine how many points should be given to such an essay; the labor of checking back and forth to find the items puts him in such a frame of mind that he may give a low grade. It has been this writer's own experience that when he finds a test paper whose answers follow an organized sequence, he often feels like giving, and does give, a higher grade than the points listed might warrant.

An easy and effective way to obtain this organization is first to jot down quickly a sketchy outline of key words that indicate the ideas to be covered. These ideas will remind the student of further ideas, which he can insert at the correct spots in his list. Writing the essay then becomes a matter of expounding on each of the ideas listed. Since the grader has to read many papers, he will appreciate any cue that will speed up his reading. It pays, therefore, to number the main points in an essay or to use a visual system, such as paragraphing or outlining, to show the organization of the answer. Often a hastily drawn diagram will do much to demonstrate that you see the relationships among the ideas being presented.

There is some correlation between length of answer on an essay question and its grade. Of course, the student who knows the most usually will write the most, but one common failing of students is to feel that a few words carry as much meaning to the teacher as they do to the student himself. A student may feel that quoting a definition from the text is enough, but the grader wonders if these words have been really understood or merely memorized. Adding an illustration helps a great deal. In a question that asks for "discussion," do not merely list points, but explain why they are important or how they are interrelated. Elaboration to show full understanding is different from "padding," which is readily recognized and resented by the grader. "Padding" consists of bringing in irrelevant points or of repeating points already made in order to fill up space. Explaining what you mean, giving illustrations, or showing the implications of your points are not padding and are much appreciated by the grader.

One surprising belief held by many students writing essay examinations is that when a page in a "blue book" is filled, the answer is good, no matter what the demands of the question itself are. Actually, the grader has a list of points that he expects the student to cover (usually the definitely indicated points made in the text or in the lecture), and he grades according to the proportion of these covered in the student's answer. If a student judges that a question is answered when the bottom of the page is reached, he is apt to leave out some of the points expected. In a question for which four points are expected, leaving out one point can result in a 25 percent drop in score.

Simple mechanics in writing examinations also markedly affect grades. For instance, in one experiment on the effect of legibility on grading papers, 43 teachers were asked to grade the same compositions at two different times; at one time the compositions were written legibly, and at the other time the same compositions were written somewhat illegibly. The compositions in legible handwriting received an average grade one level higher than the compositions in illegible handwriting (186). Examinations written in ink are more easily read than those in hard pencil. Also, take a few minutes at the end of the hour to proofread your paper. An accidentally omitted "not" or other important word may affect your grade. Be sure that the questions and their parts are numbered correctly.

It has been shown that even superior college students are surprisingly inept when asked to solve problems posed by typical multiple-choice or other types of objective questions (41). Each student in the experiment was asked to talk aloud as he thought about a question, and his methods were later classified on a four-point qualitative scale. The researchers found that no student scored at the highest level of problem solving, 7 percent scored at the second level, 74 percent at the third level, and 19 percent at the lowest level. The third level was described as "moves toward its goal, but only after a great deal of lost motion. These individuals have little in the way of a plan, seem to release much energy, make many movements quite unrelated to the end to be attained, and appear to reach their goal more as a matter of chance than of plan." When such students completed a training program on how to analyze objective questions, their performance on later tests was improved and they received better grades.

Following are certain principles that will assist in the taking of objective examinations. Since every question usually has equal weight in scoring, you should work straight through the list of questions, not hesitating too long on those whose answers do not immediately come to mind. These difficult questions should be checked in the margin and returned to later. Such a system insures that all the easy questions on the examination will be completed; later questions may remind you of the answers to the ones skipped. Be sure to go back over the examination to answer questions that were omitted the first time.

Sometimes in going back over an examination a student will come to an answer that in a second reading seems to need changing, but he hesitates because he has heard the saying that first responses are usually correct. Obviously, if a student is sure in this second reading that the answer is something other than the one given, he should change it. Even in instances in which a student is not sure but *believes* that another answer is more likely to be correct, it is alright to change the answer. An extended series of experiments on the effectiveness of changing answers versus sticking with the original choice has shown that improved scores tend to occur with such changes (35, 52, 163, 213, 227, 251).

Somewhat related to the above is the difference of opinion with regard to whether a student should answer a test quickly and without second thoughts or whether he should use all of the time he wants to go over the test in order to add more to his answers or check their accuracy. Although it would be true that students who know the material are often able to answer the quiz more quickly, many of the best papers are handed in at the end of the examination period. Studies actually show a low correlation between length of time taken and higher quiz grades (24, 51). Thus, there is no real advantage in finishing early; a student should take all the time he needs to think about the questions on his examination so that none are omitted and so that he feels sure that he has understood what the intent of each question is.

Many students also are confused about guessing on objective tests. If there is no penalty for guessing, *i.e.*, your score consists of the number of correct answers, then guess, because you will obviously get some "unknown" answers correct. If there is a penalty for guessing, and it is no more than correct answers minus incorrect answers on true-false questions, or correct answers minus one-third of incorrect answers on four-choice multiple choice, then still guess. With corrections no greater than these, you should do as well by guessing as by not answering (143). There is also good psychological evidence that you will get more than a chance number correct because certain residual memories from material read will help. If there is an "overcorrection" for guessing, such as correct answers minus two times the number of incorrect answers on true-false questions, you should leave unfamiliar questions unanswered.

Many students have difficulty believing that answering all questions, even those whose answers must be guessed at, will often raise their scores. Therefore, it seems worthwhile to give an illustration. Let us assume that a student has to take an examination containing 100 true-false items, all of which are in a strange foreign language. If he answered *none* of the questions, his score would be "zero." However, if he flipped a coin to determine the answer to each item, he would, by chance, get about 50 percent correct and about 50 percent incorrect; his score would be 50 (correct) minus 50 (incorrect), and he would again receive a "zero" score. Thus, even in this extreme instance, the student would not lose by guessing. In actual exams the questions are in English; the student can use his general knowledge in addition to what he remembers about the course in order to decide what many of the so-called unknown questions mean and thereby get *more than half* of them correct (298, 404). By guessing (or, more exactly, by reasoning) a student can get a better score than he could by omitting those answers of which he is not sure.

True-false question. If a true-false question causes difficulty, the following principle is often helpful: Most such questions are built on the pattern of briefly describing two things and their degree of relationship, *i.e.*, "Some cats are black." The two "things" in each statement (*cats* and *black* in our example) are usually true; statements are made false by changing a word so as to overstate or understate the degree of relationship. The following series of words are usually used:

All—most—some—none	Positively related—not related—
Always—usually—sometimes—never	negatively related
Great—much—little—no	Good—bad
More—equal—less	Is—is not

When a student sees one of these words in a sentence, he can usually test whether the statement is true by substituting the other words in that series. If none of them makes a better statement than the word already in the sentence, the statement is true. Thus, when the above statement "Some cats are black" is tested by substituting "All cats are black," "Most cats are black," or "No cats are black," the original statement is shown to be true. Knowing this pattern, a student can go to the key word in a true-false statement and not worry about possible exceptions to each word in the statement.

Many students have learned to look for the key words "no," "never," "every," "all," and "entirely," because they usually indicate that the statement is false; it is difficult to make any statement that is true of all items or no items to which it refers. Knowing this tendency of students to look for these specific words, however, many instructors work hard to formulate some statements in which the use of these terms makes them true, *e.g.*, "An island is entirely surrounded by water" or "All men are mortal."

Care also should be used in answering a true-false statement containing two independent clauses. If one of these is true and the other false, the whole statement must be marked "false."

Multiple-choice questions. In answering multiple-choice questions, certain choices can often be crossed out as obviously wrong. This may reduce an immediate evaluation to one or two possibilities, and if the student has to "guess" among those that are left, his chances of getting a correct answer are better that if he guesses among all the choices.

A student should read the directions given on multiple-choice tests. If they say, "Mark the *one* best answer," do not put more than one answer in the space provided. If more than one answer is listed, the item will be marked completely wrong even though one of the answers may be correct. On the other hand, if the directions for a particular multiple-choice question asks the student to list "all correct answers" or "one or several correct answers," credit will be taken away for every correct answer omitted. It is helpful in answering multiple-choice questions that ask for "one or more correct answers" to treat each choice as a true-false question; if a choice sounds true, put its number down; if it sounds false, omit its number from your answers.

Matching questions. In answering matching questions in which a given answer may be used only once, it will obviously be helpful to answer the known questions first, and then study the few remaining choices as answers to the difficult questions. Mark out the answers as you use them.

Completion questions. In answering completion questions, it is better to fill in the best answers you can think of than to leave them blank; such answers often are completely or partially correct. If the question calls for a word with a certain number of letters, use another word that carries a similar meaning if you cannot think of the correct word. If the answer is quite familiar to you, but for the moment you are unable to recall it, go on and return to this question later. Your changed point of view may assist in overcoming the previous mental block.

NEW TYPES OF EXAMINATIONS

Analysis of typical examinations shows that about 95 percent of the items deal with knowledge of facts. Though the average instructor hopes that his students are also learning certain attitudes, points of view, ways of thinking, and ways to apply information, he assumes that students who know the most facts must have these other characteristics. This is far from the truth, however, because experiments show that these latter characteristics are not likely to be learned unless there is teaching and testing for them. For these reasons many teachers are changing their testing practices to include measures of learning other than merely factual aspects (379).

Students have trouble with these new types of examinations, not only because they may not have the characteristics that the tests are attempting to measure, but also because they do not know how to take these tests. Students who are familiar with true-false examinations are often completely confused by questions that give all the data needed on the test blank and ask the student to determine with fine discrimination whether, on the basis of data given, an accompanying statement is "true," "probably true," "probably false," "false," or there is "insufficient evidence" to say. The writer has found that many students feel that they do not understand what these test items are about and so resort to guessing. On the other hand, a little explanation of how these tests are constructed has been found to increase students' scores markedly. Students at Ohio State University who analyzed their errors on a 45-item test of this type were able on the average to improve their score by 10 points on a second test; furthermore, they transferred such practice on examples in physics to similar items in zoology.

Techniques for measuring points of view, ways of thinking, and ability to apply information are not as well worked out nor as standardized as they are for the usual objective or essay examination. Therefore, the form of these tests tends to vary from campus to campus and from course to course. Two currently emphasized examples are given below as illustrations of these new types of tests. Each attempts to measure not only accuracy but also the kinds of constant errors that students make in thinking. They are known as "interpretation of data" and "application of principles" tests.

Interpretation of data tests.   An interpretation of data test gives all the necessary information in the test and asks the student to determine in terms of this whether each of a series of statements is true or false, probably true or false, or whether there is insufficient evidence to say. The test is scored not only as to the number correct, but also as to the frequency with which a student is "too cautious" or "too gullible" in handling data. That is, the test measures whether a student has learned to use data without reading too much or too little into it. In making these test items, a standard pattern is used: If a statement is directly verified or denied by the data given, it is "true" or "false." On the other hand, it is "probably true," or "probably false," if any of the following conditions exist: (1) there is a slight extrapolation of a curve, (2) there is an interpolation between points in a graph, (3) the behavior of a major part is estimated from the behavior of the whole, and (4) an experiment is repeated under comparable conditions. A statement has "insufficient evidence" under these conditions: (1) comparison is made between data given and data not given, (2) a cause is attributed for the data, (3) a value judgment is made in terms of the data, and (4) a too extended extrapolation is made. A student who know these patterns will easily recognize how a given item has been constructed and so will be able to react to it more intelligently.

"Application of Principles" tests.   In an "application of principles" test, the student not only answers a question but also checks the reasons for his answers from a list. These reasons are also constructed to fit a pattern; in this case, the incorrect ones are worded to resemble the types of erroneous arguments commonly used. These variously disguised arguments thus represent potential "booby traps" to catch the unwary thinker; some diagnosis is possible from an analysis of the types of errors that a student tends to make. Following is the pattern of errors commonly used: (a) reasoning by false analogy, (b) merely restating the conclusion, (c) reference to similar happenings, (d) appeal to authority, (e) use of ridicule, (f) teleological reasons, (g) irrelevant reasons, and (h) untrue statements. Again, it has been found that students who understand how these items are made are better able to demonstrate their ability on these tests since at least they know for what they are being tested.

Many instructors vary the form of their items from that indicated above, and other types of tests constantly are being experimented with. It is, therefore, difficult to know what types a student will encounter on a given campus. Rather than provide specific training exercises, we suggest that the student analyze his exams to see if they include items that attempt to measure these noninformational aspects and with which he has trouble. The student should have his instructor assist him in analyzing how such items are constructed; then he should make a definite attempt to improve his skill on such tests.

C. Making Use of Returned Examinations

Your score on a test does not in itself indicate how well you have done. Tests differ in length and in difficulty, so that a score of 70 may be excellent for one exam but average or failing for another. You need some standard with which to compare your score, *i.e.*, letter-grade equivalents, the average score of the class, or the range of scores in the class. Having determined your level of performance, your next step is to determine what is wrong with your attack on the questions you have answered incorrectly. Most students, however, do not take this step. Having seen their grades, they compare notes with other students, argue with the teacher that a certain question is not fair, or brood on the thought that they hate exams.

A quiz is a quick and easy way of reciting what is important in the course. The items missed are those that need further study. Questions that give difficulty are often repeated later so that the instructor can see whether or not students have mastered them. If you do not see how the correct answer is derived, ask the instructor for an explanation. In any case, use each quiz as a practice review, which shows where further study will be needed before the final examination.

Much also can be learned from a test about what the next one will be like. What kinds of questions are asked: definitions; interpretation; discussions; problems? Are they derived primarily from the text or from the lecture? Are they the ones you have expected? Of those you have not expected, where do they come from? What is wrong with your answers: not complete enough; poor distribution of time on the important parts of the test; questions omitted and careless mistakes? Very often the instructor will write on the test paper suggestions for improving your answers. If he does not, and if you cannot determine what to do, ask the instructor after class.

Number of words in this chapter: 7425

Time when chapter was completed: _____

Work rate per minute: _____

Answer the quiz on page 234.

List your work rate, comprehension accuracy, and note-quality rating on page 40.

Practice Exercises

So much for a great deal of advice; the important thing is to try these skills on actual tests to see if they work and to polish them to a high level of efficiency. Much of what is stated here ties in directly with the methods of study discussed in the preceding two chapters; skills that improve comprehension and retention are also useful with examinations. Below are some additional exercises. Set up a regular practice program along the lines of these exercises and check with your instructor for suggestions.

QUIZ PREDICTION

1. Look over the tests for Chapters 2 and 3 (pp. 231–233) to see if each question is reasonably predictable beforehand from the various typographical cues used in the text. Do the topics of these questions stand out in the text? Do they represent headings or other items set off by typographical or text cues? If a student were reading Chapter 2 or Chapter 3 for the first time and were using these cues to give direction to his reading effort, would the tests seem easier than if he had not used these cues in reading?

2. Try making question-predictions as you read later chapters in this text and as you prepare for midterm examinations in this course. Our experience in teaching this skill to students is that those who predict questions for such midterms average about 10 points better on the midterms than do those students who do not make such predictions.

In making quiz question-predictions try to do it in a way that will not take too much time and effort. Rather than bother to write out complete essay, true-false, or multiple-choice questions, merely jot down a brief sentence (or even a phrase) with a question mark at the end, *e.g.*, "What is question prediction?" or "Question prediction?" The full benefit of prediction can be obtained in this way, and much time will be saved. You will note, then, that the main phrases in your SQ3R notes actually represent these predictions. In reviewing for a quiz, change these to question form *and recite the answers*. This writer has known students to make an excellent list of question-predictions and then forget to study their answers.

3. Select an outside course for which you will make regular predictions of quiz questions. Check these predictions with your instructor for suggestions or additions and for ways to speed up making these predictions.

4. Summarize in the chart on page 68 the success (and difficulties) you have in making these predictions of quiz questions.

First attempt; course name: _____

Second attempt; course name: _____

Third attempt; course name: _____

Fourth attempt; course name: _____

Fifth attempt; course name: _____

EXAMINATION TAKING

1. What success have you had so far in taking tests in this book? Analyze these tests to see how the examination-taking skills described in the foregoing chapter might have helped.

In the true-false questions, look for the key modifiers that make a statement false or, if changed, would have made the statement false, *e.g.,* always—usually —sometimes—never. What proportion of the false statements have been accounted for by these variations in key words?

In instances in which you have not been quite sure of the right answer in multiple choice and matching tests, how effective have you been in eliminating clearly wrong choices before having to make your final choice?

Have you left any assigned questions unanswered? (You should not have, since there is no penalty for guessing.) How successful have you been when you have guessed? Have you gotten more correct than chance normally would produce?

2. Apply these same principles of analysis to other quizzes and examinations that you have taken in this and other courses. Are the same types of key words used in true-false questions? Can the process of elimination be used in analyzing many of the multiple-choice and matching questions? Does "guessing" (really, reasoning as best one can) on unknown questions give better-than-chance success?

3. Essay examinations are frequently used in courses. Do you notice that *key words* such as "outline," "contrast," "list," and so on give specific directions about the form in which the answer is to be given? Do you try to outline your answer briefly before writing, and do you use paragraphing or numbering in your answer to help the grader follow your points more easily? Do you divide your time among the various questions so you are not left near the end of the examination period with inadequate time to answer the last question?

4. If special new types of examinations are sometimes given in your school, your instructor may also give you some practice materials on taking examinations of this kind. After the principles behind the construction of these new types of tests have been explained, are you able to do better on retests?

5. Bring in available tests, essay and otherwise, from other courses for suggestions concerning improved methods of studying and of taking such tests.

"BLOWING UP" ON EXAMINATIONS

It is perfectly normal to become excited before an important examination; the condition may actually contribute to the facility with which one writes, but normally it diminishes after one gets into the examination. However, some people become so anxious that they cannot think clearly in the test situation and may at times have great trouble remembering material and organizing their thoughts. Various suggestions have been made in Chapter 4 for adequately preparing for and taking tests; if you tend to get overexcited on examinations, try these suggestions. Sometimes "blowing up" is related to a past experience in which inadequate preparation resulted in poor performance; remembering such a time can add to one's anxiety in a present test situation. A person can do little to solve this type of problem on his own, but given a chance to think it through with the help of a counselor, he can find its source and possible remedy. If you have such overemotional reactions to tests, ask your instructor where you can obtain counseling help.

Schedule of Review for Finals

Before exam week

	Wednesday	Thursday	Friday	Saturday	Sunday
8:00					
9:00					
10:00					
11:00					
12:00					
1:00					
2:00					
3:00					
4:00					
5:00					
6:00					
7:00					
8:00					
9:00					
10:00					

FINAL EXAMINATIONS

This section may be postponed until near the end of the school term when the end-of-term requirements will be clearer and the activities more relevant.

Obligations such as regular assignments, term papers, final-examination preparation, and so on, pile up near the end of the school term so that a system for getting things done is necessary. Some students try postponing these obligations as long as possible and then frantically cram the night before the final. As indicated earlier, this is ineffective because of the fatigue and confused ideas that result. Let us look at a method of scheduling for review that should not take any more time and should provide better results.

Use the charts on these two pages to plan the last 10 days of the school term. First write in your regular classes and the time for each final examination. Write in other necessary activities such as work, eating, and meetings. Now plan your study and review times. In doing this do not just write "study, study, study" in every available blank. Be specific in what you plan to do at each time. Probably

Exam week

	Monday	Tuesday	Wednesday	Thursday	Friday
8:00					
9:00					
10:00					
11:00					
12:00					
1:00					
2:00					
3:00					
4:00					
5:00					
6:00					
7:00					
8:00					
9:00					
10:00					

the first thing to put down is the study time for the last assignments in your regular classes, *e.g.,* "Wed., 7–8:30, study Chapters 17 and 18, history." Now look over available times in these 10 days for planned review for your final examinations. Early examinations would suggest earlier review times than later examinations. For each final examination set up several spaced review items each of which should be an hour or two in length. In writing these review periods on your chart, specifically indicate what course and what chapters will be covered, *e.g.,* "Wed., 9–11, Review first third history." You will want to review the night before each examination, but limit this period to a couple of hours of overview and get a good night's sleep.

This plan may make your schedule look quite full, but this is a busy time of the school year. On the other hand, such planning should leave free time for recreation and will eliminate the all-night cramming that some students finally do after not having studied enough earlier. In planning these study and review times, allow for occasional breaks of about 15 minutes, and when you get to the end of the scheduled study time, quit for the night and get some sleep. Although it may sound dedicated to say you studied until 3 A.M., little is accomplished by this kind of desperate attempt to stay awake at your desk.

Question-prediction is a second skill that should help a great deal with your final examinations. Earlier some indication was given as to the kinds of questions that are often asked. Now take at least one of your courses and make a list of all those important "question topics" that you think might be used as the basis for making up the final examination questions. Then check these with your instructor to see if you are getting the right ideas. This list can be made by jotting down just a word or phrase as key to the topic; long questions need not be written out. If you have working notes on your reading and lectures, you can go through them and check the major points with a colored pencil. Previous attempts to predict quiz questions will also be useful here, but remember that the final will tend to cover only the major points.

Rate measurement starts on page 78.

CHAPTER 5

Skills in attack and concentration

Many students complain that they have difficulty in settling down to work and in concentrating, and that in hurrying from one thing to another they seem to get very little accomplished, or that because they have so much to do they cannot relax and enjoy themselves. On the other hand, almost every underclassman admires a senior who appears to complete all his schoolwork and receives high grades, who has time for social activities and recreation, and who seems unflurried and unworried about his work. Since this senior was probably a typical freshman at one time, and since skill in concentration is acquired and not inherited, what skills must he have learned to enable him to succeed so much more easily?

Basically, much of his success is due to (1) the development of work-study skills, (2) the development of habits of using time efficiently, (3) the setting up of better study conditions, and (4) motivation. One would find that when this senior studies, he wants a quiet room, he gets right to work, he emphasizes the most important parts of his assignments rather than reading every word, and he finishes a job without unnecessary interruptions.

In this chapter we will discuss the first three of the skills that make this senior an object of envy. Chapter 6 will continue the discussion with an examination of the importance of motivation to successful concentration and study.

Work-Study Skills

The first aspect of developing ability to concentrate, the use of work-study skills, was discussed in Chapters 2, 3, and 4. It was shown that the SQ3R method helps concentration in several ways. Rapidly surveying a lesson before starting to study gives the student some notion of what it will be about and arouses his interest. Turning each heading into a question further arouses the reader's curiosity so that

73

he attends more readily to what he is reading and his mind is less likely to wander to other topics. Finally, the alternation of tasks from reading to answer a question to reciting on its answer at the end of each headed section makes it easier to keep one's attention focused. That is, when a person realizes that he has to concentrate only to the end of a headed section—maybe a page or so—he can persevere more easily than if he starts out believing that he has to concentrate constantly through-out a whole chapter. Research work in industry has shown that when workers have a job requiring close concentration they do their work better if they can alternate tasks than if they have to repeat the same task continually (68).

Self-evaluation

Since inability to get down to work or to concentrate may be due to many possible causes, an analysis of each individual's difficulties is necessary. This section includes some questionnaires in order to focus attention on the issues that are of primary importance to you. The points you miss will then give direction to your study of the following sections about study habits and study conditions.

Since reading and filling out the following questionnaires is different from the usual act of studying, the measurement of your study speed and comprehension will not be initiated until after this "self-evaluation" section is completed.

There are two aspects to this self-evaluation. First, you are asked to fill out a time chart to show how you *now* spend your time. Second, you are asked to fill out a study habits questionnaire so that you can see which of your present study methods are considered effective or ineffective.

1. In filling in the accompanying time chart select a typical school day or two typical half-days during which every hour you should mark down how you spent your time in each 15-minute interval. Be specific and be accurate: include such items as "5 minutes, smoking," "16 minutes, talking," "10 minutes, walking to class," and so on. The purpose of this exercise is *not* to indicate that you should study more (unless you have been unusually lax in this regard) but only to help *you* see how your time often is wasted. With this knowledge plans can be made that will help you study more efficiently and that probably will allow you more time for recreation.

Sometimes people like to compare their study efforts with those of others to see "if they study enough." Because every person's interests, needs, and requirements differ so much, no critical judgment can be made unless time use is extremely unbalanced, *i.e.*, all work and no play or vice versa. Table 1, which summarizes the distribution of time of several hundred women in a state university, shows that the use of time varies quite a bit among students. Similar analyses made in other universities show similar results (107, 370).

2. As a second activity you are asked to fill out the accompanying study question-naire. The questions are arranged according to areas to be discussed in the sections

Present Use of Time

(Keep careful record each hour of what was done in the preceding time.)

Day or days summarized? _____

7:00 _____	12:30 _____	6:00 _____
7:15 _____	12:45 _____	6:15 _____
7:30 _____	1:00 _____	6:30 _____
7:45 _____	1:15 _____	6:45 _____
8:00 _____	1:30 _____	7:00 _____
8:15 _____	1:45 _____	7:15 _____
8:30 _____	2:00 _____	7:30 _____
8:45 _____	2:15 _____	7:45 _____
9:00 _____	2:30 _____	8:00 _____
9:15 _____	2:45 _____	8:15 _____
9:30 _____	3:00 _____	8:30 _____
9:45 _____	3:15 _____	8:45 _____
10:00 _____	3:30 _____	9:00 _____
10:15 _____	3:45 _____	9:15 _____
10:30 _____	4:00 _____	9:30 _____
10:45 _____	4:15 _____	9:45 _____
11:00 _____	4:30 _____	10:00 _____
11:15 _____	4:45 _____	10:15 _____
11:30 _____	5:00 _____	10:30 _____
11:45 _____	5:15 _____	10:45 _____
12:00 _____	5:30 _____	11:00 _____
12:15 _____	5:45 _____	11:15 _____

TABLE 1   Week-Day Distribution of Time in Hours and Minutes of Freshmen Women; Data Given for Median, First Quartile, and Third Quartile.[a]

	Median	Q1	Q3
Sleep	8 hr 0 min	7 hr 30 min	8 hr 30 min
Meals	1 hr 13 min	1 hr 0 min	1 hr 26 min
Class	3 hr 07 min	2 hr 39 min	3 hr 35 min
Study	3 hr 05 min	2 hr 18 min	3 hr 52 min
Recreation	3 hr 26 min	2 hr 34 min	4 hr 18 min
Work	1 hr 39 min	57 min	2 hr 21 min
Personal	1 hr 50 min	1 hr 26 min	2 hr 14 min
Travel	52 min	33 min	1 hr 11 min
Miscellaneous	2 hr 08 min	1 hr 15 min	3 hr 03 min

[a] From unpublished data of M. V. Bean and E. A. Gaw. Used with permission. The times do not total 24 hours because "work" and "travel" were calculated only from those time schedules listing them.

that follow. Fill it out before you read further. The paragraph following the questionnaire tells you how to "score" your responses.

Study-Habits Questionnaire[1]

No. correct out of

38 _____

Answer each of these questions by writing in one of the following words (or its number): (1) never, (2) seldom, (3) sometimes, (4) usually, (5) always. A few questions are to be completed by writing in answers as directed.

TIME DISTRIBUTION

_____ 1. Do you have a plan of work for each day?

_____ 2. If so, do you stick to it?

_____ 3 Does your work prevent you from engaging in social activities?

_____ 4. Do you allow time for exercise?

_____ 5. Do you get enough sleep?

_____ 6. Do you have certain hours that you regularly spend talking and in recreation?

_____ 7. Do you eat at the same hours each day?

_____ 8 Do you tend to spend too much time on social and recreational activities?

_____ 9. When you study at night, how long is it usually from the time you close your book until you are in bed? (Indicate the time in minutes.)

ATTITUDES

_____10 Do you feel that you have to spend too much time studying?

_____11 Do you feel that you ought to spend as much time as possible studying?

_____12 Do you get tense and nervous when you study, or worry about your work?

_____13 Do you feel incapable of doing your work?

_____14. Do you try to complete a lesson before allowing interruptions to take place?

_____15 With a four-hour French assignment, would you try to complete it at one sitting rather than at several different times?

WORK HABITS

_____16. Do you study during the time between two classes, say between 9 and 11 o'clock?

_____17 Do you have trouble "settling down to work" at the beginning of a study period?

[1] These questions are adapted from the Study Questionnaire that appears in S. L. Pressey and F. P. Robinson, *Laboratory Workbook in Applied Educational Psychology*, 3d edition, New York, Harper & Row, 1959. Used with permission.

_____18 When you study, do you frequently get up, walk about, glance at a paper or magazine, or do other things that interrupt your work?

_____19 Do you daydream in class or when you should be studying?

_____20. Do you study a given course each weekday in the same place and at the same time?

_____21 Do you get to class or sit down to study, only to find that you do not have your notebook, pen, textbook, or other materials?

_____22. Do you get your work in on time?

_____23 Do you immediately go on to the next lesson when you have completed the one you are working on?

DISTRACTIONS

_____24 Do you prepare for bed before doing some of your studying?

_____25 Do you study some of your lessons while in bed or while stretched out on the davenport?

_____26 Is your room used for many informal meetings during the evening?

_____27 Is your room near a disturbing source of noise?

_____28 Do you have pictures or things that you like to look at on or near your study table?

_____29 Do other people in your study room distract you?

_____30 Does the temperature of your study room make you feel uncomfortable?

_____31 Is your studying interrupted by thinking about various personal problems and worries?

_____32 Is your studying interrupted by thinking about various interesting events in the near future?

MATERIALS

_____33 Do you have trouble obtaining the materials that you need for study?

_____34. How much clear table space do you have for study; that is, about how long and how wide is the free space on your desk?

FATIGUE

_____35 Do you have much glare on your book?

_____36. Does enough light fall on your book when it is in the position in which you normally have it when you study? (See directions on page 87.)

_____37. What type of lighting do you have? (a) gooseneck or study lamp, (b) overhead light, (c) indirect lighting, (d) other.

_____38 Is it generally noisy where you usually study?

The questions whose numbers are followed by periods should be answered "usually" or "always" and those question numbers not followed by periods should be answered "seldom" or "never." The answer to question 9 is "30 minutes or longer." The answer to questions 34 and 37 will be given in the discussion later. There is seldom a paragon, even among good students, who honestly can give the ideal answer to all of these. The items on which your answers differed from the ones you should have given indicate which suggestions in the following discussion will be most pertinent.

Research on students' knowledge of versus actual use of effective study methods, however, raises some interesting questions about teaching approaches. When students are asked to answer study-habits questionnaires (such as the one previously) in the manner in which ideal students would or should answer and then are asked to answer as they themselves actually study, students very quickly show that they know a great deal more than they practice (81, 90, 297, 410). Further, when a study-habits inventory is administered to entering freshmen and to the same students seven to nine months later, the latter group of freshmen are found to have poorer study habits and more negative attitudes toward college and studying than at entrance (56). Quite obviously many factors affect ability to concentrate and the bringing about of improvement (253).

Start rate measurement here; time started to read _____.

Habits of Efficient Time Use

Students' difficulties in the use of time tend to be threefold: (1) They have feelings of guilt because they think they do not study enough, (2) they waste time in moving from one activity to another, and (3) they have difficulty in settling down to work even after they have made up their minds to start.

Most students feel that they ought to study more than they do. Many have feelings of guilt whenever they stop to talk or go to a movie. But as already has been indicated, good students actually do not study more than poor students; they just study more efficiently. The primary remedy for study difficulties is more effective methods of study rather than more study time. Many good students have full, happy social lives, and it is characteristic that they usually worry less about needing to study than students with lower grades. It is not a purpose of this chapter to try to get you to study more hours, but to teach you to study more efficiently.

TYPICAL PATTERNS OF TIME USE

The average person usually feels that the hours in the day pass rapidly with too little accomplished. Part of the difficulty lies in the lack of a planned routine of activities. If a person has a continuing attitude of "What next?," he has to constantly make decisions about his next step. Such a person responds sensitively to distractions about him; he no sooner starts something than he is reminded of several other pressing matters. Since he has little or no system to his activities, everything seems to demand immediate attention. Two examples will show how, without a habitual routine, time seems to be wasted. The average student with classes at 9 A.M. and 11 A.M. behaves somewhat as follows: converses after class (10 minutes); smokes a cigarette (5 minutes); mails a letter (15 minutes); starts for the library but meets a friend (15 minutes); then, because of the time, starts for the next class. In the evening this typical student may start to prod himself to go to work immediately after supper; begrudgingly he gives himself until 7 P.M. to talk; then, with self-recrimination, extends this time until 7:30 P.M.; then, at 8 P.M.

finally drives himself to work. Once he settles down he finds that he does not know the assignment and has to find his pen; once started, he has to stop in order to help his roommate with his algebra. Study is further interrupted by the "necessity" of planning a week-end trip or of telephoning for a date. Later he decides not to go out to eat with his friends but then finds that he cannot study, so he goes out to eat alone. The next day he says he spent the whole evening trying to study.

Concrete evidence of the difficulty students have in settling down to study and then keeping at it is given in the following studies (261, 384). In one study students entering a library room were observed during their first 30 minutes after they seated themselves; it was found that only about three-quarters of their time was spent productively in study and that during the first 10 minutes only about one-half efficiency occurred.

Even when studying students do not work near their most efficient level (193). In one experiment students reading several days before a test did not know that their rate of reading was being measured (*i.e.*, similar to the usual study situation); it was found that they read only 60 percent as fast during 30 minutes as they did on similar material when they knew they were taking a reading test (300). (See Figure 9.) This same study also shows that individuals differ in the degree to which they apply their reading skills while studying. Knowing a person's rate on a test, one can predict his rate of reading during untimed study only 5 percent better than if the one predicting just guessed. It is a case of the tortoise and the hare; some read steadily along to finish first and others, more hare-brained, interrupt their work to do this and that.

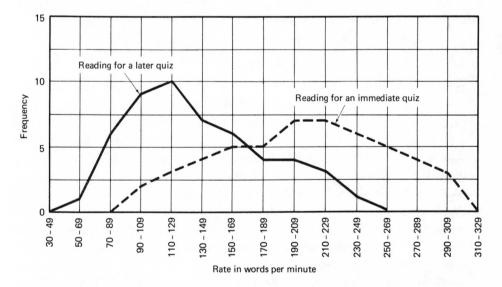

Figure 9. Rates at which students read comparable selections during 30-minute periods under different conditions: (a) reading for an immediate quiz, and (b) reading for a later quiz in an apparently untimed situation and with more study the next day seeming possible, *i.e.*, similar to normal study conditions. (Smoothed curves adapted from 300.)

Developing habits of efficient time use is somewhat different from what many students believe it to be. A person is efficient not because of superb will power used to force himself to keep to the job, but because he has developed habitual patterns or sequences of activities. A person who knows what he wants to do step by step and who gets down to work quickly, usually goes about his work with no great effort.

Two examples of activities in which most people are efficient will illustrate: the average person does not have to remind himself constantly that he must eat; even when he is engrossed in some activity his attention turns to eating at the appropriate time. He has little trouble concentrating on eating because every day at certain times he has always devoted himself to eating. Another example of efficiency built up by habit is illustrated by the greater ease one has in following a time schedule of classes that meet daily at the same time than in following a schedule that changes daily. After several weeks on a constant schedule, the student by habit goes from one class to another. He does not have to prod himself to go; he seems to follow the routine without much thought and is not easily distracted by friends and activities.

From these examples it should be obvious that the ability to concentrate and use time efficiently does not mean drudgery or following a dreary routine. As a matter of fact, skills that have become so routine that they are habits can make life more pleasant. Some people let habit get them to their accustomed eating places on time while they visit and joke. Other people, because of a habitual routine, are even able to get to an 8 o'clock class while still enjoying a half-sleep.

There are three steps in developing skills for effective time use: (1) working out an efficient time schedule, (2) following this schedule until work habits develop, and (3) applying conscious effort to certain work rules. Each of these will be discussed in turn.

Development of a time schedule. School programs are so planned that every student should be able to achieve a suitable balance among study, recreation, eating, and sleeping. If a student feels too hurried, probably he will find that rearranging his use of time—his whole time—will help. The time diary filled out earlier shows where inefficient use of time tends to occur. With this information and a little experimenting, the student can work out an efficient time schedule. One such schedule will be shown later in this chapter.

In making out such a time chart, you will find that the following steps and principles will help. First, write in those activities for which the time is more or less set—eating, sleeping, class hours, and outside work. In doing this, be sure to allow adequate time for eating and sleeping.

Next, indicate the hours during which you expect to study each subject. That is, do not simply say "Study from 7 to 11," but say "Study history from 7 to 8:30" and "Study chemistry from 8:45 to 10." Typical students average about one hour of study for each hour of class—much less than the often quoted university standard of two hours for each hour of class (107, 133). Furthermore, research shows that good students differ from poor students more in effective use of study time than in amount of study time (107, 418). In programs with time limitations and heavy work loads, e.g., engineering, it has been found that use of efficient study methods is highly predictive of whether or not bright students will make good grades (57). Rather than plan to study extra hours if you are doing poorly, you should learn to make more effective use of your time. Any student who is averaging more than two hours daily in preparing for a given subject should look to other chapters in this book for more effective study skills.

Having filled in these various activities, you will normally find that there are still some hours left. These are your reward for time well spent and should be considered "free time." Students with heavy outside work schedules may find little time left. Such students report that work normally effects hours of recreation more than anything else. Studies of part-time (up to 15 hours a week) working students show that they, with few exceptions, make as good grades and are as well adjusted socially as the nonworking student (105, 155, 385). It is also interesting to note that part-time working students usually complain less about problems of concentration than do nonworking students; the full schedules of the former require them to follow a habitual routine and so form concentration habits.

In assigning definite hours for study and recreation, you will find certain principles of assistance.

1. Normally, it is better to study an assignment immediately after the class in which it is given if the class is usually a lecture section, or just before the class in which it will be used if emphasis is on recitation or discussion.
2. If you are studying for long periods of time, stop for a few minutes between chapters or between changes of subjects (136). A period of stretching and relaxation allows one to attack the next lesson with renewed energy, and, more important, it prevents retroactive inhibition—interference with the process of remembering brought on by the immediate study of different subject matter. Furthermore, studies of eye movements of students during four hours of continuous reading show that students begin showing poorer eye movements after 30 minutes and have decreasing efficiency during the rest of the period, unless there are breaks at meaningful places (72, 169).
3. It is better to study a subject every day at the same time than to have occasional long sessions. This daily routine develops habits that facilitate planning, getting down to work, and concentrating.
4. Allow a "slowing-down" period between the end of studying and starting to get ready for bed. Such a period of relaxation is apt to make going to sleep much easier.
5. Make use of vacant hours between classes. The hour between a 9 A.M. and an 11 A.M. class, for example, is a poor time for visiting; it can be spent studying in order to reduce the evening's work.

6. From 4 to 7 P.M. is the usual period for recreation during the week. Plan to use as much of this period as possible for that purpose.

Habitual use of time schedule. Having developed an efficient time schedule for the school term, follow it until you habitually turn from each activity to the next one. It is a good idea to place the proposed time schedule where you will see it frequently, *e.g.*, in the front of your notebook or on the wall of your room. Try to follow its pattern each day. Gradually the habit of turning from one particular activity to another will develop; getting down to work and concentrating will begin to seem much easier.

It cannot be emphasized too strongly that this aspect of developing skill in concentration and effective use of time is not based on merely understanding how important it is to study, nor is it a matter of making a decision to get down to work. It is a matter of developing a habit. This habit forming will take much practice, and, to keep yourself at it, you should check your use of time occasionally.

A time schedule should not be an inflexible thing that gets in the way. When special events or opportunities occur, rearrange your schedule. During the normal course of events, however, use the basic habit pattern to guide the flow of the day's activities.

Applying work rules. The purpose of the above program is to develop a tendency to turn habitually to a next scheduled activity; a student can further develop this tendency by knowing and consciously applying certain principles of time use. As William James once said, the way to develop a habit is to do the act at the first opportunity and to let no exception take place. The proper mental attitude will help. For instance, do not wait until you are in a suitable mood before studying; begin studying at your regularly set time. Also, try to finish all your work within the time limits set; do not rob yourself of recreation time. Do not worry about all the work to be accomplished—there is a time scheduled for everything. Do not carry extra books around—you should know which ones are needed for studying. And do not waste time trying to decide what to study first—study the subject you have scheduled.

Once you are at the study table, try to go right to work; force yourself to postpone other activities until later. Check yourself whenever you start to daydream.[2] Set a time or page limit on your work, because it is easier to continue with a lesson for 20 minutes more or five pages more than it is to promise to study all evening. Try to finish your work within the time limits set; if you should finish early, take a short rest period.

[2] A study of the frequency and kinds of daydreams that college women and men have shows that there is a negative relationship between frequency of daydreams and 14 (of 24) kinds of daydreams and the grades of women. On the other hand, there is no relationship between frequency of daydreaming and grades for men, except that the more frequently the men daydreamed about achievement, the *better* they did on grades (394).

Study Conditions

Study conditions may affect the student's ability to get down to work and to concentrate in five ways: (1) Distractions tend to draw the student's attention away from his work, (2) it is more difficult to study in situations normally associated with other activities, (3) study materials not readily available cause the continuity of work to be broken while the student is hunting for them, (4) poor lighting can be quite fatiguing, and (5) physiological conditions may affect the student's ability to concentrate.

MINIMIZING DISTRACTIONS DURING STUDY

It is often difficult to concentrate on studying because it is more fun to concentrate on other things. A textbook may have to compete for interest with a photograph on the study table or a talk session in the same room, or with such attention-getters as a flickering light or a slammed door. In one series of extended observations in a women's college dormitory, it was found that only 4 percent of the students were without major distractions at the time of observation. For example, one girl was trying to study "with a radio mystery turned on, noise from the hallway, a cluttered desk and room, and talking by her roommate and friend" (162, p. 45). The library as a place to study also has its distractions; the range of these distractions is summarized in Table 2.

TABLE 2 Types and Frequency of Distractions Interrupting the Library Study of College Men and Women[a]

| | Percent of total | | |
Distraction	Men	Women	Both
Conversation	32	26	29
Aimless looking around	15	15	15
Aimless leafing through books	14	10	12
Students walking by	12	7	10
Applying makeup	0	16	8
Attracted by certain individuals	9	5	7
Daydreaming	7	5	6
Reading and writing letters	4	7	5
Arranging hair and clothes	2	7	4
Miscellaneous	5	2	4
	100	100	100

[a] Adapted from 384.

So the task is to find privacy somewhere. Surveys show that students find relative "privacy" in surprising places, *e.g.*, library stacks, music rooms, cafeterias, on the lawn, and so on (342); sometimes such selection is based on the questionable practice of trying to be "doubly efficient," *e.g.*, study and see people, or study and eat. Surveys of college students in other countries (346, 388) also show that students have a distinct preference for studying alone, but they, too, have some difficulty in achieving it.

One survey (121) shows that students who study in the library get better grades than those who study elsewhere, *e.g.*, about .4 of a grade point higher although no more intelligent. However, some effort still must be exerted to find privacy and a lack of distraction. One reason the library may be a good place to study is that this environment is one that is always used for study, so the surrounding acts as a stimulus that effects habits and attitudes of study. All necessary study materials tend to be more readily available in the library, and there is more desk space. However, some consideration has to be given to determining how distractions in the library can be diminished or eliminated. Probably the best solution is to seek a small reading room in the library, find a corner, and face the wall. Later, if the student wants social contacts he can move to the center of the main library room.

Distractions in your own room also can be diminished. It is pleasant, of course, to decorate your room. However, you should set off a quiet, unadorned area for studying. Arrange your study area so that while sitting at the study table, you cannot see any picture, souvenirs, or blotters with football schedules on them. Face your study table to the wall, not looking into the room or out the window. A book can seem more interesting if it competes only with bare surroundings. Eliminate all interesting sounds—popular music, television programs and conversations—during study hours. Arrange with fellow students to set up a few house rules to maintain quiet periods restricted for study.

In spite of these precautions some sudden sound or movement is bound to occur and will naturally tend to be distracting and affect comprehension (238). The student has two means of adjusting to such events: (1) He can deliberately return his attention to his schoolwork as soon as possible after the sudden sound occurs. If the sound seems particularly interesting, he can avoid such an interruption by challenging himself to keep at his work for the designated study period. (2) He can try to "block out" such distracting events. We have already discussed facing a wall while studying so that moving or otherwise eye-catching objects will not be seen. On the other hand, it is difficult to block out sudden sounds. In this case, many students try playing "mood music" on a phonograph or radio as a means of blocking out such distracting noises.

Students differ in their reactions to this use of music (80, 235). Sometimes it becomes a source of disagreement between roommates, so some evidence should be given concerning the conditions under which music may help (129). In one experiment, college students took a reading test and were then assigned to three groups of equal reading ability (159). Each group then took another equivalent reading test under a different condition: one group read while "classical" music was played, another group read while popular vocal music was played, and the third or control group read under conditions of the initial test, *i.e.*, while no music was played. It was found that the group reading with classical music read as well as the control group, but that the group reading with popular music comprehended only about half as well. In still another experiment (23) students did mathematics problems (1) under noisy conditions, (2) while a humorous conversation was carried on, and (3) under quiet conditions. As might be expected only the second situation caused difficulty, and it did so particularly for students who typically receive grades below their level of ability. It is easy to understand how a popular song or an interesting conversation might interfere with comprehension—they are so much more interesting. If one has an ability "to *not* attend closely" to music while studying, the playing of nonvocal "background" music may be a help, but for those who like to listen to music when they hear it, even classical music will be a distraction.

It is best to study in a quiet place, if possible, because the effort it takes to keep one's mind on his work demands extra energy and is fatiguing. Productivity can, however, remain high even under noisy conditions (157, 416). Thus, in one experiment students took one form of an intelligence test under normal conditions, and another form while bells and buzzers rang, lights flashed, barrels were rolled about on the floor above, and so on (176). The students scored equally well under the two conditions, but their behavior and reports indicated that they became much more fatigued under the noisy conditions. Although not attending to pleasant music might seem to take less energy, it still may be interesting enough so that the effort to keep one's mind on a lesson will be tiring.

Figure 10. Distracting and nondistracting study conditions. (Courtesy of Ohio State University.)

PHYSICAL SURROUNDINGS DURING STUDY PERIODS

Various physical arrangements can also be used to promote concentration. Study habits are developed and set in motion not only by time-use habits (discussed earlier), but also by keeping the same surroundings every time one studies. It has been found that if the same situation is always associated with studying, a student becomes conditioned to concentrating on his studies whenever he is in that situation. A frequently used example of this phenomenon is the manner in which a standard situation promotes sleep: Before going to bed one may not feel particularly sleepy, but changing into bed clothes, lying down on a soft pillow under the blankets, and turning out the light all produce a combination of stimuli to which people are conditioned to respond by going to sleep. Note how much harder it is to go to sleep in a strange bed and surroundings. Similarly, when studying, if a student studies the same subject in the same place at the same time every weekday, the surroundings will tend to suggest study and, therefore, help concentration. In addition, it seems evident that the place in which one studies should not also be used for letter writing, card playing, daydreaming, and so forth.

Posture can also produce stimuli that remind you of work; other postures may suggest relaxation. Take a cue from the way people behave when listening to an interesting lecture—they sit erect or even strain forward to hear each idea. Similarly, it is advisable to sit erect in a straight chair while at the study table. It is even a good practice (and not bad etiquette) to put your elbows on the table while studying. Studying demands an attitude of active work; using the posture just mentioned helps to maintain this attitude. Relaxing in an easy chair, on the other hand, is not conducive to concentration. Worst of all is dressing in pajamas before starting to study in the evening and then lying on the sofa or the bed while studying. The student, conditioned to go to sleep when in this garb and position, will have difficulty concentrating. If he learns to stay awake under these conditions, he may also tend to stay awake when he retires. Yet extended series of observations of how college students study in their dormitory rooms have shown that 47 percent study while dressed in pajamas and 41 percent try to study while lying in bed (137, 162).

ARRANGEMENT OF WORKING MATERIALS

Allow adequate space for all the materials you will have to use, and collect them before starting to study, so that they will be at hand when needed. Kraehenbuehl concluded, on the basis of a study of the needs of over 2300 students at the University of Illinois, that the "desk should be, for a single individual, approximately 30 by 48 inches in size" (204).

IMPORTANCE OF LIGHTING TO STUDY

Poor lighting is an unnecessary cause of fatigue in studying. Good lighting has three characteristics: (1) adequate and well-distributed illumination, (2) absence of glare, and (3) placement in order not to shine in the eyes. Kraehenbuehl's survey of the kinds of lights students use showed that only about 5 percent would be considered satisfactory in these terms (204). Gooseneck lamps and those with "cute" shades were the most frequently used lights and were among the poorest in lighting efficiency. Even when lamps approved by the Illumination Engineering Society were provided by one university, only 65 percent of the students studied under good lighting conditions because of their tendency to study on their beds, and so on (162).

Many studies of the effect of lighting on reading efficiency have been made; all agree that without an even distribution of light (e.g., indirect, diffused, or fluorescent lighting) it is difficult to get optimum lighting conditions (372, 406). There should not be too much contrast between the lighting on one's work and that on the surroundings; there should be an over-all illumination in the room of at least 5 foot-candles.[3] One should never study with a single gooseneck lamp over the book and with the rest of the room dark. Be careful not to have a strong light that produces glare on the pages of your book or that shines into your eyes. These studies also suggest that with such light distribution, about 15 or 20 foot-candles of light are necessary for reading with the least visual fatigue, but that increasing illumination beyond this amount will not further decrease visual fatigue (313, 372). If your illumination is inadequate and you wish to impress your landlord, the following clause, written into each housing contract at one university, may be of use: "Each man, if he so desires, is entitled to 100 watts of electric light."

Since the gooseneck lamp is so frequently the one study lamp that is available, the following suggestion is given for making it more effective. Face the lamp toward the wall at your side but tipped slightly upward and place a shiny white sheet on the wall to act as a reflector. If necessary, increase the wattage of the bulb and you will have a fairly satisfactory indirect lighting system.

EFFECT OF PHYSIOLOGICAL FACTORS ON CONCENTRATION

Conditions such as temperature, ventilation, and physical fitness have also been suggested as factors affecting ease of concentration. Although little research has been done on the effect of varying temperature on study effectiveness, many students believe that it is more difficult to study when the room is hotter or colder than usual (249). However, in one careful study done in the armed services, two equated groups of 404 men took an intensive four-week course in electronics, in

---

[3] This unit of measure is probably unfamiliar to most students, but the wattage of a lamp, e.g., 50 watts, cannot be used, because the amount of light given off will depend on the distance of the light from the book, the condition of the reflecting surfaces, the age of the lamp, and so on. However, these values can be determined quite easily with an inexpensive light meter similar to those used by photographers. Such a light meter can probably be obtained from your instructor. Although a carefully worked out illumination survey of a room is somewhat involved, sufficient accuracy can be obtained for student use by measuring the illumination that falls directly on the book and on the immediate surroundings. This is done by standing the meter vertical to the surface being read or on the surrounding surface; the candlepower will be indicated by the pointer on the meter. If the amount of light extends beyond 75 foot-candles, the extra metal plate with the small opening can be clipped over the light cell and the resulting reading should be then multiplied by 10.

which one group worked in air-conditioned rooms and the other in normal summer heat (average temperature 81 degrees) (254). It was found that both groups did equally well, although the group without airconditioning thought that its work probably had been adversely affected. A safe conclusion seems to be that equal study effectiveness is possible under the usual temperature variations found in buildings, but that if a student wants to find an excuse for procrastinating or doing less than his best, then a temperature variation from the "ideal" makes a handy excuse.

A relationship also has been found between the general level of physical fitness and grades in college (407). One explanation is that people in poor health feel so immediately worried about their condition that they give a low priority to study, and another is that their energy level is usually so low that it is difficult for them to get much studying done. In addition to this explanation, however, there is evidence that people in excellent health have more zest and energy than those in average health. Thus, the school's program of physical education, health education, and nutritional control of meals contributes to general motivation. Individual efforts along this line can also be helpful.

Under certain physiological conditions even the most physically fit student will find concentration difficult. For instance, immediately after heavy eating or coming into a warm room after exercising or being in cold weather the body makes physiological adjustments conducive to sleep. If you sit quietly reading a book under such conditions, you are likely to go to sleep. Instead, try an activity that will keep you in some action (talking or moving about). Also (and here your time schedule will be of value), you cannot study with full effectiveness after the time your body is conditioned to sleep. Time habits start physiological responses of sleepiness and it then becomes extremely difficult to stay alert while reading.

On the other hand, sometimes in searching for an excuse not to study students reason that they are "too tired" too be effective. In one experiment members of a college football squad took different forms of a difficult reading test in the morning and again in the evening after five hours of hard football practice. This was repeated for four successive days. A control group of on-campus students of equal intelligence also took these same tests in the morning and evening on four days but without extensive physical exercise. The two groups did not differ in reading performance, and the football players, if anything, did better in the evening than in the morning (156). Therefore, if motivated one can read effectively even though physically fatigued.

Motivation

The discussion so far has covered three major factors in improving ability to concentrate: (1) developing effective study skills, (2) developing efficient time habits, and (3) arranging efficient study conditions. Mention has been made of the importance of motivation in developing a willingness to study. In fact, the will to study is probably the most important determinant of effective use of time and of the ability to concentrate. This important topic has so many variables that a separate chapter (Chapter 6) will be devoted to it.

Number of words in this section: 5290

Time when this section was completed: _____

Work rate per minute: _____

Answer the quiz on page 235.

**List your work rate, comprehension accuracy,
   and note-quality rating on page 40.**

Program for Improvement

The following specific activities will help improve your time-use habits and help you arrange more efficient study conditions. Each activity calls for use of an accompanying work sheet, and reference must also be made to the precepts developed earlier in this chapter.

TIME SCHEDULE

The time schedule involves the use of the following work sheet, "Plan of Study, Classes, and Recreation." First, write in those activities for which the time is more or less set—eating, sleeping, class hours, and outside work. Next, indicate the hours during which you expect to study. In doing this be specific; do not just say "Study from 7 to 11," but say "Study algebra from 7 to 8:30" and "Study French from 8:45 to 10." Look back at some of the principles developed earlier in the chapter in assigning these various activities.

Check this proposed time schedule with your instructor and then try it. After using it for a while, you may want to revise it slightly in order to add to its effectiveness; a second work sheet, "Plan of Study, Classes, and Recreation," is provided for that purpose.

Once this general plan is worked out, it must be followed until time habits develop. *This can be accomplished only through constant and consistent use.* Although emergencies reasonably can cause deviations from your time schedule, it can become effective only as you use it until time habits develop. Remember how easy it is to eat and go to bed at specific times; try building similar time habits for studying.

ELIMINATING DISTRACTIONS

It is surprising and enlightening to see how often students are distracted as they study. Seeing this in others may make you more sensitive to distractions in your own case. For the following exercise go to a library and watch an individual for a period of 10 or 15 minutes while he studies. If it is a person in this how-to-study

I. Plan of Study, Classes, and Recreation

	Monday	Tuesday	Wednesday	Thursday	Friday	Saturday	Sunday
7:30[a]							
8:00							
9:00							
10:00							
11:00							
12:00							
12:30							
1:00							
2:00							
3:00							
4:00							
4:30							
5:00							
5:30							
6:00							
6:30							
7:00							
7:30							
8:00							
8:30							
9:00							
9:30							
10:00							
10:30							
11:00							

[a] Use red pencil to indicate classes.

II. Plan of Study, Classes, and Recreation

	Monday	Tuesday	Wednesday	Thursday	Friday	Saturday	Sunday
7:30[a]							
8:00							
9:00							
10:00							
11:00							
12:00							
12:30							
1:00							
2:00							
3:00							
4:00							
4:30							
5:00							
5:30							
6:00							
6:30							
7:00							
7:30							
8:00							
8:30							
9:00							
9:30							
10:00							
10:30							
11:00							

[a] Use red pencil to indicate classes.

Check List of Work Behavior

	Individual "A"	Individual "B"
Work activities:		
Reading		
Note-taking		
Self-recitation		
Working problems		
Distractions:		
Conversation		
Aimless looking around		
Aimless leafing through books		
Students going by		
Applying makeup		
Attracted by certain individuals		
Daydreaming		
Reading or writing letters		
Arranging hair and clothes		
Miscellaneous		
Time use:		
About what proportion of the time was spent in studying		

class, your checking will later be of use to him. It is better to choose a person at some distance from you, so that your observing will not be noticed by him. Every time there is a change in his behavior, even though it is but a brief glance around the room, tabulate it on the Check List of Work Behavior given above. This check list is similar to the list in Table 2 (p. 83): an interesting comparison can be made with it when you have completed your tabulation. You may want to make a brief study of individual differences in distraction by observing and tabulating the behavior of several individuals.

Although it is not convenient to tabulate each thing that tends to distract your own studying, you should make mental note of the things that take your attention away from studying. Possibly you can arrange with a friend to observe your studying and check the number of times you are distracted, giving some indication of the causes; or one of the other students in this course can use you as a subject for observation and show his ratings to you when he finishes.

ROOM CONDITIONS

Survey your own study room for evidence of surroundings that are distracting. Are there pictures, souvenirs, and so forth, near you when you study? Does your study table face into the room or out a window? Is a radio played or do students talk while you try to study? Also survey your room for adequacy of lighting, ventilation, and clear table space for study.

On the basis of the earlier self-evaluation questions, the above checks, and your own observations, fill in the Evaluation of Study Conditions and Plans for Correction chart that follows and note what you plan to do about them. Be specific as to difficulties and plans.

Evaluation of Study Conditions and Plans for Correction

Area	What's wrong	Specific plans
Auditory distractions in room		
Visual distractions in room		
Personal worries and interests that distract		
Auditory distractions in library		
Visual distractions in library		
Constancy of study conditions to stimulate study		
Posture while studying		
Adequacy of lighting		
Adequacy of work space		
Availability of materials		

CHAPTER 6

Motivation to study

Many students complain that if only they were interested in their courses, they could concentrate much more easily when studying. Others note that if they were sure what they wanted to do in life, they would then see the value of their courses and so be able to study more easily. Still other students put the burden of the problem on others and suggest that if instructors and textbooks were more interesting, studying would not be as difficult. Finally, many students note that if there were not so many fascinating things to do in the world and if their friends would not constantly entice them away from their studies, it would be easier to keep their minds on their work. In brief, students recognize that it is easier to concentrate on interesting activities than on uninteresting ones, and they wonder how to make studying more interesting.

As a first step in attacking this problem it is important to determine who is responsible for making courses interesting. Although teachers and textbook writers do strive to make their ideas clear and to show their application, they are actually not obligated to make their material fascinating. We may expect a professional entertainer to work hard to hold our attention and, at times, almost may dare him to make us laugh or applaud; we cannot, however, expect this of a teacher. The taxpayer, the college administration, even parents expect the college teacher to present his material clearly and efficiently and to be helpful in answering questions, but it is the student's function to make the effort to learn that material. As a matter of fact, most students dislike a teacher who tries to become popular by telling stories and jokes; they feel he is not fulfilling his teaching role.

Most students readily accept the responsibility of becoming interested in academic work, but they are puzzled about the exact methods to increase their interest. Many hope that an easy method can be found—if only there were a pill which would arouse academic interests, or if only making a vocational choice would

94

increase the attractiveness of courses, or if only the fascinating social activities of college would stay dormant when one needs to study. But no such simple solution is available; increasing academic motivation demands hard work in several areas. Not much progress is made, however, merely by realizing that the task is difficult. Let us see if we can help in this chapter by clarifying several aspects of the problem.

Studies of Motivational Factors

Many studies have been made of possible factors (in addition to academic aptitude) that affect academic achievement. Motivation is obviously one important variable. Various studies (38, 87) show that enthusiasm for learning and a general valuing of academic achievement contribute significantly to achievement. However, to deal more adequately with this area we need to make a more elaborate analysis of the skills, attitudes, and personality characteristics underlying motivation or lack of it. As a shortcut we will briefly summarize a great many experiments in Tables 3 and 4. The first of these tables summarizes a series of experiments in which underachievers and overachievers were compared on various tests of study habits and attitudes. The second table gives similar comparisons using various personality tests.

The usual test of study habits and attitudes asks a great many questions about a student's current use of time, attitudes toward specific situations, study procedures used, and so on. When the answers to these many items are correlated and then subjected to the rather elaborate statistical procedure of factor analysis, it is possible to find the few factors or components underlying the entire series of tests. This more limited list simplifies discussion. Table 3 summarizes a series of carefully done studies in which groups of underachieving, normal-achieving, and overachieving students (but of equal intelligence) were compared. The labels in each of the several columns in the table show how each study found similar factors. Column 1 refers to study skills, such as those discussed in Chapters 2 and 3 and in other later chapters. Column 2 refers to time-use skills covered in Chapter 4. The other four columns in Table 3 help give a basis for organizing our discussion of motivation.

Columns 3 and 4 in Table 3 deal with value systems. Column 3 pertains to the general vertical development of mature attitudes, which differentiate youngsters, adolescents, and adults, e.g., dependence-independence, civic involvement, vocational preparation, mate selection, and so on. Schoolwork is more related to the upper end of this developmental scale than it is to adolescent valuing of social and athletic pursuits. Column 4 represents a horizontal differentiation of values; for some areas further education is important, e.g., professional preparation, but for many areas of employment, for falling in love, and so on, it seems to have little direct relevance. So, another aspect is to explore with mature young adults to what extent a college education is relevant to their needs.

Columns 5 and 6 in Table 3 indicate another common source of motivational

TABLE 3 Factors Found Important in Differentiating Underachievers, Normal-Achievers, and Overachievers on Tests of Study Habits and Attitudes

Researcher	Column 1	Column 2	Column 3	Column 4	Column 5	Column 6
Borow, 1947	Study skills	Personal efficiency	Mature values	Curricular adjustment	Mental health	Personal relations
Brown and Holtzman, 1967	Work methods	Delay avoidance	Education acceptance	Teacher approval		
Carter, 1951	Mechanics of study	Planning; deliberation	Morale; self-confidence	School values		
Taylor and Farquhar, 1964		Activity pattern	Self-value; dependence–independence	Goal orientation	Academic anxiety	Authority relations; interpersonal relations
Waters, 1964[a]	Study skills		Motivation; knowledge of goals	Academic achievement goal	Adjustment	

[a] Water's analysis also included biographical items concerning characteristics of the family and home. These clustered as a separate factor as they did also in two other studies (57, 170b) to indicate that family traditions, experiences, and expectancies do much to shape attitudes expressed in the other factors in this table.

difficulty for students. College is relevant enough to their needs, and they want to study, but other more pressing personal problems get in the way—these may be personal anxieties (column 5) or difficulties in handling relations with other people (column 6).

Creaser tried a different approach by studying kinds of individuals rather than clusters of test items (92). He found five "kinds" of students: the Diligent, the Sophisticated, the Unconcerned, the Anxious, and the Conflicted. This approach is similar to the one used in Table 3. The Diligent student has good study skills and time use; the Sophisticated represents the student with mature interest in academic work—he knows where he is going; The Unconcerned is the immature student still engrossed in adolescent pursuits; and the Anxious and Conflicted represent two kinds of personal distress preventing these students from attending to their schoolwork.

One study offers information concerning which factors listed in Table 3 differentiate among students who underachieve, achieve normally, and overachieve (102), and another study analyzes which factors differentiate between students of marginal aptitude for college who persist through the freshman year and those who drop out early (135). Both studies used the Borow College Inventory of Academic Adjustment and found that the three factors differentiated best were: (1) personal efficiency, (2) mature values, and (3) curricular adjustment. In brief, mature students who are interested in schoolwork and who have efficient study habits do better.

Other researchers have used various personality tests to differentiate among underachievers, normal-achievers, and overachievers. Some of their results are summarized in Table 4. It will be noted that high achievers tend to be mature, like school, and are conforming in behavior. On the other hand, underachievers tend to be immature, hostile, nonconforming, and procrastinators. Part of this aggressiveness represents acting-out behavior in becoming emancipated from dependence on parents, which is transferred to all authority; part of it is due to problems of personal maladjustment. Assisting underachievers with these problems calls for counseling help.

It will be noted in these studies that achievers tend to be conformists, e.g., they do the things that are valued by the educational establishment. We might call them "organization men." Although underachievers tend to be nonconformists, the dimension is not that simple. Some of the most mature and able of college students, i.e., many present-day "activists," are nonconformists and work strenuously and creatively to change educational institutions in order to make them more attuned to social needs. Recent studies of campus activists (338, 402) show that while some may be immature and have acting-out personality problems, the really effective ones often seem more mature than the "organization men" and represent future sources of political and community leadership. The problem for college administrators is to discriminate between the mature and the immature activists. The problem is even more difficult for any reader who has a strong urge to "fight city hall," e.g., is his hostility an immature personality problem or a mature leader-

TABLE 4   Personality Characteristics of Overachievers and Underachievers

Researcher	Student sample	High achievers	Low achievers
Anderson and Kuntz, 1959	Probation		Defensive
Brown, 1960	Early dropouts		Irresponsible and nonconforming (men); withdrawn, depressed, social isolate (women)
Duff and Siegel, 1960	Achievers versus underachievers	Future oriented; positive attitude toward school; more conforming	More interested in sports and social life
Goldburgh and Penney, 1962	Underachievers		
Gough, 1964	Achievers	Responsible; socially mature; independent and adaptive achieving; efficient in the use of personal resources	Hostile toward parents and authority
Holland, 1960	Achievers	Dependent; serious; persistent; responsible; submissive; self-sufficient; self-controlled	
Horrall, 1957	Underachievers		
Irvin, 1967	Achievers	Adequate self-concept; high need for achieving	Hostile and aggressive toward authority figures
Lum, 1960	Overachievers versus underachievers	Like to study; self-confident; work under pressure	
Oakland, 1969	Achievers	Good study habits; academic motivation; social conformity	
Powell and Jourard, 1963	Underachievers		Lack of emancipation from parents; immature
Schroeder, 1965	Achievers	High conflict avoidance	
Sprinthall, 1964	Achievers	Similar values to those of teachers	
Todd, Terrel, and Frank, 1962	Underachievers		Less need to achieve; undecided on vocation; see little value in courses; lower expectancy on grades
Watley, 1965	Early dropouts		Moody; irritable; depressed; withdrawn; nonconforming
Whiteley and Hummel, 1965	Achievers	More adaptive in strategies that cope with conflict; more mature, goal oriented	
Wilson and Morrow, 1962	Achievers	Higher aspirations in grades, career, and income; See grades as compatible with being a "regular guy"	

ship role? Obviously most will place themselves in the latter category, but some thought might be given to other possible motivational sources.

In Chapter 1 it was pointed out that students today typically are reaching higher levels of achievement than a generation ago, *i.e.*, achievement tests now have much tougher norms. As noted above, many college activists who are participating in mature reform of societal conditions represent high levels of civic responsibility. Many other symptoms also show a general increased seriousness today; for example, a survey of 200 libraries showed that circulation of adult nonfiction books increased 29 percent during a recent five-year period (7). One effect of this higher developmental level is that it establishes a contrast with laggards in developmental maturity of the same age that is all the more obvious. More students, then, have become aware of and bothered by alienation from the world and are interested in seeking clarification of developing goals.

The changing world also raises questions about the present effectiveness of colleges and universities in bringing about desired educational goals. Some studies show that college programs are not fully relevant or effective. Many of the differences found in comparing colleges, or freshmen and seniors from the same college, result from the fact that students select colleges of their own type rather than are molded into that type, and many of the changes seem to be due mostly to noncurricular aspects of college life or to typical changes occurring with age (110, 203, 269, 283, 284).

Nonetheless, recent comparisons of the same individuals' scores on various tests taken as freshmen and again as seniors do show that changes take place during the four years of college (27, 117*b*, 178, 179, 184, 216, 358, 408). The results show that seniors are less authoritarian, use more reflective and critical thinking, have increased autonomy (less deference, abasement, and dependence), have a decrease in stereotyped thinking, and have an increase in aesthetic valuing.

As might be expected, these effects are not equally distributed among the entire college population. Students of high academic aptitude tend to make more changes in a psychologically positive direction than do students with less academic aptitude (285). Further, one study (117*a*) showed that in a college noted for its effective program, while one group of students made changes in desired mature directions during the four years, another group made changes in directions that had disquieting implications: an increase in authoritarianism, more withdrawal from social contacts, higher nonconformity, and, in general, a movement in a less healthy direction that might well lead to more divorces and job turnovers.

These two groups did not differ in academic aptitudes nor in majors studied. This type of finding raises at least two questions: (1) In what ways can a college more effectively work with a broader range of students? (2) What types of students who possibly should not be in college need help in making more effective choices?

Related to this has been the finding that academic accomplishment, as measured by grade-point average and as predicted by academic aptitude tests, is not necessarily related to accomplishment, talent, or creativity in many other areas (22, 395).

Achievement in many areas tends to be rather specific, and present emphasis on course achievement may not always be relevant. (On the other hand, achievement in similar activities is often predictive of later performance in that general area.) Again, attention needs to be given to making the total college program more effective, and some students may correctly decide that a college program is not best suited to their needs.

This has been a long discussion of the many motivational factors in academic achievement (beyond academic aptitude, study skills, and so on). The topic is quite complex. We have shown that underachievers tend to be immature and often have personal problems that affect their interest in schoolwork. Achievers and overachievers, on the other hand, tend to be mature for their age, see value in schoolwork, and are effective in working with others. It has also been shown that while college work and academic achievement are highly relevant for many, they may not be for many other equally mature individuals. Therefore, the remainder of this chapter will try to show ways that can help the reader sort out his own thinking about his own goals.

Possible Factors in Poor Motivation

One way to illumine the problem of motivation is to look at some of the reasons why students are *not* interested in schoolwork. Such exploration gives a basis for work on improvement in specific areas. Since this exploration will require extended discussion, it will help to list the topics of the following section and then discuss each in turn. Reasons for poor motivation are: (1) really preferring something else to attending college, (2) attending college as a means to an end other than learning, (3) distracting personal problems, (4) laziness, (5) lack of vocational choice, and (6) continuing immature values.

SOMETHING OTHER THAN COLLEGE PREFERRED

The usual approach toward discussing motivation for college work is to point out only the positive values of going to college. However, it must be recognized that some college students actually are not interested, and rightly so, in doing college work. For some, college attendance may not represent the best step toward attaining happiness and success. Encouraging these students to change their desires in order to conform to those of most other students is wrong; the goal should be to help them clarify what it is they really want to do and to help them make plans to carry this out. Some might prefer a business or trade school. These schools provide training for well-paid occupations for which some people have the ability and interest. Such training usually can be obtained in less time than four years of college, and it often results in faster advancement for these individuals than if they had attended college. In other instances, direct entry into work may be the best path toward success. In our democracy, various forms of education do not have superiority over each other; each prepares the learner for various aspects of life to which different types of persons are best suited.

It is not the purpose of this discussion to discourage anyone who really wants a college education from continuing in college, but it must be recognized that some students go to college primarily because their high school friends are going and because, at the moment, they do not give much thought to any other possibility. All through high school they have heard of the value of continuing their education and think, therefore, that college is more of the same. Only later do they realize that college work is not a program for every adolescent as is high school work; many of them want to begin to do something that is more relevant to their needs.

Others think that college will prepare them for the type of work they want to do but once they enter, they find that the curriculum is not at all what they want. Many students who are interested in electronics, for example, think that the best source of training is to major in electrical engineering in college but once they begin find that this program is abstract and theoretical and does not deal with the repair and assembly of equipment in which they are interested. In brief, some effort should be made to determine your occupational aims; this clarification will lead either to more effort or to a desire to leave college in order to find a more relevant program.

Sometimes a student realizes that it is a waste of time for him to continue in college but feels that it would be a disgrace to leave. In this case, it is only necessary to point out that the majority of students who enter college are not graduated; most of them leave voluntarily (333). One study of the academic history of freshmen entering a college at Ohio State University found that only 35 percent were graduated from the same college they had entered as freshmen, 17 percent transferred to other colleges in the university but did not all graduate, 33 percent withdrew voluntarily from the university to turn to other means of preparation, and 15 percent were dismissed. (See Figure II.3 on page 258.)

COLLEGE AS A MEANS TO OTHER ENDS

The next motivational group to be discussed is not so much interested in schoolwork as such as it is interested in the rewards obtained from being able to stay in school and graduate. Some students want to stay in school in order *not* to go to work or to be drafted. Others want to avoid probation so they will be able to participate in athletic, fraternity, extracurricular, or social activities. Still others want a college degree only because they have heard that it is necessary in order to obtain a good job and are not very interested in what they have to do in order to get the degree. In all of these instances a student may worry about his academic status and wish that studying were easier, but with his motivational pattern study will only be a chore and other interests frequently will act as distractions.

All students like social and extracurricular activities, and good students are usually active leaders in them. However, when these interests are the primary concern of a student, and when he has little or no academic interest, then college administrators are not very interested in having him stay on the campus—particularly with the sharp increase in the numbers applying for admission to college.

Later, as an adult, this person may see the need for more academic learning; if he does, an adult education program will be available to him.

The discussion thus far has emphasized the problems of students who really are uninterested in studying, but this is not true of most students. Most college students want very much to learn from their studies, but for various reasons have trouble in concentrating and need help. The remainder of our discussion will focus on possible causes of the troubles of such students.

PERSONAL PROBLEMS THAT DISTRACT FROM STUDY

In spite of a very real desire to study, many students have a particular personal problem that seems so demanding and immediate that they have trouble studying. For some it may be a health problem; for others, a financial worry, a home problem, a social difficulty, or a personality problem. Not only does the problem area differ among students but within an area such as health problems the nature of each person's difficulty is so unique that it demands individual attention. A discussion of all of these problem areas is beyond the scope of this text. Some attention can be given, however, to pointing out the importance of obtaining help for these problems. In addition, possible sources of help will be investigated, since many students do not know about some of the student personnel resources on their own campus.

Many students, while admitting the importance of these difficult, distracting problems, hope to be able to put them out of their minds while they study but recognize that they have a hard time doing so. Rather than try to ignore them they should attempt to find a solution to these problems or, at least, they should attempt to find a way of reducing their immediate insistent need. Students then can turn their attention to schoolwork. Recognizing this fact, colleges usually provide student personnel services specifically directed toward helping students with their problems. The following paragraphs discuss some problem areas of students and available student personnel services.

1. Problems of health. Although adolescence is usually one of the healthiest periods of life, students occasionally develop illnesses whose pain or cause for worry makes it difficult to study. Possibly because they fear what the diagnosis may be or worry about medical expenses, many students put off doing anything about their illnesses. They try to study because they must and because they want "to forget their troubles," but they find that their minds wander back to their illnesses because they are of such immediate importance. The university administration recognizes this problem and accepts its obligation to maintain students' well-being, and, therefore, has set up a Health Service—the first of the remedial personnel services developed by colleges. This service insures that adequate diagnostic aid is immediately available when illness strikes so that students may more quickly return to normal college activities. The regular collection of a health fee (and frequently of hospital insurance) at registration time insures that finances need not prevent any students from receiving medical help. Why, then, do some students unfortunate enough to be ill take inadequate steps to solve their problem? Some students hesitate to use this very helpful service because of dislike of medicine, unwillingness to face a possible unpleasant diagnosis, or hope that somehow "everything will come out all right." The best solution for such a student is to get his free diagnostic service; at least he can then respond to definite information rather than to his fears, and remedial help may prove not to be as difficult as he has feared.

2. Financial problems.   College is a time of incurring major expenses, as well as a time when young adults want to take on responsibility for their own care and support. In addition, other obligations may occur, *e.g.*, need to help with parental support or other family obligations, which put heavy financial pressures on some students. Frequently these students have saved money from summer jobs or have part-time jobs in school to help with this burden, but for other students the suddenness of incurring major obligations may be a cause for distracting worry in college. Again, the college administration recognizes that financial difficulties occur and has set up types of Financial Aid Offices to help with loans, part-time work, scholarships, and so on. Surprisingly, many students do not know how to go about obtaining financial aid when they need it; if you are one, inquire from your instructor or college advisor about necessary aid.

3. Problems of acceptance by other students.   Ability to get along with others is important in our crowded world. Every person wants to be liked, to become a member of some group, and to be selected for positions of leadership. With the adult world eager to have students socially adjusted and with the students themselves striving to be accepted, it would seem that little difficulty would occur. The evidence is to the contrary, however. Worries about not being liked or about not being popular are among those frequently mentioned by college students.

Although a person must adjust to many types of groups, his adjustment to his fellow students presents the most problems at the time he enters college. At this time, too, some students are going through the last stages of emancipation or are becoming independent. If a student feels secure in his social relationships, he will feel free to devote a large part of his efforts to study; if not, he is apt to be distracted from his studies.

The social structure on a campus is much different from what most persons suppose. The actual pattern is well illustrated by the results of a study, in which a sociometry test was administered in two colleges and each student was asked to list his friends (up to 15 in number) (106). When the number of choices that each person received was tabulated, the distributions that appear in Figure 11 were obtained: That is, most students received less than the average number of votes, and many received almost no votes. Although each one would like to be a popular person, most students are actually at the stage of feeling "a feller needs a friend." Furthermore, other research shows how strongly such isolates feel about their position of isolation. Whereas most students tend to pick as desired associates individuals who are somewhere near their own level of popularity, isolates and near-isolates pick not those who pick them, but the most popular individuals (as symbols of their frustrated desires).

An analysis of the factors related to popularity indicate that differences are not a result of accidents of location in the dormitory nor, particularly, to family status; differences seem in great part to spring from the personality characteristics of the individuals themselves (304, 305). What, then, are these characteristics? Surprisingly enough, intelligence is not related to popularity in college; that is, everyone is bright enough to be inoffensive to at least some other people. The factors that are related seem to be of two types: the external niceties of behavior, which make a person easy to get along with, and the worth of the person as an individual.

The niceties of behavior usually include such things as appearance, social skills, and good behavior. Though actually they are not as important as most people judge them to be, these aspects are used by everyone in making judgments about others

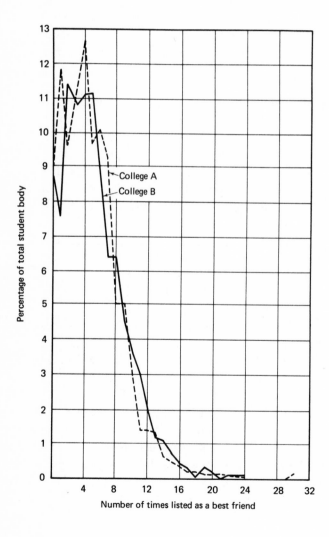

Figure 11. Distribution of popularity at two colleges (N = 1275 and 1957). (Adapted from 106).

based on first impressions. The first impression is particularly important in college because an older and different cultural group sets standards that may differ from those to which one has been accustomed at home. Freshmen become quite involved in learning to dress correctly, to use the right "language," and to know about popular activities. The observant student learns much from watching and talking with others. Most colleges, however, also provide courses, activities, and counseling concerning such things as grooming, social skills, etiquette, activities, and so on; if your Student Handbook does not provide this information, ask your instructor about it.

The judgment of worth of the individual is even more important to popularity but is more difficult to write about because of its complexity and its unique nature for each individual. What you are is the sum of many aspects of development toward which you, your parents, and your school have been working for years. Sociometric studies, such as the one described above, show that well-liked people tend to know more, to be more mature, and to be better adjusted; similarly the isolate tends to be less competent, less mature, and more maladjusted. These aspects relate to two topics to be discussed later: obtaining help with feelings of personal insecurity and inferiority and coping with problems of increasing maturity.

4. Personal problems.   Probably we all have personal problems of one type or another. In addition to worries about health, finance, and social acceptance there are frequently more personal worries about mental health, anxiety, inexplicable behavior, and so on. These worries make us inefficient by distracting our attention, by preventing normal, healthy habits of living, and by giving us a dour outlook on life. Quite often, in spite of our resolve to stop thinking about them, they keep plaguing us. Unfortunately research shows that personality maladjustment is related to academic underachievement (103, 322, 351). However, other research indicates that both individual and group counseling helps not only with the personal problems, but also with grades (122, 273, 327, 352, 369).

It is interesting to observe the way in which people sometimes try to cover up limitations that they may have; at times they seem even to be trying to fool themselves. Studies (32, 33) that have been made of people's unwillingness to accept their own limitations show that they sometimes set such extremely high standards for themselves so that they can deny any wholeheartedness in trying to achieve them, or they "protect" themselves by stating that high achievement is obtained through luck rather than effort, or they are unwilling to risk being wrong or doing poorly. Unwillingness to realistically accept one's limitations is characteristic of the underachiever. So one step to avoid this is openly to analyze one's strengths and weaknesses rather than deny them and then set up a constructive program.

Worries and fears can be dealt with so that either they are eliminated or adjustments are made. Psychologists have found that if a person talks over his problems with an adequately trained counselor, he will be benefited in two ways. First, talking over a problem with another person tends to "get it out of one's system," with quite beneficial results to one's peace of mind. Second, in spite of the common belief that each person's problems are unique, psychologists have found that most problems have certain common characteristics and that people tend to react in certain standard ways to them. With this understanding of problems and of their good and poor solutions, psychologists are able to assist people in analyzing the nature of their worries and in handling them.

Many colleges have trained people on their staff who specialize in this personal counseling. Your instructor can tell you who these counseling specialists are. Because almost everyone is reticent about having his personal affairs and problems generally known, these specialists keep all information given them strictly confidential.

LAZINESS AS A POSSIBLE SOURCE OF POOR MOTIVATION

Some students wonder if their lack of interest in studying can be due to "laziness," which they think may be inherited. After all, people sometimes say that someone "was just born lazy," and find it comforting to blame their own lack of academic motivation on their ancestors. Drives for food, water, air, curiosity, and sex are inherent in man. Eventually, conditioned learning gives rise to a wide range of interests in each individual. What is often termed "laziness" may be merely a lack of interest in immediately available school activities; students who exhibit such behavior nevertheless, may be quite interested in such other things as social activities. Laziness as such is not inherited.

Reasons other than lack of interest have also been suggested as explanations for some students being unable to develop interest in schoolwork. That is, some students not only are not interested in schoolwork but seem actively to resist it (13); in some cases it has been found that refusal to study has unconsciously been identified with solving another need—punishment of an overly demanding parent, for example—and so lack of study is actually fostered (36). One study showed that underachieving students (for their intellectual level) had difficulty in conforming to regulations and in being willing to take action in many situations outside of class work (62). For instance, fewer underachieving than overachieving students of equal intelligence bothered to check on a list of questions and answers prepared by an instructor, which he promised to include in a quiz, and fewer offered to participate in such activities as campus surveys of student opinion. Such lack of initiative would be considered a learned personality characteristic.

Finally, some conditions of complete lassitude are due to medical conditions, such as low metabolic rate, hookworm infestation, etc. In each of these instances counseling or medical help may be needed.

LACK OF VOCATIONAL CHOICE AS A SOURCE OF POOR MOTIVATION

Students may work inefficiently in college because they believe they are poorly motivated without a definite vocational goal. Assistance with your vocational planning may remove this distraction and increase your motivation for study. Research shows that students who have decided on a major study more, persist longer in college, and get better grades than those who are undecided on their major (134, 135, 413).

Psychologists cannot determine the specific vocation that a person should enter, but they can help the student to see his abilities, knowledge, and interests as they are related to the demands of various occupations. Further, they can assist him in clarifying his thinking in terms of these fields of knowledge and can show him job-hunting techniques. The final decision of job selection, however, must be left to the student.

Two types of blocks sometimes cause difficulty in choosing the best vocation: (1) Many students believe that they surely know their own abilities, and the nature of various kinds of work, and (2) they feel it is immature to change a vocational choice late in high school or afterwards. That many students do not know their own abilities or the demands of various occupations is shown by the following: many high school students with quite low intellectual ability want to prepare for professions requiring high intelligence, and about 40 percent of high school seniors indicate a desire to enter professions that can absorb only about 3 percent of the population. As for changing vocational choice, it need only be pointed out that a large group (but not a majority) of college students change their vocational choice while in college (64, 244). Studies of adults in professional work and of those who achieve eminence (the groups least likely to change occupations) showed that over one-half changed their vocational choice in or after college (306, 341).

Colleges maintain machinery for helping students to change their majors, and, if students have abilities in nonacademic areas, for helping students enter training outside of college. It is mistaken to believe that it is a disgrace to change one's mind about a chosen vocation. As a matter of fact, so many students change their major field that most colleges do not have students formally declare their major until they are juniors. If, on the other hand, a student has chosen a field and is satisfied with it, there is obviously no need to change it.

Research (93) on the many facets of development of youngsters from the fifth grade through high school shows that maturity of vocational and educational thinking are merely aspects of a general dimension of maturity. Thinking through and making a vocational choice not only provides the advantages of that decision, but it also contributes a bit to one's general progress in maturing. It also follows that if the less mature adolescent is the one apt not to have made a vocational decision, then one step in deciding on a major or a vocation may involve some general problems of growing up.

IMMATURITY AS A SOURCE OF DIFFICULTY

A sixth source of poor academic motivation is the continuation of adolescent attitudes toward school into early adult life. Although no one wants to think of himself as immature, every person has some early attitudes, which he carries into his early adult life without much notion of their source. The following discussion deals with some of these continuing attitudes that get in the way of liking to study.

If you cannot see their personal application, possibly you can see how they help explain the behavior of some of your friends.

1. Childhood interests tend to center about immediate rather than delayed goals. A nickel in the hand for candy is preferred to a dime in the bank toward a pair of roller skates. As a person grows older he becomes more aware of the importance of delayed goals. Yet, some adolescents, although highly valuing ultimate school success, are unable to resist putting off their studying when other more immediately interesting activities present themselves, *e.g.*, going along with friends to a movie instead of studying for a midterm the next day. The mature adult has the ability to weigh values in terms of his own future welfare and can plan his time and direct his energies accordingly (190, 200, 255). Such a person may study because of the future social or vocational values of the subject. It must be admitted, however, that even adults have difficulty making textbook study as interesting as some immediate goal or pleasure; for the less mature it is even more difficult.

One common misconception about good students needs to be corrected here. Good students can have good times and do not spend all their time in drudgery. For instance, fewer good than poor students answer "yes" to the question, "Do your studies tend to prevent you from participating in social activities?" An analysis of the activities of Phi Beta Kappa students shows that they belong to and are leaders in more extracurricular activities than the average student (267).

2. Young children seem to be naturally curious about the nature of things; by the time they have become high school students, however, many become hesitant about asking questions. Sometimes this reticence is a result of their having previously received too many inadequate answers; sometimes it is a result of a dislike for admitting a deficiency; at other times questions are withheld for fear they will be interpreted by other students as a form of "apple polishing." Each of these instances is unfortunate, for, as will be noted later, learning can be fun. Note how avidly graduate students, medical students, or law students read about a topic of interest to them. Are you still at the stage in which you think that being seen with a book is a handicap?

3. Personal qualities that are thought important differ at various age levels. Physical prowess is admired by young children. During adolescence physical appearance and good fellowship are apt to be weighed heavily because these traits are considered important for acceptance by a fraternity or by the opposite sex. Adults also consider the reaction of others to themselves as important but are apt to put it in a better perspective. Intellectual competence is given its greatest emphasis among adults. These trends are illustrated in Figure 12, which shows the relative degree to which various traits are admired at different grade levels.

Since a person will work hardest for what he most values, college courses may or may not appeal to a student. For the adult who desires intellectual competence, college work will seem vital and interesting; in one study this was illustrated dramatically by the intense motivation of many war veterans in college (148). At the other end of the distribution are college students who are still adolescently engrossed in belonging to a group and in being esteemed for prowess in high-school-

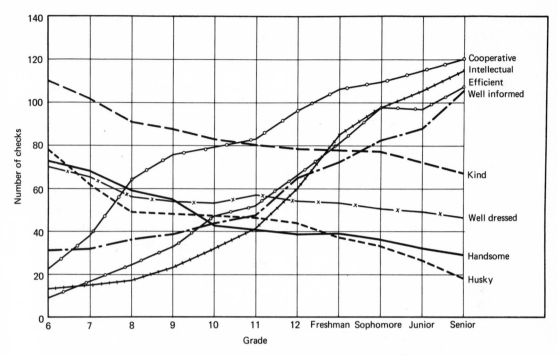

Figure 12. Changes in the degree to which traits are admired at different grade levels. (Adapted from unpublished data of S. L. Pressey.)

like activities. Such individuals are not ready for college work and will not find it interesting. Between these two extremes are the rest of the college students. Research shows that degree of maturity is related to grades (319).

That interest in schoolwork is not the strongest motive in the life of the average student is illustrated by a study comparing how hard students worked for a professor and for a fraternity (201). Ten freshmen fraternity initiates on the last evening of a very strenuous "hell week," were required to spend about two hours in working arithmetic problems; they were told that the tests were a part of their evaluation for admission to the fraternity. Later, 54 students, working under normal classroom conditions, were asked to do the same tasks. The fraternity initiates, although fatigued and harassed, did one-third more problems than the group working under normal classroom conditions.

Another interesting illustration of how differences in motives may influence studying is shown in the grades made by social fraternity initiates before and after initiation and those made by Phi Beta Kappa candidates under the same conditions (214). Fraternity and nonfraternity freshmen were matched in terms of year of matriculation, grade-point average, and hours of credit in the first semester (but *not* in intelligence). The grades of these two groups were then compared through successive semesters. Figure 13 shows that after initiation (based on grades the first semester) the fraternity students never again did as well as their matched colleagues. The broken line is inserted as a reasonable guess as to how well the fraternity students might have done the first semester had they not been interested in becoming eligible for initiation; the difference is about .2 of a grade point. Fraternity initiation standards are a useful stimulus to studying for one semester, but this experiment also shows that many college students are in great part motivated to study for reasons other than interest in knowledge and preparation for work after graduation. The Phi Beta Kappa students, on the other hand, had no such letdown after initiation. One can more nearly assume that they had an interest in learning for learning's sake.

4. A final illustration of the change in interest of a maturing individual that affects college work is the shift from the desire for parental praise to a desire to stand on one's own feet. Opportunity to obtain praise from adults is one reason among many that young children like school. Also, while the child is in school in the early grades the teacher becomes something of a parent substitute, and so the child will work under authoritarian suggestion. During adolescence adult praise becomes less important than praise from one's companions, and there may even be

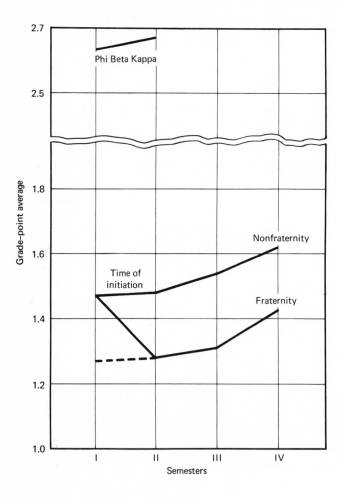

Figure 13. Effect of initiation into a social fraternity and into Phi Beta Kappa on grades in succeeding semesters. (Adapted from 214.)

a reaction against parental authority as the adolescent tries to become an independent adult. Many students unconsciously generalize the object of their rebellion to include any form of superiority—teachers, schoolwork, rules, and law (13). They feel that they know as much as adults; hence, they resent suggestions. Since they believe that they are already fully mature, this stage is characterized by a lack of interest in college work. But it is interesting to note that whereas college sophomores often feel this way, professional and graduate students rarely do.

Adolescents are typically ambivalent. They want to be independent, yet are so used to being told what to do at home and in school that many feel lost in college when someone does not "keep after" them. The writer recalls one student who announced that he had enrolled in the how-to-study course because he needed someone to keep after him since he was away from home. College authorities, however, refuse to be the "voice of conscience" for students.

Why Students Enjoy and Are Interested in Schoolwork

The preceding discussion has emphasized why students have difficulty in being motivated to study. The discussion so far would indicate that studying is one of the most difficult activities in life. Actually, this is not true for most mature students. Many students read with interest far into the night and on week ends in order to find answers to questions, organize a research project, or prepare a paper. Hundreds of millions of books and magazines are sold to adults each year because they *like* to read. It is important, therefore, that the value and pleasure of reading for information be pointed out.

In the first place, everyone is curious about the way things are, the way they have been, and the way they may develop in the future. A child can ask questions of "What?" and "Why?," but adult queries usually concern issues beyond the knowledge of people immediately around them. Only in books can one find answers to many questions at the time one wants to know them.

In addition to simple curiosity about unknown phenomena, every person has many other needs with which reading and knowledge from reading can be of help. Reading helps one prepare for and keep up to date in one's profession; it provides information about home and hobbies; it is a pleasant and often profitable way to fill leisure hours; and, finally, ability to read is a status symbol—every illiterate in our culture has a marked emotional problem growing out of feelings of inferiority about his disability.

This writer does not propose to write at great length about the values of reading, because many of the values are already known and because reading interests differ so much from person to person. In fact, reading is one of the prime ways one can develop his own uniqueness (and, at the same time, discover his kinship with others).

Every college student probably knows that reading can be fun; his difficulty occurs when other things become more threatening, more immediately important, or are easier to do. The problem is to help him find ways to focus his interest in reading (and eliminate distractions) so that attention can be maintained. The suggestions in the next section deal with this topic.

Methods of Focusing Interest on College Work

1. Since the abstract nature of textbooks makes it difficult for them to compete in reference to interest with football schedules, photographs, or talk sessions, you can study better if these distractions are eliminated from the immediate study environment. Methods of eliminating them were discussed in the preceding chapter (pp. 89–93).

2. Students sometimes find that clarification of their vocational aims increases interest in courses related to their vocational preparation. This topic was discussed earlier in this chapter, and a later "Self-Evaluation" section (pp. 115–117) contains some helpful queries to guide your thinking.

3. Make practical applications of the material you are studying. Try to see the relationship between the facts you study and the problems you will face in your chosen vocation. If you are not able to do this, ask your instructor for assistance in making such applications. All too often students approach courses as so much memory work, rather than as storehouses of interesting and valuable facts. Rote memorization is rarely of interest, but understanding is.

4. Persons who have had work experience are usually more highly motivated than others. Work experience apparently makes the vocational goal seem more clear-cut and better understood and, therefore, more immediate. Also, read all you can about your chosen vocation; it will help to focus your interest on college work.

5. Techniques of imagining more immediate goals assist in focusing interest more sharply. Studying as though there will be a quiz in a few minutes may be hard on your blood pressure but it will arouse your interest in preparation. Setting time limits for study, as outlined in the preceding chapter, sets the immediate goal of completing your work within the time limit. This also helps you to resist recreational distractions.

6. The story behind the discovery of facts is often as interesting as any adventure tale. Unfortunately, the stories get dried out by the time they appear in a textbook, but the library contains books of real interest about the work you are doing. Often this kind of motivation is the purpose of collateral reading.

7. The analysis of errors makes a problem seem much simpler and, therefore, easier and more interesting to overcome. For instance, it would seem more interesting and challenging to improve writing the letters "o" and "n" if these accounted for 50 percent of a person's illegibilities, than it would be to try without such a diagnosis just to write more clearly. Thus, in this and in other courses find the cause of your difficulties and you will become more interested.

8. Knowledge of progress makes work seem much more interesting. Try to obtain even rough measures of how well you are doing, and make a graph of your

progress. You will probably be surprised to find how interested you are in making the line on the graph increase. Set a goal on the graph and move your line toward it as you complete the units.

9. The technique of asking questions, discussed in Chapter 2, arouses curiosity as you read and makes the material seem more interesting. Another technique is to make up problems to solve; this will not only increase your interest but will also insure that you comprehend the material.

Number of words in this chapter: 8353

Time when chapter was completed: _____

Work rate per minute: _____

Answer the quiz on page 236.

List your work rate, comprehension accuracy, and note-quality rating on page 40.

Exercises in Self-Evaluation

The above discussion gives some notion of how different motives affect student behavior and of the changes that take place in their emphasis as a person grows older. It is difficult to evaluate one's own pattern of motives, because the average person has not given much thought to it and wants to think as well of himself as he can. Moreover, motives are so nebulous as to be difficult to evaluate. In fact, it is usually easier to recognize others' motivational patterns than one's own. It will be helpful, however, to attempt an evaluation. Some may discover that they have been fooling themselves with verbalizations about vocational preparation, whereas they really have more important interests. Others may realize that they have been continuing activities based on earlier interests and are not giving their present values much consideration.

The following analyses are easy to complete but difficult to answer frankly. Unless you are candid with yourself, however, they will be of little value.

1. In order to make more concrete how motives conflict, 10 situational questions are listed below. Do not answer them the way you think your instructor wants you to, or the way your mother would want you to, or even the way you think you ought to. The "correct" answer to all these questions may well be "yes," but the writer has found few undergraduates who could honestly answer all of them that way. The value of the "no" answers will be to suggest how motivational patterns may conflict with schoolwork.

Motivational Conflicts

Yes No   1. You discover at 7 P.M. that you have no assignments to prepare for the next day, but you remember that you do have a midterm exam the day after tomorrow. Normally in such a situation, would you study for it?

Yes No 2. A regular two-hour laboratory class is canceled one day because of difficulty with plumbing. Normally in such a situation, would you study?

Yes No 3. When you spend an evening in study, do you spend more than three-fourths of the time in actual reading and study?

Yes No 4. A basic but not required course in your major is given only at 8 A.M.; another course that is acceptable in the major but actually not quite as good for your needs as the other is available at 10 A.M. Would you take the 8 A.M. course?

Yes No 5. Do you spend more time a week (not including Sunday) in studying than in all types of social recreation?

Yes No 6. You have not been home for three weeks, and there is as much schoolwork for the coming weekend as usual. Would you stay on the campus and study?

Yes No 7. If an instructor asks if there are any questions about what he has just presented, would you ask about something that you do not understand?

Yes No 8. You would rather raise your grade-point average .5 of a point than be elected to a well-known, semihonorary campus organization.

Yes No 9. Twins of your own sex and with pleasing personalities are in your class. You would rather have as a friend the one who is outstanding as a student than the one who is popular with the opposite sex and in social activities.

Yes No 10. Assuming that it would take an equal amount of effort and would produce an equally successful result, you would rather write for publication a short paper in your major field than manage the campaign of a candidate for president of the student government.

2. *Why do you want to make good grades?* A list of typical reasons given by students as answers to the question, is indicated below (120).[1] Which ones of these most motivate your schoolwork? Which are least important? Rank these reasons in their order of importance as they affect your schoolwork. This order need only be approximate, since it is difficult to interpret and weigh these values carefully. Although such a rating device is too unreliable for accurate measurement, it will tend to stimulate your thinking.

I Want to Make Good Grades

_____ To secure a better future recommendation for a job.

_____ To indicate that I am actually learning something: new facts, how to think, and so forth.

_____ To win in a competition with another person or persons.

_____ To please my family.

[1] You will note that this and the following sections begin by asking questions. These questions may be used to put you in an enquiring frame of mind as you read; they may also be used fruitfully as topics for essays to clarify your thinking on these issues.

_____ To be eligible for initiation and student activities.

_____ To uphold a reputation already gained among my associates and friends.

_____ To win special honors and recognition.

_____ To meet the requirements for a degree.

_____ To gain the respect of my instructors.

_____ It is a matter of little interest to me.

3. *What would you miss if you could not return to school next term?* It is interesting to note that in response to this question many college freshmen list such things as "seeing friends," "the social life," "the athletic events," and so on, but never mention anything related to academic work. Are such students only fooling themselves when they say they are in school "to prepare for a vocation" or "to get a liberal education"? Be honest with yourself when you list some of the things you would miss and note where unhappiness at losing scholastic learning falls in your list. If in all honesty you cannot list it among the primary things that would be missed, then you should give some thought to why you actually feel you need to stay in college at your parents' and the taxpayers' expense. If you would miss your classwork, then the following exercises may help illumine your problem.

4. *Are any personal problems, e.g., health, finances, home, social problems, or emotional problems bothering you, which keep you from being able to study effectively?* Everybody has problems of one type or another and, for many, some particular problem may be so pressing that it makes concentration on schoolwork difficult. Although it is probably true that any problem this disturbing is not easily solved, there are two reasons why it would be helpful to talk over the nature of your problem with some trusted adult. The very act of describing your problem often helps give it a new perspective and suggests ideas for solving it. Also, because the other person can see the problem more objectively, he can often suggest useful resources that you might not think of. Possibly your instructor has had you fill out a problem check list as a means of informing him about some of your problems. You should feel free to talk with him or with some trusted adviser or counselor on the campus if you want help.

5. *Are your vocational goals defined clearly enough to give definite direction to your study efforts?* Some students know quite clearly what field they are planning to enter after graduation and look with interest at the possible application to it of the content of their courses. Many other students, as was noted earlier, have not decided what vocation they want to enter but are at a stage at which they want to make this decision. If you are one of the "undecided," some thought may well be given to the following points.

Which fields have some interest for you? Have any work experiences, class activities, or hobbies given you a notion of types of jobs you would possibly like to work at? With these several vocations in mind, check them against the following elements that are usually considered in evaluating probabilities of success in a chosen vocation.

a. What is your academic aptitude test score? Your college probably gave you such a test at admission as a basis for selection and as a basis for prediction of academic grades. Although such test results do not predict grades perfectly (actually only 20 percent better than chance), they help a person estimate how well he may do (see Tables 5 and 6). These test scores also are used on admission blanks for professional and graduate schools. Table 5 shows that on one of these academic aptitude tests persons at various levels make every type of grade; note, however, the tendency of those in the high percentile on the aptitude test to make better grades, in contrast to those of lower aptitude who are less likely to make high grades. Similarly, Table 6 shows that students at all levels of aptitude graduate from college but that those in the top fifth are about five times more likely to graduate than those in the lowest fifth. Your aptitude test score will give you a basis for estimating your chances of doing well or of being selected for admission in each of your possible fields of preparation. If your chances look poor, some thought should be given to what further steps you need to take. Your instructor or a college counselor will be glad to help you learn about your score and its interpretation, and he will assist you with other helpful vocational tests.

TABLE 5 Percent of University Freshmen in Each Third (Approximate) on the Ohio State Psychological Examination Who Made Various Grade Records at the End of One Year's Residence[a]

| O.S.P.E. percentile | Grade-point average | | | | |
	Drop out	0.0–.99	1.00–1.99	2.00–2.99	3.00–3.99
66–100	21%	2%	17%	41%	19%
30–65	24%	4%	36%	32%	14%
1–29	39%	3%	42%	15%	1%

[a] Adapted from 115.

TABLE 6 Level of Intelligence of Students Getting Degrees from a Large University Over a Ten-year Period. The Percents Indicate the Proportion of the Graduating Class in That Fifth[a]

| Graduates' level of intelligence on entrance to university | Degrees earned | | | |
	B. Arts	B.S. in Education	B. Engineering	B. Laws
Top fifth	39%	31%	32%	41%
Fourth fifth	25	25	24	23
Middle fifth	17	21	21	15
Second fifth	12	17	13	14
Bottom fifth	7	6	10	7
	100%	100%	100%	100%

[a] Based on unpublished data of H. A. Toops and R. H. Bittner, Ohio State University.

b. Interests are a second factor that should be considered in choosing a vocation. Do you know what fields are of greatest interest to you? Do you know what occupational group has interests most similar to yours? The evidence indicates that a person whose interests and outlook on life coincide with those of active members of some occupation will be most successful in that occupation. The Strong Vocational Interest Test indicates which occupational groups a person's profile of interests tend to resemble the most. The Kuder Preference Record also indicates a person's profile of interests. If you would like to take either of these tests, ask your instructor for a copy. Other rough measures of your interests include the courses in high school and college that you have liked best and least.

c. Not only do previous work and hobby experiences provide a basis for deciding whether or not you would like a field of work; those experiences also give you a head start if you take up a related occupation. For example, a person who has lived on a farm has such a fund of knowledge about animals that colleges of veterinary medicine in selecting students give priority to those persons with such previous experience. Have any of your previous work or hobby experiences given you a basis for selecting an occupation, or have they given you a head start in a particular field?

d. A fourth major factor in choosing an occupation is any unique opportunity that you may have. In addition to previous knowledge that gives you a head start in a field, are there opportunities that exist for you because of friends or relatives who are in a particular field, because of unique opportunities where you live, or because of particular strengths of the college you are attending, and so on?

e. Finally, in addition to knowing yourself, do you know much about the fields of work that you are considering? Actually, most students know very little about the jobs they are considering as their future vocation. Students usually overestimate the average income in their chosen field by 100 percent to 200 percent. They know little about the actual activities demanded on the job and have scant knowledge of the factors leading to promotion and the speed with which it takes place (309, pp. 48–51). Can you answer the following questions concerning your preferred job?

What is the average income five years after entering?
What steps have to be taken or what jobs must be held before you obtain the job you want?
How crowded is the field of your chosen occupation?
How much training is necessary?
How much money does it take to get started, *e.g.,* buying equipment, etc.?
What are the opportunities for further advancement?
Is the occupation stable, growing, seasonal, or on the decline?
What are the duties of this job?
What is a person's status on the job when he reaches 40 or 50 years of age; do the opportunities increase; do the opportunities decrease?

Specific information concerning occupations of interest can be obtained from the occupational information library on your campus.

6. *How mature are your academic interests?* Although this is a difficult area in which to make self-estimates, four areas of immaturity have been discussed earlier in the chapter.

a. Immediate goals are much stronger than delayed vocational goals.

b. Curiosity is inhibited.

c. Characteristics other than scholarship and intellectual development are valued most.

d. Emancipation from parental supervision is not complete.

Look back over things you used to enjoy or thought were important; see how much you have grown. Do you have to go back many years before you can see a change? Compare yourself to college seniors and to other adults; are you able to see comparable steps to further growth?

7. Finally, on the positive side, *What do you like about your courses? How interested are you in doing your class work? Are you looking forward to some courses in your major area? What are some of the reasons for these areas of in-*

terest? It is improbable that an undergraduate student will respond to this analysis with a realization that as soon as he jumps out of bed in the morning he wants to grab a book, but such an analysis should clarify some reasons for studying, should show some of the conflicting interests that all people have, and should give some notion of the care that each student will have to use to keep distractions to a minimum.

CHAPTER 7
Classroom skills

Because students learn through class participation, and their work is evaluated from it as well, it is important that they have effective classroom skills. Although listening skills are in many ways related to reading skills, there are important differences. Careful statistical analysis shows that quite separate listening skills exist, which are related to academic achievement; in fact, some studies have shown that listening skills are more important than reading skills in determining grades (230, 318, 350, 392).

Students frequently feel inadequate in these skills. Many students are afraid to recite in class and are even more terrified to volunteer in discussion or to ask questions. Most students have difficulty in determining what should be learned in a lecture and know no good way to remember what they do learn. Some students write as rapidly as they can to record what is said, but because of such a secretarial attitude, scarcely understand what they have written; others write nothing. Still other difficulties arise because some students do not understand that certain classroom mannerisms and practices offend the teacher and can act as a detriment. Principles relating to these problems will be presented under four headings: (1) improving ability to handle lectures, (2) improving ability to discuss and recite in class, (3) improving class manners, and (4) having conferences with the teacher.

Improving Ability to Handle Lectures

Very little instruction on how to listen to classroom explanations or lectures is given in the schools. Studies made of the comparative efficiency of listening to and reading the same type of selections show little difference during elementary school, but after, with continuing instruction in how to read, reading becomes much more effective than merely listening to something being presented (28, 187, 220, 367).

119

The ability to listen seems to show little change during secondary school because of this lack of training.

Comparative studies of the kinds of errors made in listening and reading show that although listeners had fewer omissions in their reports, they did have many more distortions in what they reported (173, 174). A study made of the relevance of student thoughts to the class work showed that "the lecture is much less successful than a discussion method in holding the students' thoughts to the immediate situation" (39, p. 167). Furthermore, there was a correlation of .61 between the relevancy of students' thoughts in the classroom experiment and his score on an end-of-the-quarter comprehensive examination.

Quite obviously students need help in learning how to listen to lectures efficiently. Furthermore, studies of attempts to teach listening skills show that this can be effective (104, 113, 229, 412).

A first step in developing classroom skills is to sit where you can hear the lecture easily. This point may seem obvious, but many students disregard it to the detriment of their classroom efficiency. Many students, for example, gravitate toward the back of the class or sit next to a door or beside a window. In all three of these places students are subject to many distractions. Those at the back of the room have to look past all the other students in order to watch the instructor; their attention is constantly distracted from the lecturer as these intervening students squirm in their seats, whisper, or drop things. Students sitting by a door or window are distracted by occurrences outside the classroom. Studies of students' preferences as to seat locations and of the relationship between classroom position and grades show an advantage in sitting at the center of the room or toward the front (123, 311). Also sit where material on the blackboard can be seen easily. If you have difficulty in hearing, sit where you can hear better and where you can watch the speaker's lips.

Students have as much or more difficulty in picking out what is important and remembering it in lectures as they have in reading (207). Various factors enter into this: For one thing, lectures are not as well organized as books. As noted above, students also lack skill in listening. Certain characteristics of personality also enter into this (53). For example, one study showed that people who had particularly strong beliefs on an attitude test did poorly on a comprehension test after listening to a lecture to which these attitudes might relate, i.e., they may have refused to listen to something with which they disagreed (58). Finally, another study showed that in listening to a short lecture the students had the most trouble on an immediate comprehension test with items taken from the middle of the talk and least trouble with items taken from the end of the talk (188).

One basis for the solution of this problem of picking out what is important in a lecture can be found in an appreciation of the two purposes of a lecture: (1) to present important material not otherwise easily available to students, and (2) to explain important points that might cause difficulty or that warrant elaboration. Since a teacher's class time is limited, he must use great selectivity in determining what is to be discussed. Whatever is said in class should, therefore, be important.

Even a rambling or loosely organized lecture may, however, contain illustrations of important points in the textbook. The crux of the problem in learning how to listen to a lecture is: How can one determine what is important and how can one remember it? (2).

This sounds familiarly like the problem in reading textbooks. Both textbook writers and lecturers try to make only a few major points in a chapter or a lecture but have to use a great deal of explanatory detail in order to make these major points clear. The student's problem is to learn how to spot these major points. A lecture usually contains fewer cues than a textbook, and, presented extemporaneously, the cues are not so clearly emphasized. Even though such organizational cues as inflection, topic sentences, and summary statements may be skillfully presented, the average student is not trained to spot them. Just as most students pay little attention to headings in books, so most students know little about typical cues used in lecturing. To begin with, the average student usually has a mistaken notion of how much is covered in a lecture. He usually thinks that many points are covered, whereas actually they will range from a couple of major ideas to half a dozen minor ones.

Students usually go to one of two extremes—both bad—in approaching this problem. Some students, feeling that everything said is important, write madly, trying to put everything down; those who know shorthand feel prepared. These persons are so busy, however, that they scarcely understand a thing that is said. They may feel that they can study their notes later, but they seldom do so, and if they do, they have done twice the work necessary. At the other extreme are those students who say that it is impossible to both listen and write and that it is difficult to know what to write. They feel that the best approach is to listen and watch carefully so as not to miss anything; note-taking would be a distraction. These individuals may understand the lecture while it is being presented, but they usually do not isolate the main points and have no basis for a later review. Actually, in one study it was found that there was no difference in achievement on a later test between one group who took notes during a lecture and another group who waited until the end of the lecture to jot down a summary (116). One possible reason for this finding is that these students were untrained and, therefore, ineffective in their note-taking methods.

With lectures, as with textbooks, the core ideas are important. A student needs to isolate these core ideas and to see the explanatory material as such. This he should do by watching for cues that the lecturer gives. In one experiment it was found that when a group took two forms of a listening test they did much better on the form that was preceded by a prefatory remark, than they did on the selection that had no prefatory remark (54). A lecturer often starts a section with a topic sentence, and he may close a topic with a summary statement. He usually indicates the number of important subpoints by such cue statements as "the three parts," "the five results," and so on. Lecturers may use an inflection in their voice to make a point stand out; they may often repeat important points, pause significantly, or even precede a statement by saying, "This next point is important." A student then should listen attentively and, through such cues as the above, try to determine what main point is being developed. When this is decided, he should write down a brief note summarizing the point. He then should listen again until the next point is made. By the end of a class hour possibly not more than a half page of notes should have been taken. The writing will not have been laborious, and the several statements written will be very helpful later for review.

Insofar as possible, try to show organization in your notes. Label them as to major topic and indent subpoints so that the major ones stand out. Since it is sometimes difficult to determine the exact organization as the lecturer proceeds, it is worthwhile to take a few minutes at the end of the class or during the evening of the same day to glance over the class notes so as to mark important points, indent subpoints, and so forth. In such revising it may also become obvious that in your haste too little has been written; in such a case, add further clarifying statements. Typing class notes, on the other hand, is generally a waste of time. Typing is hard work for most students, and legibly written notes would do just as well.

Notes that show organization make major points stand out and are more easily visualized later, but the usual scribbled notes have been found to be of little value (59, 232). In order to make indentations, which enhance this visual pattern, it is necessary to have a large notebook; they cost little more than the smaller notebooks. Furthermore, the ideas from one or several lectures can be put on one large page so their relationship can be seen more easily. Little notebooks are cute and easy to carry but are inefficient for class notes. Worst of all is the use of backs of envelopes and odd sheets of paper for note-taking; these are difficult to organize and keep collected.

As was true with notes on readings (Chapter 2), an outsider's evaluation and coaching often quickly suggest worthwhile ways to simplify and improve classroom note-taking. Have your instructor check your notes, and then try to improve your technique of taking notes. Successive ratings should show improvement in your notes, and lectures should begin to have more organization for you.

Improving Ability to Discuss and Recite in Class

Almost every teacher devotes some time to class discussion and student recitation; some teachers devote most of their class time to it. There are several reasons for this practice. The give and take of discussion increases student interest and emphasizes understanding rather than memorization of ideas. Students have been found to have more relevant thoughts when listening to a discussion rather than a lecture (39). Recitation, as was shown in Chapter 2, tends to fix ideas in one's memory so they are forgotten less rapidly; class discussion plays the same role. Through listening to questions and ideas presented the teacher can evaluate what students know. The following experiments give an indication of how important discussion is in schoolwork. In one experiment an accurate count was kept of how many times each student participated in classroom recitation and discussion, and in another the teacher rated each student's "quality of class participation"; these scores were found to be highly related to the grades each student received at the end of the school year (39, 73). Of course, it may be assumed that the students who knew the most might have tended to recite the most, but this is not the complete explanation. In another study, college students were measured on their ability to influence each other in discussion (335). When this ability of students was compared to their success in class, it was found that "students able to influence their classmates most in discussion situations were also able to influence their teachers most favorably and get the highest marks" ($r = .38$) (335).

Fear of reciting or discussing in class is one of the most frequent problems mentioned by students. In a checklist of ninety items in which students were told to rate how they compared to other students in their class, more students put themselves in the bottom fifth on the item, "speaks up in class discussion" than on any other item (428). Another indication of this same problem is obtained from the use of a "Guess Who" test. In this type of test a descriptive statement is read and the students guess who in the class it best describes. When the item "This is the student who is most afraid to discuss in class" is read, more students usually mention themselves than on any other item.

Why are students afraid to participate in class discussion? A large number of college students, when asked to analyze why it was difficult to obtain discussion in class, listed 25 different causes ranging from teaching procedures to student attitudes (197). Among the most important were the four student attitudes listed in Table 7. Characteristic of all these student attitudes is a fear of appearing inferior to others. This fear is not simply limited to what the teacher may think, because fear of what classmates may think is probably an even greater deterrent. For instance, many students are willing to ask questions after class but not during class.

TABLE 7 Student Attitudes That Inhibit Student Questioning in Class[a]

These attiudes affect recitation:	Seldom or never	Sometimes	Frequently	Very often
Students fear ridicule	2%	19%	46%	33%
Lack of preparation	2%	8%	38%	52%
Dislike to expose ignorance	1%	16%	41%	42%
Timidity	—	14%	44%	42%

[a] Adapted from 197.

Analysis of class discussions tends to indicate that students fall into three types: (1) the "off-the-beam" or "disturber" type, (2) the quiet unknown, and (3) the leader. Fear of being classed in the first of these categories inhibits many students; unluckily, they then fall into the second class, unknown to teacher or students. Evidence of these student types is obtained through use of a "Guess Who" test, which contains a series of items ranging from "this student can't say what he means" or "this student seems most timid in class discussions" to "this student's discussion is interesting and to the point" or "this student is easily heard and understood." The test is scored in two ways: (1) the total number of times each student's name is mentioned, and (2) the number of times each student's name is mentioned for favorable items minus the number of times it is mentioned for unfavorable items. The results from administering such a test to two small classes are summarized in Figure 14. It will be noted that the distribution falls into a **V** shape. At the left are the individuals who received many but almost entirely negative votes. In the middle are those whom scarcely anyone remembered when thinking about the class (it is surprising to note how many "nonentities" can exist even in small classes). At the right are the accepted leaders of the groups.

What can be done to help students participate in discussions? The primary difficulty to overcome is the fear itself. The procedures suggested below seek to give students a feeling of assurance so they will venture comments in class. Once they start, most students have little difficulty thereafter.

1. Since it is obvious from the above results that most students feel that they are less able than others to speak up in class and secretly admire those who do, there is

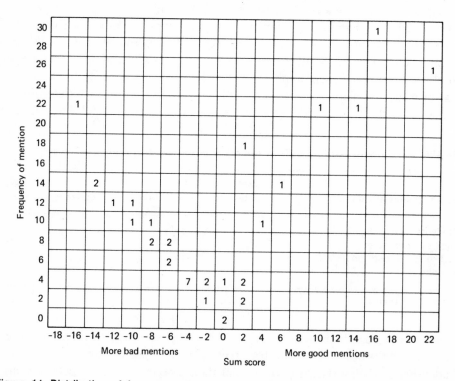

Figure 14. Distribution of frequency of mention and sum scores on a "Guess Who" test dealing with classroom behavior of students in two small classes. (Based on unpublished data of the author.)

good reason to try making a comment. When a student realizes that other students are not the critical judges he thought, it is less difficult for him to participate in class discussions.

2. Since most instructors follow their textbooks rather closely, one can usually predict what will be discussed in class. Prepare yourself on a few items that will surely come up; then, seize the opportunity to recite when these topics are introduced.

3. When class discussion emphasizes an exploration of points of view on an issue, give your own opinion. Such discussions move forward only when there are differences of opinion to clarify the point at issue. In such a situation your opinion is probably as good as the next person's. The previously mentioned study of student influence on others also showed that students with definite opinions influence others more than those who are not sure and, of course, more than those who do not speak up.

4. A good way to read is to apply what you are studying to different practical situations. A good form of class participation is to suggest such applications and, if you cannot think of any, to ask how such material might apply in a given situation. An instructor is pleased to find students thinking rather than memorizing in a course.

5. Start participating in class discussion early in the school term. At that time the class is not yet organized, so that even questions that are digressive are acceptable. Once you have started speaking out in class, you will probably have little difficulty thereafter in that class.

6. When you do not understand something, ask questions. Instructors know that students do not understand everything in their lessons; many of them ask from time to time if there are any questions in order to clarify issues before they are included in tests. If the instructor does not ask for questions, he will usually be happy to help outside of class.

7. An important maxim in college life when a teacher asks for persons to work on special projects, is "Volunteer." When special projects are used in a class, they are usually planned so that all students eventually will have something to do. Those who volunteer early impress the teacher with their interest in the work; moreover, early acquaintance with the instructor actually does much to liven the work during the rest of the term.

As indicated earlier, the main problem is getting started. An analogy to the treatment of stuttering may be helpful here. Stutterers' emotional fear of stuttering, especially in social situations, increases their tension so that they are even more likely to stutter. One aspect of treatment is to get them accustomed to speaking in strange situations; many such experiences tend to reduce this emotional tension and so decrease the tendency to stutter. Stutterers also have trouble getting started, so some clinics send them out with slips of paper and tell them not to come back until they have talked to someone and have had the paper signed to prove it. Such drastic treatment need not be used on you, but a first step is to resolve to discuss in one class you have today.

Improving Class Manners

One approach to "winning grades and influencing teachers" is to be considerate in class. This does not mean excessive politeness but, rather, common courtesy. Just as rules of etiquette make it easier to be comfortable and get things done at dinners and social gatherings, so the following simple rules of behavior in the classroom make life easier for students and teacher. Teachers work hard and tend to become irritated by students who constantly violate these rules.

1. Do not cut classes. You will miss part of your instruction. Teachers occasionally react negatively toward chronic cutters. Studies show that number of absences is highly related to grades (15). Figure 15 indicates that for a large number of students in a midwestern university not only did persons earning low grade-point averages tend to cut classes much more than most students but there was a linear relationship between number of absences and quality of grade. Merely attending class every day will not insure a B average, but, conversely, it can be said that cutting frequently may make getting a B average difficult.

2. Be on time. Some people have difficulty getting to class on time. Sometimes this is due to the fact that the preceding class is too far away; if so, be sure to tell your instructor. Others find it hard to get to places on time. In one study a record was kept of what time students arrived at their 8 A.M. classes. When the grade-

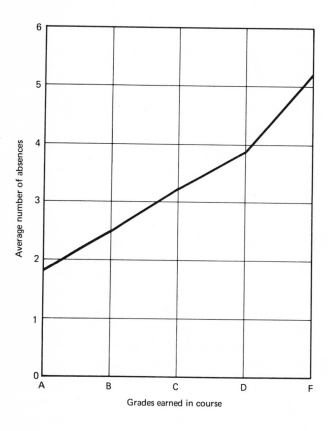

Figure 15. The number of absences of 2654 students who earned certain grades in university classes. (Adapted from 15.)

point average of students who were on time or even early was compared to the average of those who were late, it was found that "the early students had a grade of B, whereas the late students had a grade of C plus" (111). Figure 16 shows the typical distribution of time of arrival at class; most students come a few minutes early, but a minority straggles in for some time after the bell rings. These late-comers are a distraction to the class and to the instructor.

3. Participate in class. On a hike you would not let someone else carry your pack. In class do not take the attitude of daring the instructor to try to interest you. When the instructor opens an issue to discussion, do not let everyone else discuss but take some responsibility for moving the discussion along. The more quickly it is discussed, the more quickly the class can move on.

4. Classes, like many activities, sometimes are boring, but you should not show that you are bored. It is all right to look at your watch, but only occasionally, and do not check to see if it is running. Do not stack your books and put your coat on before the bell rings, because the commotion will disturb the rest of the class. Don't whisper to others in a lecture class; whispered comments are interesting to those in the room and so distract them. If you have ever talked to someone who while you are talking, continually looks about as if his mind were on other things, you know how instructors sometimes feel in class.

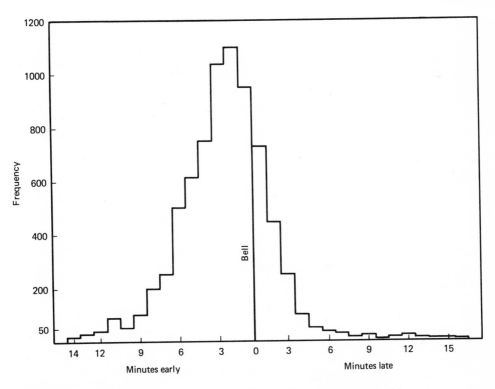

Figure 16. Distribution of time of arrival at 8 A.M. classes. (Adapted from 11.)

5. Get reports in on time or earlier. Most students put off writing reports until the last minute (if not a few days after that). But a theme takes no longer to write on time than later. Teachers appreciate getting reports on time, or even early, because they plan their work to handle these papers. Since a late paper means a special session of grading, the irritation is usually sufficient to cause the teacher to give a lower grade.

Having Conferences with the Teacher

Many students feel that an instructor will think they are "apple-polishing" if they ask for a conference. Actually most instructors enjoy the opportunity to work with and know their students individually. Part of their job is to hold conferences with students from their classes. Certain courtesies are helpful, however.

1. If the instructor has time, questions can be asked before or after class. This informal opportunity makes it easy to have conferences without much effort.

2. If a conference has to be arranged at another time, make an appointment with the instructor and then *be sure to keep it*; teachers' schedules are too full to be used up by missed appointments.

3. Questions can be asked in several ways, some more effective than others. In discussing a quiz, it is not as effective to ask "Why did you give me a low grade?" as "What type of material should I have included?" The latter will usually bring a sympathetic approach to your problem.

In summary, then, classroom skills are as important as study skills in determining college achievement. Special attention should be given to improving your skill in the four areas discussed in this chapter: (1) ability to handle lectures, (2) ability to discuss and recite in class, (3) classroom manners, and (4) having conferences with instructors. Attention should be given to the following exercises as means of improvement.

Number of words in this chapter: 4341

Time when chapter was completed: _____

Work rate per minute: _____

Answer the quiz on page 237.

**List your work rate, comprehension accuracy, and
   note-quality rating on page 40.**

Practice Exercises

1. How does your usual classroom behavior rate? Answer the following questions by writing in the word (or its number): (1) never, (2) seldom, (3) sometimes, (4) often, or (5) always.

_____ 1. Do you take notes on your lecture classes?

_____ 2. Do you keep your notes in one notebook at least 6 x 9 inches in size?

_____ 3 Do you recopy your notes after a lecture?

_____ 4 Do you write as fast and as much as you can during a lecture?

_____ 5 Do you use shorthand in taking notes?

_____ 6. Do you look over and edit your notes after class?

_____ 7 Do you sit near the back of the classroom or near a door or window?

_____ 8. Do you participate when there is classroom discussion?

_____ 9 Do you feel nervous and afraid when you have to participate in class discussion?

_____ 10. When you do not understand something that has been explained in class, do you ask questions when given the opportunity?

_____ 11. When the instructor calls for volunteers, do you yourself volunteer?

_____ 12. When reviewing for a quiz, do you try to predict from your class notes what will be asked?

_____ 13. When you are having trouble in a course, do you try to talk to the instructor after class or to have a conference with him?

_____ 14 Do you cut classes during a school term?

_____ 15 Are you late to class?

_____ 16 Do you stack your books or put your coat on just before the bell rings?

_____ 17 Do you whisper to other students while the teacher is lecturing or leading a discussion?

_____ 18. Do you hand in term reports and other papers on or before the due date?

The questions whose numbers are followed by a period should be answered "often" or "always," and those without periods should be answered "seldom" or "never."

2. Take notes on sample lectures given in this class and have them evaluated by the instructor. Have your lecture notes in other classes evaluated for suggestions on how to improve them. A look at the notes of other students in your classes may also give you some useful ideas.

3. Make a definite effort to start participating in classroom discussions. It is easier to discuss with some teachers than with others; "break the ice" in an easier classroom discussion and then see how easily participation skill can be developed.

4. Notice what things students do in your classes that distract other students from the lecture or discussion. It is an interesting class exercise to make lists of these behaviors and summarize them in class.

It is also interesting to make a list of instructors' habits and mannerisms that distract students, _e.g.,_ tossing chalk, constantly looking out the window, gesturing while speaking, and so on. Although this list will not help your grades, it may make you feel better.

5. If you are having trouble in any of your courses, have a conference with the instructor.

CHAPTER 8

Preparing reports[1]

Term papers are a typical part of many college courses. They should consist of more than a few pages of quotations copied and brought together; in upper-division courses they should be rather extensive treatises. Because instructors have to pass rapidly over many interesting points, they assign papers and oral reports so the student can dig out the information he wants and also obtain credit for it. College reports are, therefore, real investigations of interesting topics by inquiring minds. Sometimes such papers are good enough to be published.

The expected makeup of a report varies somewhat from course to course, but three general characteristics are desired by all teachers: (1) evidence that the student has studied different sources in order to stimulate his thinking, (2) presentation in an acceptable form, and (3) evidence of original thinking. As with most activities, a report may be done the hard way, or easy short cuts may be used. This chapter proposes to demonstrate these short cuts so that better reports can be written with no greater expenditure of effort or time.

The first of these desired characteristics is evidence of resources studied. Much energy is often wasted in inefficient search. This writer has found that even in advanced classes some students will work much harder on papers than the average students but will get lower grades because they do not know about the simplest library aids. The first part of this chapter deals with library resources and short cuts in using them.

With regard to the second characteristic, correct form, students are often concerned about the form in which a term paper should be presented and are ignorant of any peculiarities of style expected in a given subject field. The teachers, on the other hand, expect the reports to be in good form—the historians want the reports

[1] The remaining chapters are not set up to obtain measures of work rate and comprehension accuracy as you read, because diagnostic tests have been introduced into the text of each chapter. Practice of the SQ3R method, however, should be continued on other reading assignments.

styled as historical essays and the scientists want them to be scientific discussions. Facts presented in correct form receive higher grades than the same facts presented in the usual English essay form. The second part of this chapter indicates resources that give simple directions for writing reports.

With regard to the third characteristic, evidence of original thinking, much depends on the ability of the student. However, any student who finds it easy to obtain resource material, who is stimulated by that material, and who has a plan for writing his paper, should have the time and energy to do some original thinking. Some suggestions will also be made, which will foster such originality in reports.

Use of the Library

The primary resources for college work, in addition to textbooks, are books and periodicals. Because of the large number of these reading materials that have to be used, a system of cataloguing and rules for use are necessary; yet, these very systems are unfamiliar to most students and so may act as barriers rather than as aids.

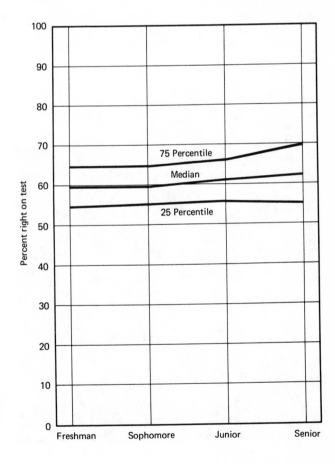

Figure 17. Success of students on a test of "beginning working knowledge in the use of the library"; the median and the range of scores for the middle 50 percent are shown for each college year. (Adapted from 224.)

Acquaintance with library books is often limited to the reserve room, where a student's request for an assigned book is all that is necessary. Such students do not know of the wealth of material that the school supplies; they do not know one of the best and simplest ways of finding materials for term papers; and, probably worst of all, they miss interesting books and articles on topics about which they are curious.

Concrete evidence showing that knowledge of the library is related to school success and that even the average senior does not know enough about the library is shown by a study made at Ohio University (224). The experimenters, with the aid of other faculty members, constructed a test of essential information about the library. Its items represented "beginning of a working knowledge in the use of the library." When 441 students took the test, it was found that knowledge of the library was related to grade-point average even when the effect of intelligence on both scores was canceled out. Other studies corroborate this finding (359, 393). The results summarized in Figure 17 also show that the average students, even among the seniors, know only about 60 percent of these essential items, and little, if any, growth in knowledge of the library takes place during the four years in college. The small range in scores between the first and third quartiles indicates that most of the students are about equally ignorant concerning the use of the library. It is evident that students do need training in use of the library.

SELF-EVALUATION

How much do you know about the library? You may feel that you can use it well, since you are familiar with public and school libraries. Three tests are provided on

Figure 18. Some commonly available library aids for use in building bibliographies for term papers in the social studies field.

the next few pages to measure your skill and also to act as training units. Each has been made carefully so as to cover the essential aspects of library service, which every student ought to know. Much more technical and professional aid can be found in a library, but it seems best to limit these diagnostic tests to minimal essentials. The first test covers information concerning what is in the library. The second test measures your skill in the actual use of library aids. After scoring these two tests and studying your weak spots you will be ready to try your skill on the third test— preparing a bibliography for an actual term paper. It will show how library aids can be used as short cuts in the writing of good term papers.

I. TEST OF INFORMATION ABOUT THE LIBRARY

This test covers the important aspects of the library, which the typical student needs to know. The test is divided into four sections: A. Dictionary Card Catalogue; B. Parts of a Book; C. Indexes and Abstracts; D. How to Use the *Readers' Guide*. The key for scoring your answers is on page 283 in Appendix III.

Place your score (the number correct) in the appropriate norm box.

Norms

Lowest quarter	2d quarter	3d quarter	Top quarter
44	48	52	
Q_1	Md.	Q_3	

A. DICTIONARY CARD CATALOGUE

What will be the alphabetic order of the following title references in the dictionary card catalogue? Indicate the proper order by numbering (1, 2, 3, 4, or 5) on the proper line to the left.

_____ 1. *A Manual of Determinative Mineralogy* (by J. V. Lewis).

_____ 2. *Social Organization and Disorganization (*by S. A. Queen).

_____ 3. *The American College* (by A. F. West).

_____ 4. *Annotated Bibliography on Adult Education* (by V. M. Proctor).

_____ 5. *A Syllabus on Vocational Guidance* (by V. A. Teeter).

If a statement is true, circle "T"; if it is false, circle "F."

T F 6. All classified books are listed in the dictionary card catalogue.

T F 7. The location of a book in the library is indicated by the call number on the dictionary card.

T F 8. The arrangement of the dictionary card catalogue is the same as that of books on the shelves.

T F 9. A card in the catalogue saying "Robins, *see* Birds" means that there is nothing in the library on robins.

T F 10. A student interested in the American Revolution can begin preparing a bibliography by looking up any of the following subject headings in the dictionary card catalogue: American Revoluton; Revolution, American; U.S.—History—Revolution.

T F 11. A book written by Samuel Clemens should be listed in the dictionary card catalogue under the name "Mark Twain," since he is more
widely known by that name.

T F 12. A book written by Zorro and translated by Kiesow would be entered
in the card catalogue under both names.

T F 13. Cross references (i.e., *see* and *see also*) in the dictionary card catalogue and in periodical indexes are for the technical use of the li-
brarian and, hence, are of little use to the student.

T F 14. Library books assigned by an instructor will usually be found on
reserve and will always be listed in the dictionary card catalogue.

Find the best answer in the right-hand column for each statement on the left.
Write the letter of that answer on the line to the left of each statement.

———15. The card in the dictionary card catalogue   A. Author card
on which you would find listed a book by   B. Index card
John Ruskin.   C. Title card

———16. The card in the dictionary card catalogue   D. Subject card
on which you would find a book called   E. Bibliography card
The Tides of Life.

———17. If you wanted information for a paper on   A. Arrowheads
"Indian Arrowheads," what would be the   B. Bow and Arrow
best topic to look up?   C. Indians of North
     America
———18. If you wanted information for a paper on   D. Indians of North
"The Religious Music of Indians," what   America—implements
would be the best topic to look up?   E. Indians of North
     America—music
———19. If you wanted information for a paper on   F. Indians of North
"Pocahontas," what would be the best   America—religion and
topic to look up?   mythology
   G. Music, sacred
   H. Pocahontas

RC 530
A4   **Alvarez, Walter Clement,** 1884–
     Practical leads to puzzling diagnoses: neuroses that run
through families.   Philadelphia, Lippincott ₍1958₎

     490 p. illus. 24 cm.

     Includes bibliography.

     1. Neuroses.   I. Title.   II. Title: Puzzling diagnoses.

   RC530.A4   616.85   58–11879 ‡

   Library of Congress   ₍10₎

Answer the following questions about the facsimile catalogue card on page 134.

_____20. The location of the book in the library is indicated by (1) the author's last name, (2) the number in the upper left-hand corner, (3) the title, "Practical leads to puzzling diagnoses."

T F 21. The number in the upper left-hand corner is based on the Dewey Decimal system rather than the Library of Congress system.

_____22. The book was published in what year?

T F 23. This book contains a bibliography that could be used for further reading.

_____24. In how many different places will cards for this book appear in the dictionary card catalogue of the usual library?

T F 25. A card for this book will be found if you look up the subject "Neuroses."

T F 26. A card for this book will be found if you look up the subject "Diagnoses."

B. PARTS OF A BOOK

Find the best answer in the right-hand column for each statement on the left. Write the letter of that answer on the line to the left of each statement.

_____27. Part that gives an outline of what the book contains.

_____28. List of references given at the end of a chapter or at the end of a book.

_____29. Page on which name of publisher appears.

_____30. Place to look up location of minor but, nevertheless, important topics in the book.

_____31. Section that states why the author wrote the book.

_____32. Part at end of book containing additional information not in the text proper.

_____33. Statements in small print at the bottom of some pages.

A. Glossary
B. Copyright
C. Preface
D. Footnote
E. Bibliography
F. Title page
G. Index
H. Appendix
I. Table of contents

C. INDEXES AND ABSTRACTS

Following are some indexes, abstracts, and other bibliographical sources commonly found in college libraries.

a. *Readers' Guide to Periodical Literature*
b. *International Index to Periodicals*
c. *Agriculture Index*
d. *Art Index*
e. *Education Index*
f. *Bibliographic Index*
g. *Chemical Abstracts*

h. *Psychological Abstracts*
i. *Biological Abstracts*
j. *Cumulative Book Index*
k. *New York Times Index*
l. *Book Review Digest*
m. *Biography Index*
n. *Vertical File Index*

In answering the following use the list of reference works given above. Place the letter of the correct title on the line to the left of each phrase.

_____34. The best place to find recent articles on "intelligence testing."

_____35. Articles containing bibliographies on various topics.

_____36. Articles for a paper on "mural painting."

_____37. Articles for a paper on "the divorce problem."

_____38. Articles for a paper on "testing cows."

_____39. Where to find the date on which a recent major event occurred.

_____40. Where to find the publisher and cost of a book not in the library.

_____41. Where to find a summary of critical evaluations of a book you have not seen.

If a statement is true, circle "T"; if it is false, circle "F."

T F 42. Some books contain bibliographies; this information is listed on the dictionary card for that book.

T F 43. Bibliographies on some topics are published as separate bulletins; these are listed in the dictionary card catalogue.

T F 44. The alphabetical entries in typical periodical indexes are listed by author and subject, although both are not always included.

T F 45. *The Readers' Guide to Periodical Literature* usually enters an article in its alphabetical listing by author and by subject.

T F 46. *The Readers' Guide to Periodical Literature* lists new books as well as magazine articles.

T F 47. The best way to obtain a bibliography of books from the dictionary card catalogue is to use the title cards.

T F 48. Good, modern encyclopedias contain well-written articles on many topics assigned for papers or studied in college classes.

D. HOW TO USE THE READER'S GUIDE AND OTHER INDEXES

Directions: In the excerpt from the June 25, 1969, issue of the *Readers' Guide,* line numbers have been added at the left to help in identifying the material to be used in answering the questions below. Answer each question in terms of the line or lines referred to.

_____49. The number that appears *before* the colon ":" within the number sets in each listing refers to (1) the year, (2) the page on which the article starts, (3) the volume number of the magazine.

_____50. The number that appears just *after* the colon ":" within the number sets in each listing refers to (1) page number, (2) year, (3) volume number.

T F 51. The magazine referred to in lines 7 and 8 appears once each month.

T F 52. The word "see" in line 13 means that additional references may be listed under the topic "Vietnamese war, 1957- —Guerrillas."

_____53. The symbol "por" in line 18 indicates that (1) there is a picture of Che Guevara, (2) there is a picture of M. Ray, (3) the article is written in Portuguese.

T F 54. The symbol "il" in line 18 means that the article contains illustrations.

_____55. In line 16 Ernesto Guevara is (1) the author, (2) the subject of the article listed.

Excerpt from *Readers' Guide* (June 25, 1969)

T F 56. The article in lines 32–34 appears in two installments in the April and May issues of the *New Republic* magazine.

T F 57. The article by Fulbright listed in lines 50–52 contains a bibliography of further writings on this topic.

_____58. How many acticles are listed as dealing with "Guerrillas in Latin America"?

T F 59. Any article about hi-fi systems will be found under the topic "High-fidelity sound systems."

_____60. In line 67, Desmond Guinness is (1) the author, (2) the subject of the article listed.

_____61. The symbol "+" in line 72 means that (1) the magazine appears late in May, (2) the article is particularly good, (3) part of the article appears on later pages in that issue, *i.e.,* back among the advertisements.

T F 62. To check for articles by J. E. Haas (line 82), one should look under "T. E. Draback" in this issue of the *Readers' Guide*.

II. LABORATORY PROBLEM IN THE USE OF LIBRARY AIDS

Your how-to-study laboratory is equipped with various sample library aids. The next step is to see if you can actually use them correctly. The second test has been prepared especially to fit the college situation; when you are ready for it, ask your instructor for a copy. This exercise will cover the use of the dictionary card catalogue, the *Book Review Digest,* and various indexes, abstracts, and encyclopedias. If any part causes trouble, the instructor will be glad to help you.

PROGRAM FOR IMPROVEMENT

1. Did you know how to use the library? How did you compare to other college students? Even though you may have scored higher on these tests than the average student, the honor is a dubious one, since it has already been shown that the average student knows little about the library. A more realistic goal is to understand everything in these tests, since each item has been selected carefully as a basis for undergraduate work.

Read up on those items that you missed. One of the following references will provide an excellent source of information about the library. Your classroom or college library will have some of these (and probably another booklet describing the local library setup), which will help answer your questions.

Aldrich, E. V., *Using Books and Libraries*, 5th ed. Englewood Cliffs, N.J.: Prentice-Hall, 1967.
Alexander, C., and Burke, A. J., *How to Locate Educational Information and Data*, 4th ed. New York: Bureau of Publications, Teachers College, 1959. (See especially chaps. 4, 7, and 10.)
Cook, M. G., *New Library Key*, 2d ed. New York: H. W. Wilson, 1963.
Downes, R. B., *How to Do Library Research*. Champaign, Ill.: University of Illinois Press, 1966.
Hook, L., and Gaver, M. V., *The Research Paper; Gathering Library Material and Preparing the Manuscript*, 3d ed. Englewood Cliffs, N.J.: Prentice-Hall, 1962.
Turabian, K. L., *Student's Guide for Writers of Term Papers, Theses and Dissertations*, 3d ed. Chicago: University of Chicago Press, 1967.
Williams, C. B., and Stevenson, A. H., *A Research Manual for College Studies and Papers*, 3d ed. New York: Harper & Row, 1963.

2. Study a map of your library in order to familiarize yourself with the locations of resources, particularly the card catalogue, indexes, and general references. Take time to browse in the reference section in order to see where these resources are located.

3. When these two steps are done, and only then, try the following "real library project." It tests your ability to use your knowledge of the library in preparing for an actual term paper. To try this project before completely understanding the library setup will result only in confusion and waste of time. On the other hand, if you are familiar with the basic use of the library, this part of the chapter will be quite easy.

III. TERM PAPER LIBRARY PROJECT

Parts A, B, and C can be filled out in class; Part D must be done at the library. Do this project on your own; do not bother the librarians. If you need help, ask your instructor or other students (if you feel they know the answer).

A. Select a topic for a term paper in an area in which you are interested. (If you have a paper to write in some course this term, or if you know of a topic that can be used in a later course, use that topic.) The topic is:

B. Under what headings would you expect to find references to articles and books dealing with your topic?

1.	4.
2.	5.
3.	6.

C. What reference sources would it be best to use? (When this section is filled out, star the three resources that probably will be of most value for your topic.)

1. What index or abstract journals would be best to use?

2. Will the dictionary card catalogue be of much help?

3. Will an encyclopedia be of much help? If so, which one?

4. Will you have special problems with regard to biographical data, current events, statistical data, small items of necessary information? If so, where should you look to solve those problems?

D. List below at least 10 references for your topic. You can use the three sources you have "starred" in the preceding questions and more if you wish. Include books as well as journal articles. Do not list just any references on your topic; be selective in order to list a well-rounded selection of the best sources.

Writing the Paper

You have now taken an early and major step toward writing a report by completing the previous library projects; you have a complete bibliography, or at least a good portion of one, for a term paper. Writing the paper itself, however, also presents difficulties for many students. Some find it difficult to express their ideas in writing; some have to labor so hard over grammar and punctuation that little energy is left for creative writing. Others have trouble with organizing their ideas.

Still others have problems with the format expected on a term paper. Approaches to these difficulties are discussed here.

SELF-EVALUATION

The only way to measure your skill and difficulties in writing term papers is actually to analyze some you have written. The following will give a basis for determining where remedial work is needed.

1. What grades have you received on previous term papers? What comments were written on them?

2. If you have the opportunity, read term papers that have received good grades. In what ways do they differ from yours?

3. Ask your instructor to review some of your former papers and to make suggestions as to specific ways in which they might be improved. Old essay exams also offer a basis for constructive suggestions on writing. Primary areas of difficulty should be checked below:

_____Legibility   _____General form
_____Spelling   _____Length
_____Grammar   _____Bibliography
_____Punctuation   _____Headings
_____Capitalization   _____Paragraphing
_____Sentence structure   _____Organization
_____Specific errors in format   _____Development of ideas

PROGRAM FOR IMPROVEMENT

With what aspects of writing term papers do you have the most difficulty? Suggestions for improvement will be presented in three sections: English usage, form, and organization and writing of the paper. Emphasize those sections that are the most pertinent and then complete step 4 (p. 143).

1. If one of your difficulties lies in correctness of written expression, see Chapter 11 (pp. 179–202). Most persons with this difficulty have seen comments like "poor English" or "poor spelling" written so often on their papers that they feel they will never become proficient. Chapter 11 will show, however, that college students who have such difficulties really know most of the rules of English usage but frequently

have trouble with just a few rules. When a student sees that two or three simple rules account for over one-half of his errors, a remedial program will seem easy and feasible to him.

2. Other students have difficulty in deciding what the correct form is for a term paper. Details as to length, expected divisions, use of headings, bibliographical form, form for quotations, use of footnotes, and so on, cause confusion and make it difficult to devote full energy to expressing one's ideas. An easy way to help with this difficulty is to study a model term paper and then refer to it as problems of form arise. The references by Turabian, by Hook and Gaver, and by Williams and Stevenson listed earlier (p. 138) give actual samples of such term papers. Since the form of term papers sometimes varies from one subject field to another, one should also find out what requirements the instructor has and, if possible, look over former term papers in that course.

3. The major difficulty for some students lies in organizing a term paper. They scarcely know where to begin or end; thus, some begin writing, continue merely adding material, and stop when the paper seems long enough. Since a job plan helps in expediting any type of work, the following plan should do much to make your approach to writing a term paper easier and more systematic.

a. Select a topic. It should be broad enough to provide plenty of material for writing but not so broad as to be suitable for a book. Look up several tentative topics in an index, such as the *Readers' Guide,* and select the one that has the best available bibliography.

b. Build your bibliography. As suggested in the first part of this chapter, use indexes, abstracts, the dictionary card catalogue, encyclopedias, and so on, to obtain a select bibliography; read these for ideas. Keep notes on your readings so that later they can be referred to, making unnecessary a return trip to the library. If these notes are kept on cards, they can later be put in some topical order and will help in the organization of writing.

c. Keep an idea page. A paper is usually assigned some time before it must be written. During this interval various ideas often come to mind that ought to be included in the paper. If these are not jotted down at once, they are often forgotten by the time you start writing the paper. Use a page in your notebook to jot down these ideas; then, when you are ready to write, these brief notes will serve as reminders. Instances of things to jot down are news events and stories that illustrate your points and new angles on your topic that occur to you. A premium is placed on originality in a paper, so this device will do much to increase the quality of your paper.

d. Outline your paper in detail. It was suggested that in writing essay examinations you jot down a brief outline before starting to write, which would produce a better answer. This is even more true in writing term papers, because the wealth of material to be covered makes it impossible to organize as one writes. This outline should be very complete: Each idea to be covered should be mentioned in the outline.

Use cue words and phrases rather than complete sentences. If rearrangement seems necessary, scratch out items and place them in better locations. Finally, when the outline is completed, the organization of the paper will stand out clearly. The major points in the outline will represent the headings for sections of your paper. With each point in its place in the outline, the job of writing will merely require that each point in turn be changed into a sentence or short paragraph.

e. Write the paper; dash it off from the outline and polish it later. It is difficult to keep many things in mind as you write. Devote your initial writing efforts to getting your ideas stated; you can go over this initial draft later in order to correct English mistakes and to put in headings, references, and footnotes. Dashing this first version off helps a writer keep his attention on his theme and not get lost in details, and the sentence ideas tend to flow into each other much more smoothly. Usually all necessary corrections can be inserted in this first draft, but, if necessary, parts can be cut out and pasted in order.

f. Type or rewrite the paper. Legibility and good form in a paper have a great deal to do with the final grade. As was indicated in connection with writing essay examinations, papers legibly written will average 10 percent higher grades than the same papers written somewhat illegibly. Reread this final version to be sure that a word or phrase has not been accidentally left out and to correct misspellings or illegibilities.

g. Submit the paper in an attractive form, since the over-all impression also influences the instructor. Put the paper in a binder. Put the title, your name, and the course number or name on the front. Number the pages. Finally, hand the paper in on time.

4. Do you have any papers to write this term? If so, the material on library usage earlier in this project will have given you a start. Discuss your plans for this paper with your instructor; he will be glad to assist in evaluating your outline and written report. The instructor who assigned the paper and your English instructor will also be glad to answer any questions you may have. Very often papers for your English course and for other courses can be combined.

CHAPTER 9
Foreign-language study

Whereas some students find the study of a foreign language easy and interesting, others find it one of their most difficult subjects. Some in this latter group spend hours each day studying the strange language, only to find that they have made little progress. Difficulty or lack of difficulty of foreign-language study is, in part, due to differences in facility for linguistic learning, but learned factors also determine success in language courses (91, 330). While occasionally a student may feel that he is incapable of learning foreign languages, the causes actually lie elsewhere and are usually remediable.

Some indication of the nature of these difficulties is shown in a series of experiments on factors related to success in German classes (208, 421, 422). In the first experiment two groups of students, equal in ability but differing markedly in their success in German, were measured in a large number of characteristics that might be related to success in language. The only areas in which the two groups showed significant differences were: English proficiency, desire to master a foreign language, daily preparation of lessons, habit of studying corrections made on their papers, and reading German for ideas rather than translating words. In a second experiment, an analysis was made of the methods that students use in studying German. The results showed that: (1) The poor students tended to postpone study, but the good students mastered each lesson and actually studied German when they sat down; (2) the poor students said they had a great deal of trouble with English grammar, but the good students did not and said they saw grammar as a means rather than as the end purpose of their course in English; and (3) the poor students said they made no special effort to study declensions, but the good students did. The latter also had a plan to use in attacking new German sentences and studied any corrections that the instructor made on their papers.

In brief, these factors are of three general types: motivation, English training, and special skills in foreign-language study. Each type of factor will be discussed in turn.

1. Some students have difficulty because they really are not interested in foreign languages and only study them to fulfill requirements for a degree. Even for those who are interested, the necessary routine practice does not provide interesting new facts such as the budding scientist finds in his study of chemistry. It is little wonder that a student sometimes prefers to study other more interesting courses first and finds it difficult to keep his mind on his language study. As a first step in making language study easier, a student must clarify in his own mind the values he expects to obtain from the study of a foreign language (108). Since this whole problem of getting down to work and learning to concentrate is the topic of Chapter 6, turn to that chapter if you are having trouble with language study.

2. Training in English, more specifically in English grammar, is another important factor that determines success in studying a foreign language (247). Because greater use is made of grammar terminology in teaching a foreign language than in teaching English, experiments show that knowledge of English grammar is actually more highly related to success in studying a foreign language than to success in studying English.

However, the necessary grammatical terminology is not as extensive as the size of a grammar book might indicate. On page 146 is a list of grammatical terms that analysis shows are frequently used and that teachers consider important in foreign-language study (292). (Of course there are many additional grammatical terms that a college student would know from his work in English composition.) Test yourself on these terms to see if you can think of an illustration for each. Any terms that cause difficulty can be looked up in an English grammar book or a dictionary.

Other practice materials dealing with English usage will be found in Chapter 11; turn to it if you feel that English usage is a factor in your language-study problem.

3. Special techniques for language study are also important. The suggestions that follow deal with the twin problems of learning to read for meaning and learning vocabulary and conjugations. A first suggestion is to read constantly for meaning rather than plod along looking up English equivalents (43, 78). Some students feel that they have read their lessons if they have dutifully looked up each word, but such translating gives little meaning and does not develop habits of expecting meaning; it is not really learning to read. Since reading for meaning is difficult the first time through a lesson, an immediate rereading provides this experience and helps fix the material in your mind. Further practice at reading for meaning can be obtained by reviewing previous lessons and by reading easy stories and newspapers in a foreign language.

Another suggestion is to study any specific aspect of the language that causes trouble. Even in chemistry it is important to study the technical vocabulary, but in a foreign language it is imperative to put special emphasis on vocabulary, conjugations, and idioms. Much of this is learned in reading selections, but some additional practice is necessary to fix in mind the meaning of frequently recurring foreign terms. Self-recitation practice on such word lists is extremely valuable. Whereas

TECHNICAL VOCABULARY IN FOREIGN-LANGUAGE COMPOSITION

1. masculine gender
2. feminine gender
3. neuter gender
4. possessive pronouns
5. possessive adjectives
6. relative pronouns
7. interrogative pronouns
8. demonstrative pronouns
9. definite articles
10. indefinite articles
11. transitive verbs
12. intransitive verbs
13. regular verbs
14. irregular verbs
15. nominative case
16. objective case
17. impersonal verbs
18. reflexive verbs
19. auxiliary verbs
20. infinitives
21. predicate nouns
22. indirect objects
23. negatives
24. interrogatives
25. prefixes
26. suffixes
27. positive degree
28. comparative degree
29. superlative degree
30. imperfect tense
31. perfect tense
32. pluperfect tense
33. active voice
34. passive voice
35. subjunctive mood
36. imperative mood
37. indicative mood
38. inverted word order
39. syllable
40. declensions
41. conjugations
42. inflection

only brief use of self-recitation was shown to be very effective immediately after reading a headed section in history, in learning such things as foreign vocabulary or poetry it is most efficient to spend as much as four-fifths of your time in self-recitation. That is, in learning a foreign language much time will be spent in actual reading and rereading, but that part of the time spent in vocabulary study should emphasize reciting from memory rather than mere reading of definitions (326).

A good way to practice self-recitation is to prepare a pack of vocabulary cards: On one side of the card write a foreign term and on the other side write its English equivalent or the desired declension or conjugation. Such cards can be made for important or frequently recurring words. Drill is carried on by looking at the foreign terms, thinking of their meaning, and then checking on the reverse side. Keep separate for a second trial the cards for those words that were not known; put cards for known words in a separate pile and review them occasionally.

Still another technique in foreign-language study is the development of a three-level plan of attack on new material.

 a. Try to foresee what is going to happen in the selection. Before starting to read, it is helpful to read the title and briefly skim over the selection; this general orientation greatly helps in recognizing the meanings of words or in guessing the meanings of entirely strange words. And as you read further in a selection, the story or theme becomes clearer so that anticipation is easier; this attitude should be maintained throughout the reading.

b. Techniques of attack on sentences are also important. In some languages the sequence of subject, verb, and object differs from the pattern in English; the student should have this pattern clearly in mind and, with difficult sentences, make it a practice to look for the words in that sequence. The position of modifiers in some languages also differs from their position in relation to nouns and verbs in English; attention to this detail also helps with difficult passages. With sufficient practice or with easy material, however, the student will find the language so familiar that he can get the sense of the sentence as he reads straight along, much as he does with English.

c. The third level of attack concerns methods of dealing with unknown words. Very often the context of a selection can indicate the probable meaning of a strange word; use the context to guess at words and finish the sentence or paragraph before using the dictionary to verify your estimate. Very often a familiar word root will represent part of a strange word, or a known word may be linked with other unknown words to form a compound word. In either instance, such analysis of the unknown word may be sufficient to suggest the correct meaning, which can later be verified. Guesses as to what a word means are correct so often that you should trust your first attempts at guessing and read straight along for general meaning; later you can check for more exact meanings. This practice is more effective than translating each word, which involves continually turning to the back of the book or to a dictionary.

Foreign languages are taught by different methods and with different emphases. For instance, some instructors emphasize grammar or exact translation, whereas others emphasize rapid reading for whatever meaning can be obtained. Some emphasize reading ability, whereas others emphasize pronunciation. It is obvious that each emphasis demands a somewhat different approach in studying. If you are having trouble with a language course, ask your instructor for suggestions concerning the best methods of learning the language.

PART TWO
Educational Deficiencies Affecting Schoolwork

Deficiencies in the three Rs affect the success of many students in college. For instance, tests show that some college freshmen read no better than the average fourth-grader, that some cannot do a single problem in long division, and that some cannot recognize pronouns in a sentence. Difficulties such as these prevent otherwise capable students from completing their lessons, from doing physics problems correctly, or from translating a foreign language easily.

Studies have shown that these difficulties are often limited to a few specific errors or bad habits and that with individualized help quite astounding gains can be made. For instance, rate of reading can be doubled, improving the writing of four letters will account for over 50 percent of legibility difficulties, and learning a few specific constructions or words will eliminate a large percentage of grammatical or spelling errors.

With this in mind, it is proposed that you make a survey of your basic skills (you have already completed some of the tests) in order to determine in which areas, if any, you need particular assistance. Because many of these tests are quite long, in order to provide adequate diagnosis, most of the tests for Part Two are grouped together in Appendix II. Page references are made for these tests as they are needed.

CHAPTER 10

Reading ability

Because of the great emphasis placed on long assignments in textbooks and reference books, reading ability is an important determinant of school success (37, 237, 339). For this reason, higher-level skills in reading were discussed at length in Chapters 2 and 3. Some students are prevented from making full use of such higher-level skills because in certain aspects of basic reading skill they have serious deficiencies, *e.g.*, word-by-word reading, poor habits of comprehension accuracy, inadequate vocabularies, or inability to read graphs and tables. The present chapter is devoted to the diagnosis and treatment of deficiencies in these four aspects of reading skill. Tests for self-evaluation are included in this chapter and in Appendix II so that you can determine which sections will be of most interest.

GENERAL CHARACTERISTICS OF READING

A discussion of three general characteristics of reading provides a basis for understanding the diagnostic sections into which this chapter is divided.

1. There are many reading abilities, not just one (98). A person who is expert at reading fiction may not be proficient at reading nonfiction for information. Since student lessons deal primarily with the latter, reading nonfiction is emphasized here. Skill in reading different types of nonfiction may also vary because of differences in vocabulary, style of writing, and what is wanted from the selection. It is important, therefore, that reading diagnosis be carried out on textbook-like materials, *e.g.*, nonfiction assignments that include graphs and tables and that are followed by quizzes.

2. Students show different levels of reading skill, which vary not only quantitatively, as in rate, but also qualitatively. Four such levels are here described:

a. The most inefficient level is word-by-word reading. Here the reader goes at an exceedingly slow rate and makes little, if any, adjustment to the difficulty of the reading material. For instance, in one experiment with such readers in college it was found that they read a selection from an easy elementary school reader at the same rate as one from a difficult graduate textbook (12). Such students usually have high intelligence and vocabulary; their difficulty seems to lie in certain perceptual-motor habits of perceiving one word at a time. Students reading at this level present a special problem in rate training.

b. Most students are at the second level of reading skill—flexible adjustment of rate to changes in difficulty and purpose (210, 240). The nature of this skill is well illustrated by the bottom three lines in Figure 19. They show that students' rate of reading over 9 minutes was adjusted to differences in difficulty in the three selections. Further, it shows that these readers started at a good rate but gradually adjusted their rate to the difficulty of the text; word-by-word readers, on the other hand, made no such adjustment and read straight along at the same rate. The dip in the Geology line is a further example of rate adjustment, in this case to a difficult table in the text. Not all readers have to slow down in this way on these selections; for instance, students who have a background of training in art can read the Art Reading Test straight along without slowing down. So one approach to remedial work is to increase a student's background of information, *i.e.*, vocabulary and information in his subject fields. A second ap-

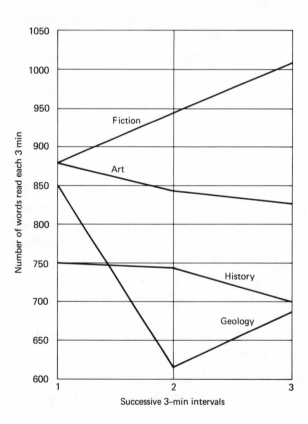

Figure 19. Change in rate of reading different subject matter during three successive 3-minute intervals. (Adapted from 310.)

proach is to provide training in qualitatively different, higher-level readings skills such as are described in the next two levels (336).

c. The third level is the use of the context of a story to precomprehend what is coming (263). The Fiction line in Figure 19 illustrates this. This fiction story was easy to comprehend, so about one-half of the readers read straight along at the same rate for the entire 9 minutes; other students, comprehending the story, however, used their ability to guess what was going to happen to speed up their later comprehension. Such precomprehension is very useful in reading.

d. The fourth and highest level of reading skill is the ability to benefit from typographical and writing cues in the text; the SQ3R method is an example of such a skill. Not only does the preliminary survey of headings aid in precomprehension (level 3) but the use of typographical cues while reading also indicates what must be read carefully and what can be skimmed or skipped.

As consideration is given to the very top levels of reading skill, some misconceptions or misunderstandings may occur concerning their nature and what is possible. Maximum rate of reading is one such example. Sometimes it is stated that a person can learn to read at a thousand or more words per minute. In such an instance, however, he would be *skimming*, not doing straight reading (177, 373, 380). Although skimming, *i.e.*, quickly reading topic sentences but skipping over large sections of material, is a useful skill, it should not be confused with straight reading (145, 217). Similarly one would not try to increase walking efficiency by practicing running. Studies made of persons known to be outstanding readers have shown that the maximum rate of straight reading is around 500 words per minute (262). This rate is twice as fast as most students read and is certainly a worthwhile goal to aim for. There are occasions when facility in skimming is also worthwhile. The difference is noted here so that the reader will not be confused in his expectations.

3. Finally, there are basic factors or components in reading that should be considered in making a diagnosis (98, 349). These factors are well shown in an experiment in which 100 college students took 25 different reading tests and other types of tests (150). The results on each test were correlated with every other test and these several hundred correlations were then subjected to a rather involved method of statistical treatment known as factor analysis. Through this technique of mathematical analysis the educational psychologist is able to determine how many different, independent traits are involved in determining the scores on all of the original tests. In addition, a study of the factors that each test tends to measure enables him to describe these traits that have been isolated. The following factors were found and identified in this experiment; below each factor is listed the tests in this book that measure it.

1. Rate of comprehending material

   Rate on Canadian History Reading Test: Words per minute _____
   Percentile _____

2. Attitude of comprehension accuracy

> Comprehension Accuracy on Canadian History Reading Test:
> Percentile _____

3. Vocabulary

> General Vocabulary Test: Percentile _____
>
> Dictionary Test: _____ Percent correct (100 percent correct expected)

4. Ability to read nonverbal material

> Table Reading Test: _____ Percent correct (100 percent correct expected)
>
> Chart Reading Test: _____ Percent correct (100 percent correct expected)
>
> Map Reading Test: _____ Percent correct (100 percent correct expected)
>
> Formula Reading Test:_____ Percent correct (100 percent correct expected)

DIAGNOSING YOUR READING ABILITY

The first step in this project is to complete these tests so that you may have a profile of the abilities that determine your reading skill. With the exception of the General Vocabulary and the Dictionary Tests that appear later in this chapter, all the other tests referred to in the preceding section are located in Appendix II. Directions are given with each test, although some assistance in timing will have to be given for the Canadian History Reading Test. When they are completed, each test should be corrected with its key in Appendix III. Norms for the History Reading Test are given in the following paragraph, and norms for the other tests are included later in this chapter. When you have completed these tests, write your results in the blanks given in the preceding section, as a general summary of this chapter.

Some special directions are needed for scoring the History Reading Test. The number of the line marked at the end of the 10-minute interval gives the average number of words read per minute. Table 8 shows how well a student's rate compares with that of other college students (superior readers in the general population) in terms of percentile ranks. Thus, if a student's words per minute on the History Reading Test were 207, his percentile rank would be 50, or equal to that of the average college freshman. If his rate were 181 words per minute (this number is halfway between 176 and 186 or the 20th and 30th percentiles on the table), he would interpolate and say that 181 words per minute is equal to the 25th percentile.

Comprehension accuracy in reading is determined by dividing the number of questions a student answers correctly by the number of questions asked about the material he has read. That is, if a student got 10 questions correct out of the 20 questions asked about the material he read on the History Reading Test, his percent correct would be 50. (Students who wish to save themselves some work in long division will find that the table on page 253 can be used to translate fractions into percent.) This score of 50 percent correct, however, does not indicate how he

TABLE 8 Percentile Ranks for Rate Scores
and for Comprehension Accuracy Scores
on the Canadian History Reading Test

Percentile	Rate in words per minute	Comprehension accuracy in percent right
99	375	95
95	314	90
90	279	87
80	251	80
70	234	75
60	217	71
50	207	67
40	196	63
30	186	58
20	176	53
10	163	44
5	152	37
1	104	22

compares to other students; to find his percentile rank, compare the percentage score in the right-hand part of Table 8 with the percentile column at the left. It will be seen that 50 percent correct on the History Reading Test is about equal to the 16th percentile.

PLAN OF THIS PROJECT

Did you have difficulty with any of these tests? What are the characteristics of your reading difficulty? You will be interested in finding the causes and methods for treating them. The subdivisions of this chapter are arranged to fit the above analysis, *i.e.*, (A) Rate of Reading, (B) Comprehension Accuracy, (C) Vocabulary, and (D) Special Reading Skills for tables, charts, maps, and formulas. If a test has shown that you have difficulty in any of these fields, you will be interested in the remedial exercises suggested in that section.

A. Rate of Reading

The two aspects of reading that show the greatest improvement during the freshman year in college are rate of reading and vocabulary. Rate of reading is intimately related to the number of fixations that the eyes make as they move across the page. A record of such eye movement patterns is shown in Figure 20. Such a record is obtained by photographing the eyes as they move across the page and then projecting the film on the original text where the location of each fixation is marked. Each vertical line, therefore, represents a fixation; the numbers at the top of the lines indicate their sequence, and the numbers at the bottom indicate their duration in thirtieths of a second. It will be seen that good readers make fewer fixations and regressions than poor readers do.

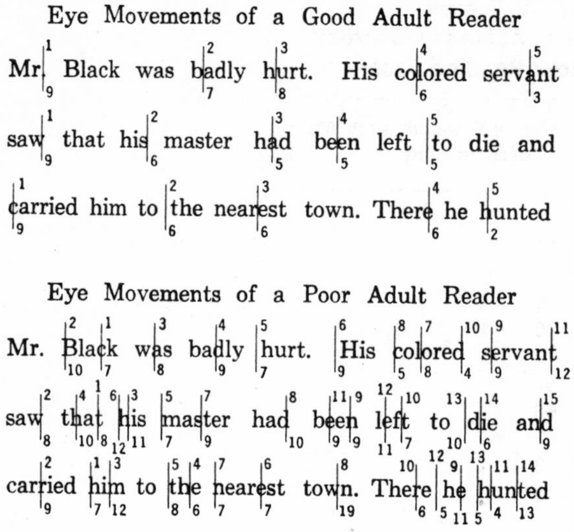

Eye Movements of a Good Adult Reader

Mr. Black was badly hurt. His colored servant
saw that his master had been left to die and
carried him to the nearest town. There he hunted

Eye Movements of a Poor Adult Reader

Mr. Black was badly hurt. His colored servant
saw that his master had been left to die and
carried him to the nearest town. There he hunted

Figure 20. Eye movements of a good and a poor adult reader for the same material. (Adapted from G. T. Buswell, How adults read, *Supplementary Educational Monographs*, 1937, no. 45. By permission of The University of Chicago Press.)

If conditions can be set up by the individual so that he makes fewer stops and, therefore, longer jumps, he will read at a much faster rate. Reading rate is primarily determined by comprehension facility, which will be discussed later in this chapter (347). The present section deals with a specific condition that seems to cause a slow rate, even though comprehension ability is good; that is, a carrying over of oral-reading habits into silent reading. Such a carry-over often makes an individual look at one word at a time and so develop a habit of reading slowly. This word-by-word reading was the lowest of the four levels of reading ability described above.

SELF-EVALUATION

1. Is your rate percentile quite low (lowest 10 percent)?

2. Do you tend to read the History selection at about the same rate during each time interval? The first number marked shows the amount read during the first 3 minutes, the difference between the first and second number equals the number of words read during the second 3 minutes, and 75 percent of the difference between the last number and the second will give the rate for the third 3 minutes.

Tabulate these results here:

First 3 minutes _____

Second 3 minutes _____

Third 3 minutes _____

3. Do your lips move while reading?

PROGRAM FOR IMPROVEMENT

If the preceding evaluation shows that you have a habit of reading slowly, the following remedial suggestions will be of value. If your slow rate seems to be due to comprehension difficulties, however, you should turn to Sections B and C of this chapter for remedial suggestions.

1. Practice reading more rapidly than you do now, and in a short time you will develop a habit of reading faster. You must be careful in pushing your rate in order not to skim and miss the meaning of the selection. The way to read might be best illustrated by the way a student would read if he discovered that in 10 minutes there would be a quiz on a lesson that he had not read. Such a student would read very rapidly, yet would get all that he can out of the lesson. At first, reading in this way may be fatiguing. If so, take short rests to write notes on what you have read. Later, a faster rate will become habitual. Read all your work in this manner; halfhearted practice is of little value. Use any free time you have in this classroom for practice on rate.

The simplicity of this method of improving reading rate may seem easy. Continued effort must be exerted, however, to produce gains. You will have to plan a definite program of practice each day and carry it out faithfully.

Because it is sometimes difficult to remember to keep pushing your rate as you read, it may be helpful occasionally to use one of the "speed reading" devices; these mechanical devices can be set to expose (or cover up) reading material at different rates so the reader has to keep pushing his rate in order to keep up (see Figure 21). The rate of reading can be determined with a little computation from the dial of the instrument and so a record of progress in increasing rate is easily obtained.

Figure 21. A "speed-reading" device. The shield over the book can be moved at varying speeds, thus making the person read faster. (Courtesy of Ohio State University.)

There has been some argument as to whether these instruments are uniquely effective in increasing the reading span (or the amount seen at each eye fixation). A great deal of recent research has shown that continued practice in merely trying to read faster (while comprehending) is as effective as the use of any of the mechanical devices (49, 189, 206, 259, 356, 368). However, it is clear that the devices are interesting to use, reduce the effort of trying to read at a faster rate, and are, therefore, a motivating device for some students (31, 314, 374). Since there are many kinds of instruments, ask your instructor for information about how to operate the type that is available.

2. It is difficult for a person to determine his improvement day by day because of the tendency for his rate to fluctuate with the change in difficulty of the material, and without a record one is unable to remember his earlier scores. Hence, it is important to measure rate of reading several times each week and summarize these results on the following chart. Fluctuations in rate can be kept at a minimum, and optimum practice can be given in increasing reading span if interesting, easy material is used from magazines, novels, and nonfiction. In time the rate at which you read during these practice sessions should gradually increase. Such evidence of improvement gives encouragement to carry on further practice and also indicates when a satisfactory rate has been attained. At the end of the term another standardized Rate and Comprehension Test will be given, so that gain from practice during the term can be shown from two comparable tests.

In estimating the amount read, count the words on a full page and multiply this by the number of pages read. Divide this number of words by the number of minutes it takes to read the selection.

Care must be taken, while measuring rate, to make sure that you are comprehending as you read. Comprehension can be checked by writing a summary paragraph about what you have read when measuring rate. These summary paragraphs may also be used to evaluate your ability to summarize.

3. Lip movement, whispering, and pointing with the finger while reading all prevent rapid reading. These acts do not aid comprehension and should be eliminated.

4. Since comprehension difficulties are usually the main determinants of rate of reading, exercises to improve vocabulary, to learn to read for questions, and to improve organization will result in faster as well as better comprehension. The methods for improving these are given in the following sections of this chapter. Practice with the SQ3R method also usually results in improved rate of reading. All these should be practiced in addition to the rate exercises.

Instances of "supernormal" reading rate.   Within recent years a great deal of publicity has been given to commercial training programs that produce individuals who can read at a thousand or more words per minute. It has been pointed out in earlier chapters that students have more difficulty with comprehension and remembering than with speed of reading. Experiments cited earlier show that people

Reading Rate Practice

Date	Material and pages read	Rate in words per minute	Date	Material and pages read	Rate in words per minute

normally read more slowly when reading books than when taking a reading test. Further, when individuals who have taken a reading test are asked to read another comparable selection "as fast as they can," they make even higher rate scores (50, 210, 252). The effect that mere change in attitude has on reading rate helps explain part of the gains made from pre- and posttesting in training programs, *i.e.*, not a real, habitual difference.

Nonetheless, in our culture a general admiration for speed of doing things and a desire to get work done quickly so time will be available for other things leads many individuals to want to know more about these "fantastic" readers. One research worker defined "supernormal reading ability" as ability to read at or above 1500 words per minute on the Survey Section of the Diagnostic Reading Test with comprehension at 70 percent or better (3). He found only 12 cases out of 2000 in a good training program who met this definition. His further analysis showed that they were excellent readers before training. Some evidence cited earlier indicates that these supernormal readers moved into a type of skimming skill and were not doing straight reading.

Many of these speed reading programs make statements about the nature of the reading process (perception, eye movements, neurology) that are not actually true. Thus, in one analysis of 20 reading improvement programs it was found that 18 included statements contradictory to research about the nature of eye movements and perception in reading (31, 146, 365). Also, careful evaluative studies of the outcomes of these programs show that the gains made are not as substantial nor do they persist and transfer as well as sometimes claimed (222, 348, 363).

In brief, supernormal speeds do not particularly help with schoolwork, and many exaggerated claims are made. These supernormal speeds involve learning techniques of skimming in which learning to spot key phrases and summary statements is an important element—a comprehension technique to be discussed later in this chapter. Thus, skimming is not a universal solution to study problems, but developing competence in it can be useful for scanning reference books for a needed item of information, getting a general impression of a book, and so on.

B. Comprehension Accuracy

Students read in order to comprehend and be stimulated by the ideas in a selection; the major emphasis in training should, therefore, be on improving comprehension (389). Within recent years there has been a marked shift in college reading training programs from an emphasis on rate of reading to improving comprehension (89, 234). The characteristics of effective comprehension vary with the requirements of the situation, so a first step is to define the nature of the undergraduate task.

Analysis of undergraduate textbooks and quizzes shows that they are primarily trying to put across a limited number of basic concepts in each subject field. The great amount of detail in a text is there to elaborate and illustrate these essential concepts.

1. A first characteristic of the student's task is, therefore, to select and comprehend these basic concepts.

2. A second characteristic is to complete this comprehension within a reasonable amount of time. Students frequently complain that their lessons take too long to read and, consequently, they seek ways of increasing their speed of comprehension.

3. A third and related characteristic of the reading task is to adopt a level of comprehension accuracy in order to efficiently complete the assignment, *i.e.*, sufficient depth of understanding to answer the question, but not such great depth (unless called for) that extra time is taken and an attempt is made to retain confusing detail. In brief, one needs to learn how to be selective in comprehending.

4. If comprehension skill can exist at several levels, then an expert reader should develop several levels of reading skill and be intelligent and flexible in using the comprehension mode that is most relevant (46, 181, 211, 312). Much as a person who plays golf recognizes that golf consists of more than just hitting the ball each time and, therefore, buys different clubs and learns different swings for the varying situations he meets on the course—so a student should develop several ways of going about comprehending at different levels (skimming, getting main ideas, following directions, careful analysis, and so on) and then learn to use these methods flexibly in the appropriate situations.

These four characteristics of the student reading task are treated more fully in the Program for Improvement Section that follows.

However, when studies are made of how flexible readers are (elementary school through college, good readers versus poor readers in college, readers in this and other countries), it is found that the great majority are "Johnny-one-notes"—they read everything in the same way (47, 217, 239, 260, 337). As might be expected, such flexibility cannot come through working on other aspects of reading, such as rate or vocabulary (240, 390) but from direct training.

As noted above most college assignments do not (possibly unfortunately) call for much careful analytical or critical reading. Recently, however, much more emphasis is being placed on carefully defining the nature of critical reading and in devising programs for teaching it; some of these programs are proving quite effective (48, 223, 334, 381).

SELF-EVALUATION

The History Reading Test provides two measures that are of interest here. The rate of reading score, except in that instance in which it would be abnormally low because of word-by-word reading, is in reality a measure of the speed with which you were able to comprehend the selection. That is, it provides a measure of how rapidly your background of vocabulary, knowledge of these fields, intelligence, and so on, permitted you to read this selection. Is your rate of comprehension for non-fiction material at a satisfactory level for you?

Although it is generally true that when a student reads more slowly and carefully his comprehension accuracy tends to increase and when he skims his accuracy score tends to go down, the History comprehension accuracy test actually measures an aspect of reading that is uniquely different from the factors measured by the rate test. The directions ask the student to read in the manner in which he normally studies his assignments. The comprehension accuracy score then represents a measure of the level of comprehension accuracy that the student thinks is sufficient to answer quizzes, *i.e.*, it is a measure of his *attitude* toward study material. (The rate test indicates how fast he can comprehend at *that* level.) It is important that a student learn to adjust the level of comprehension accuracy with which he reads to an efficient level for college assignments.

Now look over your reading rate and comprehension test scores and note if either the rate or the comprehension accuracy scores indicate need for remedial work on this section.

PROGRAM FOR IMPROVEMENT

1. Selecting and comprehending the main points. Effective study consists of "reading with one's head instead of one's eyes." The student must learn to read with an active attitude of seeking what is important and subordinating what is merely explanatory. He must rise above rather passive comprehension of each succeeding sentence and paragraph. The SQ3R method, which was discussed in Chapter 2, is the main approach to this aspect of the reader's task. Chapter 2 should be reread if this area is a problem for a student.

2. Increasing speed and depth of comprehension. Students read more rapidly in those fields with which they are familiar. Although the text of a chemistry book is usually more difficult than the text of a sociology book, chemistry students can usually read the former text at the faster rate. They would more than likely say, because of their background of vocabulary and chemical knowledge, that the chemistry selection was the easier of the two. A basic approach to improving comprehension, either in speed or depth, is to increase vocabulary and understanding of the basic ideas in a student's subject fields (172). (See Section C for a discussion of procedures here.) Techniques that help the reader focus his attention on the main ideas in the selection tend to keep him from becoming engrossed in detail and so speed up his reading. Techniques of using a preliminary survey and the thread of the argument thus far to precomprehend what is coming can also help in speeding up comprehension.

3. Developing an effective level of comprehension accuracy. In general, the higher the level of comprehension accuracy the better it is for the student; this is not always true, however. Obviously a person who scores very low on the comprehension accuracy test should work to increase his accuracy in order not to miss so many essential ideas as he reads. Since the questions in the History test are based on important ideas in the selection, the student who comprehends more of them than another student is usually the better reader. Sometimes, however, students reveal a combination of extremely high comprehension accuracy with an exceedingly slow rate. These students misunderstand what college studying means. Their attempts to dwell meticulously over each idea so slows them down that they waste time. Although their immediate memory may be good, the large number of ideas often seem like a mass of unorganized detail and are rapidly forgotten. Thus the slow learner often tends to be the rapid forgetter. Both the inaccurate reader and the slow, meticulous reader will be discussed here.

The inaccurate reader often does not understand that a deeper comprehension is required in college work. Awareness of how his accuracy scores compare to those of other students will do much to make him read more carefully. Even more effective is adoption of a method of checking his comprehension of essential ideas after he reads each section. This can be done by changing a heading into a question, reading to answer it, then checking to see if he can answer the question from memory. If so, he can be sure he is comprehending the essential ideas. A third technique for raising comprehension accuracy is to increase a student's vocabulary and background of information so that the ideas can be comprehended more deeply and accurately. One common cause of inaccuracy and difficulty in reading is failure to understand basic material that came earlier in the book. Later parts of a textbook usually make use of basic concepts explained earlier; thus, a student who does not get these early basic ideas is lost in the later material.

The problem of the slow, meticulous reader cannot be solved simply by having him speed up his reading until rate and accuracy are in a better balance. Basically such a reader is going about his lessons incorrectly, and a distinct shift in method may be necessary. He is like the housewife who was found dusting the inside of the piano when the guests arrived; both should be admonished to keep important goals in mind. A slow-reading student should turn to the material on the SQ3R method and to the preceding section on reading to select and comprehend the main points. Much practice will be needed to develop this new skill so it can be substituted for his present method. In working on this, a student should use easy reading material, such as the *Reader's Digest*. He should look at the title to orient himself, read the article rapidly, and then recite briefly on it. Such practice will gradually develop an effective substitute skill.

4. Deeper, critical comprehension. In addition to learning how to read (attitude and skill) for major points in an assignment, one must also develop many other kinds of comprehension skill and learn how to use them flexibly to suit the situation, *e.g.*, skimming, appreciating literature, following directions, critical comprehension, and so forth. The last of these—critical comprehension—needs to be discussed further because it is one of the most difficult kinds of comprehension and is of importance in upper-division and graduate work. This type of reading, however, is still not reading "to comprehend and remember everything." One still looks for the major theses developed in various paragraphs and sections, but one now more carefully judges whether each major point follows from the details presented in that section and whether the flow of logic in the succeeding sections or paragraphs rings true or seems to take unwarranted jumps.

Such careful reading demands many skills, high intelligence, and a well-adjusted personality. The reader must have the vocabulary to understand the words used, he must be familiar with the many meanings that a word may have and select the correct one in that sentence, he must be able to determine what the main ideas are that are being presented, he must have the background of experience to judge whether the ideas coincide with reality, he must be bright enough to grasp the argument presented and to judge it, and he must be well-adjusted so his personal biases do not interfere with an objective evaluation. Thus, it is little wonder that when a careful survey of adult readers was made in a large midwestern city, few, if any, were found who were able to read at the maximum of all the scales used in studying "the mature reader" (144).

When comparative studies are made of the personalities (good versus poor adult readers), it is found that good readers tend to display mature, well-developed personalities, e.g., trust, autonomy, initiative, positive self-concept, and lack of anxiety (18, 66, 266, 426). Poor readers, on the other hand, are characterized by anxiety, pessimism, intolerance, abasement needs, negativism and immature ego development (166, 221, 426). Not only does personality maladjustment keep the reader from thinking as effectively as he might, but it also affects how he perceives the main characters in the story, e.g., he may project his own needs on to the character (29, 168, 195, 345). When other studies are made of the cultural background of good versus poor readers, many differences are found, e.g., parents of good readers read more books and magazines, carry on more intellectual discussions in the home, value the importance of an education, and the children have had a wider variety of experiences to provide background (79, 165, 194, 340). In brief, not only must skills be taught but attention must be given to providing each youngster with opportunities for adequate general development.

C. Vocabulary

As indicated above, vocabulary is another important aspect of college reading (321). An analysis of college quizzes, especially in freshman and sophomore courses, indicates that they frequently call for definitions of words. The vocabulary necessary for comprehending even newspapers is quite large. For instance, it is estimated that a vocabulary of 50,000 words is necessary to understand fully an edition of The New York Times. A large vocabulary of usable words is also an aid in making precise statements. Most students have experienced occasions when they have searched rather unsuccessfully for words to express exactly what they mean.

College students show surprising unfamiliarity with words important in their work. The vocabulary test later in this book carefully samples the 20,000 most frequently used words out of several hundred thousand in an unabridged dictionary, but the average college freshman gets only about half of the words correct. A study of 2000 freshmen in seven colleges in Great Britain showed that they knew only about one-half of a group of words carefully selected as important in reading college selections and which "ideally all students should know" (198). Words that were common at one time, and known by professors, may currently be unfamiliar. For instance, a group of 425 adults (21–30 years old) who were children during World War II had trouble with words current at that time, e.g., "gobbleygook" was thought to be a fast eater for some and a Korean turkey for others (375).

As cited in Chapter 1, few students know how good their vocabulary is in comparison to other students. Without such information a student scarcely knows how hard he should work in this area.

SELF-EVALUATION

A power test is provided for measuring your general vocabulary. It is based on a thorough sampling of words according to their frequency of use. You are not expected to know all the words included; but with this sampling method it can be assumed that if you know a certain percentage of these words you will also know a like percentage of all words of equivalent frequency of use. This test will be taken by everyone in the class at the same time. After you have worked 20 minutes, the instructor will read the correct answers, or you may turn to pages 284–286 to score your test. Then use Table 9 to translate your score into a percentile rank. If your

TABLE 9 Percentile Ranks for Scores on Vocabulary Test

Percentiles	Scores
100	80
95	65
90	56
80	49
70	44
60	39
50	36
40	33
30	30
20	26
10	21
5	18
1	10

rank is lower than you would like, read the suggestions in the section Program for Improvement (pp. 173–177). In this case, however, do not study the specific errors you made on the test.

In addition to a general vocabulary, each person has to master the basic technical vocabulary in his fields of interest (382). Thus, the doctor and the lawyer use many words in common, but each has a list of technical words in his own field. One of the great difficulties faced by the college student is the necessity of mastering the basic technical vocabulary in each of his courses, e.g., the terms from history, from geology, from mathematics, from social science, and so on (185). Unless he knows these concepts, all the explanations in text and class will be "over his head."

Your competence with such technical vocabulary in your courses can most easily be measured by marking the technical words that are used in headings or that are italicized or in boldface type in the body of your textbooks. Then see if you can briefly define or explain each one. Any missed should be listed on page 176 and studied. Previous quizzes are another source of important technical terms. Whenever you find a question missed because of your not knowing the terms used, list them along with the technical terms found in your textbooks.

The dictionary is an extremely important tool in learning about concepts used by authors. Yet many students do not know how to use a dictionary effectively, nor are they in the habit of using it often. Use the following Dictionary Test to measure your skill in dictionary usage. When all of the questions have been answered, use the key on page 286 to correct your test. Place your score (percent correct) at the top of the test. Remember that 100 percent correct is the expected norm.

A General Vocabulary Test[1]

Score _____ Percentile _____ Date _____

In this test you are to show that you know the meaning of the following words. In the parentheses at the left, write the number of the word which means the same as the word to be defined. Note the example; then proceed at once to the test. Work rapidly.

Example

(5) reply: (1) show (2) reason (3) call (4) rejoice (5) answer

1. ( ) illustrious: (1) clever (2) famous (3) odd (4) sensitive (5) wicked

2. ( ) confident: (1) sensible (2) confiding (3) sure (4) expectant (5) enthusiastic

3. ( ) allegiance: (1) safety (2) respect (3) loyalty (4) honesty (5) honor

4. ( ) covet: (1) hold (2) usurp (3) seize (4) refuse (5) desire

5. ( ) pensive: (1) meditative (2) quiet (3) mistaken (4) earnest (5) relieved

6. ( ) discreet: (1) secret (2) prudent (3) opposite (4) brief (5) separate

7. ( ) amiable: (1) loving (2) sad (3) satisfied (4) agreeable (5) clever

8. ( ) fatigue: (1) weariness (2) pain (3) sorrow (4) remorse (5) bitterness

9. ( ) loathe: (1) dislike (2) recall (3) hinder (4) refrain (5) detest

10. ( ) absurd: (1) peculiar (2) sick (3) ridiculous (4) laughable (5) queer

11. ( ) decade: (1) fortnight (2) a score of years (3) ten years (4) one hundred years (5) one thousand years

12. ( ) bewilder: (1) perplex (2) lose (3) soothe (4) deceive (5) chasten

13. ( ) alien: (1) opposed (2) special (3) menacing (4) foreign (5) mysterious

14. ( ) fidelity: (1) faithfulness (2) enthusiasm (3) strength (4) forbearance (5) veneration

15. ( ) dissension: (1) hypocrisy (2) elongation (3) discord (4) misery (5) discussion

16. ( ) eccentric: (1) crazy (2) odd (3) intellectual (4) sensible (5) conventional

17. ( ) latent: (1) punctual (2) late (3) dormant (4) easy (5) impossible

18. ( ) heretic: (1) communist (2) pagan (3) insane person (4) atheist (5) dissenter

19. ( ) eminence: (1) nearness (2) distance (3) greediness (4) distinction (5) generosity

20. ( ) judicious: (1) unusual (2) earnest (3) wise (4) lawful (5) bold

21. ( ) arduous: (1) endless (2) passionate (3) light (4) easy (5) difficult

22. ( ) incredulous: (1) faultless (2) surprised (3) dutiful (4) insincere (5) skeptical

23. ( ) propitious: (1) sympathetic (2) favorable (3) clever (4) odd (5) ugly

24. ( ) penury: (1) power (2) debt (3) poverty (4) graft (5) credit

[1] Devised by S. L. Pressey and used by special permission of the Ohio State Department of Education.

25. ( ) acquit: (1) liberate (2) adjourn (3) stop (4) condemn (5) refuse

26. ( ) contentious: (1) mean (2) bitter (3) harmonious (4) mild (5) quarrelsome

27. ( ) impertinent: (1) diffident (2) modest (3) polite (4) disrespectful (5) unreasonable

28. ( ) benign: (1) aged (2) indignant (3) kindly (4) sad (5) celebrated

29. ( ) complacent: (1) snobbish (2) delighted (3) satisfied (4) dull (5) stubborn

30. ( ) ludicrous: (1) weird (2) appalling (3) weak (4) laughable (5) insane

31. ( ) appreciable: (1) perceptible (2) welcome (3) honest (4) small (5) valuable

32. ( ) instigate: (1) sense (2) make public (3) prowl (4) start (5) find out

33. ( ) palpable: (1) readily perceived (2) safe (3) erroneous (4) fatuous (5) weak

34. ( ) adroit: (1) lucky (2) reserved (3) playful (4) deceitful (5) dexterous

35. ( ) diffident: (1) unruly (2) small (3) eager (4) silly (5) reserved

36. ( ) menial: (1) pious (2) servile (3) exalted (4) devoted (5) angry

37. ( ) candid: (1) frank (2) weak (3) clever (4) absurd (5) deceitful

38. ( ) enigma: (1) laxity (2) sentence (3) decoration (4) puzzle (5) religion

39. ( ) interim: (1) likewise (2) meantime (3) during office (4) space (5) age

40. ( ) refund: (1) guarantee (2) exchange (3) discount (4) receive (5) pay back

41. ( ) blatant: (1) evident (2) strange (3) noisy (4) wild (5) foolish

42. ( ) juvenile: (1) soft (2) weak (3) legal (4) young (5) amusing

43. ( ) anathema: (1) result (2) warning (3) blessing (4) irony (5) curse

44. ( ) contiguous: (1) smooth (2) comparable (3) distant (4) even (5) adjoining

45. ( ) adherent: (1) follower (2) cynic (3) old man (4) hermit (5) prejudiced

46. ( ) emolument: (1) flattery (2) decoration (3) theft (4) pay (5) honor

47. ( ) munificent: (1) rich (2) large (3) ideal (4) joyful (5) generous

48. ( ) litigation: (1) business organization (2) partnership (3) law suit (4) fight (5) clandestine affair

49. ( ) preamble: (1) procedure (2) introduction (3) command (4) hypothesis (5) law

50. ( ) cogent: (1) right (2) stated (3) convincing (4) absurd (5) real

51. ( ) inundate: (1) flood (2) extinguish (3) release (4) charge (5) moisten

52. ( ) veracity: (1) fear (2) wisdom (3) truth (4) courage (5) earnestness

53. ( ) abrogate: (1) annul (2) initiate (3) reduce (4) prepare (5) demur

54. ( ) dogmatic: (1) faithful (2) positive (3) religious (4) clear (5) radical

55. ( ) loquacious: (1) heavy (2) sorrowful (3) foolish (4) talkative (5) witty

56. ( ) anomalous: (1) poor (2) incognito (3) nameless (4) unimportant (5) abnormal

57. ( ) necromancer: (1) poet (2) sorcerer (3) orator (4) author (5) minister

58. ( ) soliloquy: (1) tirade (2) adage (3) conversation (4) monologue (5) cadenza

59. ( ) decorous: (1) sad (2) elegant (3) proper (4) obsequious (5) fashionable

60. ( ) mediocre: (1) good (2) odd (3) mistaken (4) ordinary (5) lax

61. ( ) comity: (1) beauty (2) humor (3) courtesy (4) godliness (5) faith

62. ( ) ascetic: (1) invalid (2) medicine (3) savior (4) athlete (5) recluse

63. ( ) nonpareil: (1) matchless (2) pacific (3) unwritten (4) foreign (5) extravagant

64. ( ) duplicity: (1) stealth (2) candor (3) deception (4) consistency (5) weakness

65. ( ) habiliment: (1) property (2) garment (3) home (4) habit (5) accessory

66. ( ) exigent: (1) departing (2) urgent (3) safe (4) timely (5) late

67. ( ) vertigo: (1) alertness (2) metamorphosis (3) action (4) speed (5) dizziness

68. ( ) charlatan: (1) prostitute (2) savior (3) servant (4) quack (5) mystic

69. ( ) amelioration: (1) calm (2) prayer (3) peace (4) penance (5) improvement

70. ( ) desiccate: (1) burn (2) cut down (3) destroy (4) remove (5) dry up

71. ( ) taciturn: (1) wise (2) loquacious (3) bashful (4) reserved (5) quarrelsome

72. ( ) chanson: (1) song (2) feat (3) noble deed (4) penalty (5) sacrifice

73. ( ) nonchalant: (1) bored (2) happy (3) indifferent (4) conceited (5) suave

74. ( ) replica: (1) antique (2) necklace (3) resemblance (4) painting (5) duplicate

75. ( ) flagitious: (1) facetious (2) villainous (3) simpering (4) repulsive (5) militant

76. ( ) recondite: (1) delinquent (2) criminal (3) pensive (4) ideal (5) profound

77. ( ) abnegation: (1) authority (2) veto (3) renunciation (4) refusal (5) surrender

78. ( ) fatuous: (1) obvious (2) celebrated (3) heavy (4) silly (5) impossible

79. ( ) amenity: (1) pleasantness (2) praise (3) correction (4) improvement (5) misunderstanding

80. ( ) ubiquitous: (1) learned (2) selfish (3) omnipresent (4) departed (5) wicked

Left column labels:

angle bracket
12.1

author quoted
12.2.1

binomial
13.1

boldface type
1.1, 19.1

capitalization label
5.1

centered period
1.6

cognate cross-reference
1.7.3

comb form
3.3, 18.

definition

directional cross-reference
15.1

double hyphen
1.6.1

equal variant
1.7.1

etymology
7.

functional label
3.1

homographs
1.4.1

hyphened compound
1.1

inflectional forms
4.1, 4.2

lightface type
1.1

lowercase
5.1

main entry
1.1, 19.1

often attrib
6.

open compound
1.1, 2.6

pl but sing in constr
4.3

prefix
3.3, 18.1

Right column entries:

⁴**save** \(ˌ)sāv\ *conj* **1** : were it not : ONLY — used with *that* **2** : BUT, EXCEPT — used before a word often taken to be the subject of a clause ⟨no one knows about it ~ she⟩ **3** : UNLESS ⟨~ they could be plucked asunder, all my quest were but in vain —Alfred Tennyson⟩

scar·a·bae·us \ˌskar-ə-'bē-əs\ *n* [L] **1** *pl* **scar·a·bae·us·es** *or* **scar·a·baei** \-'bē-ˌī\ : a large black or nearly black dung beetle (*Scarabaeus sacer*) **2** : a stone or faience beetle used in ancient Egypt as a talisman, ornament, and a symbol of the resurrection

scar·a·mouch *or* **scar·a·mouche** \'skar-ə-ˌmüsh, -ˌmüch, -ˌmau̇ch\ *n* [F *Scaramouche*, fr. It *Scaramuccia*] **1** (*cap*) : a stock character in the Italian commedia dell' arte drawn to burlesque the Spanish don and characterized by boastfulness and poltroonery **2 a** : a cowardly buffoon **b** : RASCAL, SCAMP

sce·nog·ra·phy \sē-'näg-rə-fē\ *n* [Gk *skēnographia* painting of scenery, fr. *skēnē* + *-graphia* -graphy] : the art of perspective representation applied to the painting of stage scenery (as by the Greeks)

sceptic *var of* SKEPTIC

schiz- *or* **schizo-** *comb form* [NL, fr. Gk *schizo-*, fr. *schizein* to split] **1** : split : cleft ⟨*schizo*carp⟩ **2** : characterized by or involving cleavage ⟨*schizo*genesis⟩ **3** : schizophrenia ⟨*schizo*thymia⟩

scho·las·ti·cism \skə-'las-tə-ˌsiz-əm\ *n* **1** *cap* **a** : a philosophical movement dominant in western Christian civilization from the 9th until the 17th century and combining a fixed religious dogma with the mystical and intuitional tradition of patristic philosophy esp. of St. Augustine and later with Aristotelianism **b** : NEO≠ SCHOLASTICISM **2** : close adherence to the traditional teachings or methods of a school or sect

¹**scru·ple** \'skrü-pəl\ *n* [ME *scriple*, fr. L *scrupulus* a unit of weight, fr. *scrupulus* small sharp stone] **1** — see MEASURE table **2** : a minute part or quantity : IOTA

²**sculptur e** *vb* **sculp·tur·ing** \'skəlp-chə-riŋ, 'skəlp-shriŋ\ *vt* **1 a** : to form an image or representation of from solid material (as wood or stone) **b** : to carve or otherwise form into a three≠ dimensional work of art **2** : to change (the form of the earth's surface) by erosion ~ *vi* : to work as a sculptor

sea-maid \'sē-ˌmād\ *or* **sea-maid·en** \-ˌmād-ᵊn\ *n* : MERMAID; *also* : a goddess or nymph of the sea

se·clude \si-'klüd\ *vt* [ME *secluden* to keep away, fr. L *secludere* to separate, seclude, fr. *se-* apart + *claudere* to close — more at SECEDE, CLOSE] **1 a** : to confine in a retired or inaccessible place **b** : to remove or separate from intercourse or outside influence : ISOLATE **2** *obs* : to exclude or expel from a privilege, rank, or dignity : DEBAR **3** : to shut off : SCREEN

¹**sec·ond·hand** \ˌsek-ən-'\ *adj* **1** : received from or through an intermediary : BORROWED **2 a** : acquired after being used by another : not new ⟨~ books⟩ **b** : dealing in secondhand merchandise ⟨a ~ bookstore⟩

²**secondhand** \ˌsek-ən-'\ *adv* : at second hand : INDIRECTLY

secretary–general *n*, *pl* **secretaries–general** : a principal administrative officer

²**seer** \'si(ə)r\ *n*, *pl* **seers** *or* **seer** [Hindi *ser*] **1** : any of various Indian units of weight; *esp* : a unit equal to 2.057 pounds **2** : an Afghan unit of weight equal to 15.6 pounds

²**seethe** *n* : a state of seething : EBULLITION

¹**seg·ment** \'seg-mənt\ *n*, *often attrib* [L *segmentum*, fr. *secare* to cut — more at SAW] **1 a** : a piece or separate fragment of something : PORTION **b** (1) : a portion cut off from a geometrical figure by a line or plane; *esp* : the part of a circular area bounded by a chord and an arc of that circle or so much of the area as is cut off by the chord (2) : the part of a sphere cut off by a plane or included between two parallel planes (3) : the finite part of a line between two points in the line **2** : one of the constituent parts into which a body, entity, or quantity naturally divides : DIVISION **syn** see PART — **seg·men·tary** \'seg-mən-ˌter-ē\ *adj*

selling race *n* : a claiming race in which the winning horse is put up for auction

se·man·tics \si-'mant-iks\ *n pl but sing or pl in constr* **1** : the study of meanings: **a** : the historical and psychological study and the classification of changes in the signification of words or forms viewed as factors in linguistic development **b** (1) : SEMIOTIC (2) : a branch of semiotic dealing with the relations between signs and what they refer to and including theories of denotation, extension, naming, and truth **2** : GENERAL SEMANTICS **3 a** : the meaning or relationship of meanings of a sign or set of signs; *esp* : connotative meaning **b** : the exploitation of connotation and ambiguity (as in propaganda)

semi- \ˌsem-i, 'sem-, -ˌī\ *prefix* [ME, fr. L; akin to OHG *sāmi*- half, Gk *hēmi*-] **1 a** : precisely half of: (1) : forming a bisection of ⟨*semi*ellipse⟩ ⟨*semi*oval⟩ (2) : being a usu. vertically bisected form of (a specified architectural feature) ⟨*semi*arch⟩ ⟨*semi*dome⟩ **b** : half in quantity or value : half of or occurring halfway through a specified period of time ⟨*semi*annual⟩ ⟨*semi*centenary⟩ — compare BI- **2** : to some extent : partly : incompletely ⟨*semi*civilized⟩ ⟨*semi*independent⟩ ⟨*semi*dry⟩ — compare DEMI-, HEMI- **3 a** : partial : incomplete ⟨*semi*consciousness⟩ ⟨*semi*darkness⟩ **b** : having some of the characteristics of ⟨*semi*porcelain⟩ **c** : quasi ⟨*semi*governmental⟩ ⟨*semi*monastic⟩

CHART

Notes of Webster's Seventh New Collegiate Dictionary, beginning on page 7a.)

stato·blast \'stat-ə-,blast\ *n* [ISV] **1 :** a bud in a freshwater bryozoan that overwinters in a chitinous envelope and develops into a new individual in spring **2 :** GEMMULE

stat·ol·a·try \,stāt-'äl-ə-trē\ *n* **:** advocacy of a highly centralized and all-powerful national government

stead·ing \'sted-ᵊn, 'stēd-, -iŋ\ *n* [ME *steding,* fr. *stede* place, farm] **1 :** a small farm **2** (*chiefly Scot*)**:** the service buildings or area of a farm

²steer *vb* [ME *steren,* fr. OE *stīeran;* akin to OE *stēor*- steering oar, Gk *stauros* stake, cross, *stylos* pillar, Skt *sthavira, sthūra* stout, thick, L *stare* to stand — more at STAND] *vt* **1 :** to direct the course of; *specif* **:** to guide by mechanical means (as a rudder) **2 :** to set and hold to (a course) ~ *vi* **1 :** to direct the course (as of a ship or automobile) **2 :** to pursue a course of action **3 :** to be subject to guidance or direction ⟨an automobile that ~s well⟩ **syn** see GUIDE — **steer·able** \'stir-ə-bəl\ *adj* — **steer·er** *n* — **steer clear** ⟨**:** to keep entirely away — often used with *of*⟩

stel·late \'stel-,āt\ *adj* **:** resembling a star (as in shape) **:** RADIATED ⟨a ~ leaf⟩ — **stel·late·ly** *adv*

³stint *n, pl* **stints** (*also* **stint**)[ME *stynte*] **:** any of several small sandpipers

²stipple *n* **:** production of gradation of light and shade in graphic art by stippling small points, larger dots, or longer strokes; (*also*)**:** an effect produced by or as if by stippling

¹stom·ach \'stəm-ək, -ik\ *n, often attrib* [ME *stomak,* fr. MF *estomac,* fr. L *stomachus* gullet, esophagus, stomach, fr. Gk *stomachos,* fr. *stoma* mouth; akin to MBret *staffu* mouth, Av *staman*-] **1 a :** a dilatation of the alimentary canal of a vertebrate communicating anteriorly with the esophagus and posteriorly with the duodenum **b :** an analogous cavity in an invertebrate animal **c :** the part of the body that contains the stomach **:** (BELLY, ABDOMEN) **2 a :** desire for food caused by hunger **:** APPETITE **b :** INCLINATION, DESIRE **3** (*obs*)**a :** SPIRIT, VALOR **b :** PRIDE **c :** SPLEEN, RESENTMENT

¹strike \'strīk\ *vb* **struck** \'strək\ **struck** *also* **strick·en** \'strik-ən\ **strik·ing** \'strī-kiŋ\ [ME *striken,* fr. OE *strīcan* to stroke, go; akin to OHG *strīhhan* to stroke, L *stringere* to touch lightly, *striga, stria* furrow] *vi* **1 :** to take a course **:** GO **2 :** to deliver or aim a blow or thrust **:** HIT **3 :** CONTACT, COLLIDE **4 :** DELETE, CANCEL **5 :** to lower a flag usu. in surrender **6 a :** to be indicated by a clock, bell, or chime **b :** to make known the time by sounding **7 :** PIERCE, PENETRATE **8 a :** to engage in battle **b :** to make a military attack **9 :** to become ignited **10 :** to discover something **11 a :** to pull on a fishing rod in order to set the hook **b** (*of a fish*) **:** to seize the bait **12 :** DART, SHOOT **13 a** *of a plant cutting* **:** to take root **b** *of a seed* **:** GERMINATE **14 :** to make an impression **15 :** to stop work in order to force an employer to comply with demands **16 :** to make a beginning **17 :** to thrust oneself forward **18 :** to work diligently **:** STRIVE (~) *vt* **1 a :** to strike at **:** HIT **b :** to drive or remove by or as if by a blow **c :** to attack or seize with a sharp blow (as of fangs or claws) ⟨*struck* by a snake⟩ **d :** INFLICT **e :** to produce by or as if by a blow or stroke ⟨*struck* (~) off flints⟩ **2 a :** to haul down **:** (LOWER) **b :** (**:**)to dismantle and take away

strin·gent \'strin-jənt\ *adj* [L *stringent-, stringens,* prp. of *stringere* to bind tight] **1 :** TIGHT, CONSTRICTED **2 :** marked by rigor, strictness, or severity esp. with regard to rule or standard **3 :** marked by money scarcity and credit strictness (**syn** see RIGID) — **strin·gent·ly** *adv*

strong \'strȯŋ\ *adj* **stron·ger** \'strȯŋ-gər\ **stron·gest** \'strȯŋ-gəst\ [ME, fr. OE *strang;* akin to OHG *strengi* strong, L *stringere* to bind tight — more at STRAIN] **1 :** having or marked by great physical power **:** ROBUST **2 :** having moral or intellectual power **3 :** having great resources (as of wealth) **4 :** of a specified number ⟨an army ten thousand ~⟩ **5 :** effective or efficient esp. in a specified direction **6 :** FORCEFUL, COGENT **7 :** not mild or weak **:** INTENSE: as **a :** rich in some active agent (as a flavor or extract) ⟨~ beer⟩ **b** *of a color* **:** high in chroma

syn STRONG, STOUT, STURDY, STALWART, TOUGH, TENACIOUS mean showing power to resist or to endure. STRONG may imply power derived from muscular vigor, large size, structural soundness, intellectual or spiritual resources; STOUT suggests an ability to endure stress, pain, or hard use without giving way; STURDY implies strength derived from vigorous growth, determination of spirit, solidity of construction; STALWART suggests an unshakable dependability and connotes great physical strength; TOUGH implies great firmness and resiliency; TENACIOUS suggests strength in seizing, retaining, clinging to, or holding together

stron·tia \'strän-ch(ē-)ə, 'stränt-ē-ə\ *n* (NL,) fr. obs. E *strontian,* fr. *Strontian,* village in (Scotland) **1 :** white solid monoxide SrO of strontium resembling lime and baryta **2 :** strontium hydroxide Sr(OH)₂

sty·loid \'stī(ə)l-,ȯid\ *adj* **:** resembling a style **:** STYLIFORM ⟨— used esp. of slender pointed skeletal processes (as on the temporal bone or ulna)⟩

sub·ac·id \-'as-əd\ *adj* [L *subacidus,* fr. *sub-* + *acidus* acid] **1 :** moderately acid ⟨⟨~ fruit juices⟩⟩ **2 :** rather tart ⟨~ prose⟩ — **sub·ac·id·ly** *adv* — **sub·ac·id·ness** *n*

²sun *vb* (**sunned; sun·ning**)*vt* **:** to expose to or as if to the rays of the sun ~ *vi* **:** to sun oneself

Label	Section
primary stress	**2.2**
pronunciation	**2.**
regional label	**8.3.4**
run-on entry (derivative)	**16.1**
run-on entry (phrasal)	**16.2**
secondary stress	**2.2**
secondary variant	**1.7.2**
sense divider	**11.4.2**
sense letter	**11.2**
sense number	**11.1**
small capitals	**15.0, 15.2**
status label	**8.**
subject label	**9.1**
swung dash (boldface)	**3.2**
swung dash (lightface)	**12.1**
symbolic colon	**10.**
synonymous cross-reference	**15.2**
synonymy cross-reference	**17.2**
synonymy paragraph	**17.1**
uppercase	
usage note	**14.**
verbal illustration	**12.1**
verb principal parts	**4.5, 4.6**

Test of Dictionary Usage

Percent Right _____

(Use the sample dictionary page on the preceding pages to answer these questions.)

1. In many definitions, as in the one for "save," the angle brackets (< >) are used to enclose a sample sentence in which the defined word is used.   T   F

2. In many definitions, as in the one for "save," a swung dash (~) is used as a short designation that the defined word is to be inserted there.   T   F

3. In the word "scarabaeus" the centered dots between the boldface letters indicate where the word could be broken (divided or hyphenated) to be carried over from the end of one line to the beginning of the next.   T   F

4. In the pronunciation section for the word "scarabaeus" the symbol " ' " means that the second syllable is stressed or given more emphasis in pronunciation.   T   F

5. In writing about a single scarabaeus either of two spellings is acceptable.   T   F

6. In spelling the word "scaramouch" either of two spellings is acceptable.   T   F

7. If the word "scaramouch" is used to represent a standard character in Italian comedy it is capitalized.   T   F

8. The definition of "sceptic" is found under the listing "skeptic."   T   F

9. The use of the word "seclude" to mean to expel someone from a rank or privilege is now obsolete.   T   F

10. The plural form of "secretary-general" is secretary-generals.   T   F

11. The word "seer" when used as a unit of weight has the same meaning in India and in Afghanistan.   T   F

12. Further synonyms for the word "segment" will be found under the word entry for "part."   T   F

13. In a "selling race" the winning horse is put up for auction.   T   F

14. If a writer wants to use the word "semantics" in a singular form, he should write it "semantic."   T   F

15. In the word "statoblast" the symbol " ' " before "stat" in the pronunciation guide means that the first syllable is stressed or emphasized.   T   F

16. The word "statolatry" means to emphasize a decentralized or federalized government.   T   F

17. The use of the word "steading" to mean service buildings on a farm is commonly used throughout Europe.   T   F

18. The intransitive verb form of the word "strike" has how many meanings? _____

19. Meanings for the transitive verb form of the word "strike" are indicated both by numbers and by letters. Both symbols indicate equally distinctive meanings.   T   F

20. If you would like to find some synonyms for the word "stringent" in this dictionary, you should look up what word? _____

21. The entry for the word "strong" gives several synonyms and furthermore differentiates some of their meanings more specifically.
   a. If you wanted a word to indicate ability to withstand pain, it would be best to use the word (1) stout, (2) strong, (3) sturdy, (4) tenacious, (5) tough. _____
   b. If you wanted a word to represent firmness and resiliency, it would be best to use the word (1) stout, (2) strong, (3) sturdy, (4) tenacious, (5) tough. _____

PROGRAM FOR IMPROVEMENT

A student should be selective in setting out to increase his vocabulary. He should learn new words that will help him the most in his schoolwork and in his daily living. The following two bases are best in making such selections. (1) He should note words and phrases used in lectures, conversations, and reading that say better what he may have tried somewhat ineffectually to say. List these on page 176. (2) Even more important for schoolwork, he should learn as early as possible the unknown words (especially the technical terminology) that occur frequently in his textbooks. To the beginning student the percent of unfamiliar words in some science textbooks is higher than in some foreign language textbooks (where the vocabulary burden is more carefully controled). However, a tabulation of the actual words used shows that the number of different unfamiliar technical terms is not particularly large. They are used frequently. Learning these words as they occur the first time saves a lot of vague comprehension later as they reappear again and again.

1. As part of your self-evaluation, you were asked to make a list of technical terms you did not know. Make it a regular practice to mark new technical terms as you come to them in your textbooks or list them with the others on page 176 (182). It will also be useful to take one of your courses—the one with which you are having the most difficulty, if you wish—and list all the basic technical terms that have occurred (omit terms that are obviously included in the explanatory material and do not recur again). Some students may feel that such a list of technical terms in a textbook might be almost endless, but only the basic technical terms are meant here, *i.e.*, those that are used again and again. Thus, in one text 63 percent of the technical terms were used only once and would not be considered in preparing such a basic list. On the other hand, 82 words (7 percent of the technical words) were used more than 10 times in over 400 pages (88). These words can usually be spotted rather easily from their location in headings or because they are italicized in the text. Your list over a part of a course should turn out to be surprisingly small. Notice in your later lessons how frequently these terms recur. And if you study these terms, your new assignments should seem much easier.

2. The next step is to learn these selected words on both lists (everyday vocabulary and technical vocabulary). One technique is to read down the lists or through your checkings of such terms in your texts and see if you can define each one. Look up those that cause difficulty. These words must also be made functional for you so

they can be used on tests and in discussions. Try using them in discussions and explanations. There is a saying that a word used three times is yours forever. If you make a conscious effort to learn and use a few new words each week, your vocabulary will develop with surprisinging rapidity.

3. Wide reading tends to broaden one's background so that ideas in lessons seem more familiar. Also, the context of what is being read tends to develop some familiarity and understanding of new terms presented. Frequent encounters with these words will gradually build up an understanding of them. A program of regular recreational reading will do much to increase your vocabulary. It must be said, however, that although reading the sport page and the comics will increase your vocabulary, such sources do not develop an understanding of terms frequently used in college work.

4. When a new word is encountered in reading, certain techniques for understanding are more helpful than others (60). It is a good practice *not* to stop reading when you come across an unknown word; finish the paragraph first. The meaning of the paragraph may be enough to indicate the meaning of the word so that you will not have to look it up. Reading to the end of the paragraph also keeps the unfamiliar word from interrupting the main idea that you were trying to grasp. If the word still seems important and unknown, try analyzing the word in terms of word roots, prefixes, suffices, and so on (74). If all of this has not worked, look the word up in a dictionary. However, note here that word analysis techniques may often save some effort in use of a dictionary.

Several ways have been worked out that enable a reader to guess what a word means by using certain clues in the text (11, 149, 236). Sometimes authors will add to a strange word its definitions or synonyms, or the whole context of the paragraph may indicate its meaning. Good students tend to use these clues more than poor students, and any student can be helped who learns consciously to look for such clues when he has difficulty with a word. Various types of clues, with an example of each, follow. Can you guess what the word omitted in each blank space means?

a. Definition: "A _____ is a large, cat-like animal."
b. Experience: "as _____ as a boy or girl before a first date."
c. Comparison or contrast: "Eskimos have _____ing eyes like the Chinese."
d. Synonym: "When Jim heard about the trip, he was _____. He was glad there was to be no school that day."
e. Familiar expression or language experience: "harder than _____."
f. Summary: "His knees shook and his eyes seemed to pop as he looked all around, for he was very much _____."
g. Reflection of mood or situation: "He hopped and skipped and danced about and whistled _____ly to himself."

It is interesting to analyze portions of different textbooks to see how many of these devices an author uses. Of course, the more he uses, the easier comprehension is for the trained reader.

5. Since most multisyllabic words combine certain recurring prefixes, suffixes, and word roots, a knowledge of these elements may help in determining the meaning of strange words (275). By the time a student is in college he has learned what many of these elements mean, *e.g.*, "pre," "de," "multi," "ology," "ment," and so on. A dictionary will give further information about other prefixes and suffixes, and a perusal there of word origins will show how many words have word roots similar to known words.

6. If the meaning of a word cannot be quickly determined by the above techniques, look it up in a dictionary. Good readers, even the most highly educated, make very frequent use of a dictionary. In fact, the better the reader, the more likely he is to use the dictionary. Many students are inefficient in using a dictionary, however, and often do not know about its many values. If you missed any items on the Dictionary Test, use the keyed answers and the boxed legends at the edge of the sample dictionary page to learn how to read a dictionary. Every question in this test dealt with an aspect of dictionary usage that every student should know; therefore, it is worthwhile to study every item that you may have missed.

Important Words to Learn

It may sound strange, but a dictionary can be an interesting book—not to read straight through, but to browse through. In addition to giving the meaning of a word, a dictionary also indicates spelling, pronunciation, source, synonyms, and occasionally antonyms. You will also be interested in the number of meanings that many words have—for instance, there are over one hundred meanings for the word "run." Pages 7a to 14a of *Webster's Seventh New Collegiate Dictionary* or pages 15a to 20a of the Third Edition of *Webster's New International Dictionary* give further information about how to use a dictionary.

D. *Special Reading Skills*

Tables, graphs, formulas, and maps are devices that aid comprehension. Yet, most poor readers skip them with a sigh of relief. Tables summarize and unify a wealth of data so that you can see possible relationships and trends; graphs picture these trends even more readily for you; formulas are a shorthand method of stating involved relationships in a simple manner; and maps, of course, picture geographic relationships. Reference to the importance of these forms of presentation was also made earlier in Chapter 3.

Difficulty with these comprehension devices springs from two causes: (1) lack of knowledge of how they are constructed and interpreted, and (2) lack of appreciation of the fact that these devices cannot be read at normal reading speed but must be studied.

SELF-EVALUATION

Tests of four types are included in Appendix II: reading tables, reading graphs, reading maps, and reading formulas. Each test contains simple examples of the kinds of material typically found in textbooks; the questions measure your ability to get *basic* information from these materials. Since these are simple examples of basic materials, your goal should be ability to answer *all* of these questions as well as ability to understand nonverbal materials that occur in your studies. The keys for correcting these tests are on pages 292–294 in Appendix III.

PROGRAM FOR IMPROVEMENT

1. Correct and understand the test items that you miss.

2. Practice reading all graphs, maps, tables, and formulas that you find in your lessons. They emphasize and illustrate important points; effort spent on them is very worthwhile. Your instructor will assist you in interpreting any of these comprehension aids that give you difficulty.

Modern textbooks are using graphs and charts more and more; rather than being simply a supplement to the text, they are now frequently used as the basic means of presenting ideas. Within recent years, types of visual aids new to undergraduate courses have become popular, *e.g.*, wiring diagrams, blueprints, three-dimensional drawings, weather maps, topographical maps, pictorial maps, and so forth. Ability to read these has become basic to schoolwork and to everyday living.

E. Summary

The several sections and their interrelations indicate a need for a summary of the activities listed in this chapter. Look over your reading test results again and decide which areas seem most in need of remedial training. Then, in the following outline of suggested remedial activities, check those that you plan to carry out.

A. Rate
 1. Practice daily and record results
 2. Use speed-reading device
 3. Stop lip movement and line-following with finger
 4. Improve comprehension

B. Comprehension accuracy
 1. Learn to select and comprehend main points
 2. Increase background of information and knowledge of technical terms
 3. Practice SQ3R method
 4. Learn to use context of story to precomprehend what is being read
 5. Build an efficient attitude of comprehension accuracy

C. Vocabulary
 1. Make and study lists of technical terms and vocabulary of courses
 2. Make list of everyday words and use them
 3. Read widely to broaden background and vocabulary
 4. Practice techniques of figuring out meaning of unknown words
 5. Learn to use dictionary more effectively

D. Special reading skills
 1. Study errors made on tests
 2. Analyze tables and charts in textbooks to find any difficulties in reading
 3. Make it a practice to study all tables and charts in lessons
 4. Obtain training in reading new types of charts

Summarize briefly below further details of your proposed training program in reading.

CHAPTER 11

Writing skills

A large part of our endeavor to affect the behavior of other people is done through writing. If an account is poorly written, the reader has difficulty in comprehending it and also tends unconsciously to lower his estimation of the writer's authority (377). Good writing is, therefore, effective writing.

The essential abilities for a clear and concise written message are classified here into (1) English, (2) spelling, and (3) handwriting. A section in this chapter is devoted to a discussion of diagnostic and remedial procedures for each of these divisions.

A. English

Knowledge of language form is basic to good writing. If a writer chooses effective words and presents them in correct English form, one is able to read right along. Training in this field is usually the province of English courses. The purpose of this unit is to provide a description of each student's abilities. Such an analysis usually shows that a student is not generally poor at grammar or punctuation, but rather that most of his difficulty results from a few rather specific errors. Two or three rules do not seem difficult to master, so a student is more motivated to attack such an apparently simple problem (242).

SELF-EVALUATION

The area of English is divided into the following diagnostic divisions: grammar, capitalization, punctuation, and sentence structure. Tests to measure your skills in these areas are given on pages 264–272 in Appendix II. These tests do not represent a random sampling of all the many rules of English but are based on the 40 rules that research has shown most frequently cause trouble in writing. Every item, therefore, deals with an important point.

TABLE 8 Percentile Ranks on English Survey Tests

Percentile	Grammar	Capitalization	Punctuation	Sentence structure
100	80	80	80	80
95	78	78	75	78
90	76	76	70	76
85	74	74	68	73
80	73	72	62	70
75	72	71	58	67
70	71	70	55	64
65	70	69	53	61
60	69	68	51	59
55	67	67	48	57
50	65	66	45	55
45	62	65	42	54
40	59	64	39	53
35	56	63	36	52
30	53	62	33	51
25	49	60	30	49
20	45	58	27	47
15	41	56	24	45
10	37	53	20	43
5	33	50	16	40

Follow the directions printed on the tests. When these tests are completed, correct them and then translate their scores into percentile ranks by using Table 8. Write these percentiles in their respective places in the following summary list. Choice of words is an important aspect of good writing; in fact, a wider selection of words is used in writing than in speaking (147, 296), so write in your percentile from the General Vocabulary Test, which you took in the preceding chapter.

Grammar _____percentile rank   Sentence structure _____percentile rank

Capitalization _____percentile rank

Punctuation _____percentile rank   Vocabulary _____percentile rank

The percentile ranks indicate your standing relative to other students; but what is the nature of the specific errors that you make? Since a student's errors tend to "constellate" in certain areas, the extent of his remedial work may be limited. In order to find these areas, the following procedure is suggested. Each time you mark a wrong answer, copy the symbol (S1, C6, and so on), which is beside the answer on the key.[1] This symbol refers to the rule in this chapter that has been violated

---

[1] The meaning of these symbols is as follows: "G" stands for grammar, "C" for capitalization, "P" for punctuation, and "S" for sentence structure. The numbers refer to specific rules under each of these headings. Thus, "G5" refers to the fifth rule under the Grammar heading, which says that the verb "to be" should agree with the subject and not with the predicate noun.

and will expedite your looking it up in the rule section that follows. Since each of the test items, correctly written, has been placed under the rule indicated by the symbol, you can tabulate your errors quite easily. Merely check under the rule the correct form for each item you missed. When this checking is completed, a glance at the list of rules will show where the errors tend to "constellate." If you master these few rules, your performance should show marked improvement.

Organizational skill and style of writing are also important in effective writing. These were discussed in part in Chapter 8; further help can be obtained from your English instructor. This chapter deals only with certain mechanics of English.

One further point. These tests tend to measure your peak performance, but many students do not use their full skill in everyday class work. Various essays and examinations that you have written should also be analyzed to determine the errors you make in such writing.

Rules of English[2]

GRAMMAR

AGREEMENT OF VERB WITH ITS SUBJECT

1. A subject composed of two or more nouns (either singular or plural) joined by *and* requires a plural verb. A subject composed of two or more singular nouns joined by *or* or *nor* requires a singular verb.

   _____ 12. Neither Martha nor John *is* older than I.
   _____ 16. Algebra and geometry *have* been easy for me.
   _____ 28. Neither Jane nor I *was* able to play basketball.
   _____ 31. Basketball and baseball *are* what I am going to take.
   _____ 76. Either dramatics or athletics *is* going to be my specialty.

2. The number of the verb is not determined by a noun or pronoun that intervenes between the subject and the verb.

   _____ 25. The price of supplies *is* high.
   _____ 55. The price of the tickets *was* two dollars.

3. The number of the verb is not changed by adding to the subject words introduced by *with, together with, as well as, like,* and so forth.

   _____ 63. The referee, like the other officials, *was* dressed in white.
   _____ 69. Mary, as well as the other girls, *has* asked me to tell about the game.

4. *There is* or *there are* should be used according to the number of the subject that follows.

   _____ 56. There *were* about 30,000 people there.
   _____ 72. There *are* several reasons.
   _____ 77. There *are* several things to choose from.
   Another example: There *is* a man at the door.

---

[2] Adapted from the pamphlet, "Student's Handbook of Essentials," published by the Ohio State Department of Education and used with permission.

5. The verb *to be* should agree with its subject and not with its predicate noun.

    ————— 17. The greater part of the curriculum *is* English subjects.
    ————— 23. The weakest part of our school *is* the materials in the laboratories.
    ————— 78. Sports *are* the best part of any school.

6. The verb *does* or *doesn't* is used with a third person singular subject.

    ————— 10. Jack *doesn't* remember the other schools.
    ————— 22. Martha, . . . *doesn't* go to school.
    ————— 32. Jane *doesn't* go to school.
    ————— 75. The curriculum *doesn't* matter so much to us.

7. The pronouns *each, every, everyone, everybody, anyone, anybody, either, neither, no one, nobody* demand a singular verb. The word *most* when used in such phrases as "most of us," "most of them" demands a plural verb.

    ————— 2. Each of us pupils *greets* the teacher.
    ————— 15. Each of us *was* told to register.
    ————— 35. Most of us *have* a very good time playing basketball.
    ————— 51. Most of us *prefer* the schools. . . .
    ————— 71. No one in our crowd *has* seen a big game.
    ————— 79. Everybody *doesn't* agree with me.

AGREEMENT AND CASE OF PRONOUNS

8. Pronouns that refer to other nouns or pronouns should have the same number. (Note especially that the pronouns listed in No. 7 are singular.)

    ————— 9. Teacher has told each one to do *his* part.
    ————— 18. The greater part of the curriculum is English subjects, which *are* very uninteresting.
    ————— 39. No one wants her on *his* (*her*) team.
    ————— 58. Everyone shouted as loud as *he* could.
    ————— 61. Each player took *his* position.

9. Pronouns have a different form when used as the subect of a clause than when used as the object of a verb or preposition. The following are some specific situations that often cause trouble:

    a. When words come between the pronoun and the word that governs its case.

        ————— 73. Our teacher told Mary and *me.*

    b. When *who* and *whom* are used in the first position in a sentence or clause.

        ————— 13. The teacher wanted to know *who* my father was.
        ————— 14. I told her . . . *whom* I was living with.

    c. When the pronoun follows *as* or *than* it has the same case as the noun or pronoun with which it is compared.

        ————— 36. Jane is taller than *I.*
        ————— 37. She used to play baseball better than *I.*
            Another example: I see him more often than *her.*

d. When the pronoun follows the preposition *like* it must be in the objective case.

    _____ 40. She is fourteen, like Mary and *me*.
    _____ 80. Mary prefers athletics, like Frances and *me*.

e. When a first person pronoun stands with a noun, it has the same case as the noun.

    _____ 1. Each of *us* pupils greets the teacher.
    _____ 45. *We* girls are going to the same college.

TENSE OF VERB

10. The following verbs are frequently misused, either bcause the wrong tense form is substituted or because a similar but unacceptable form is substituted. The past participle is used with the auxiliary verb "to have."

Present	Past	Past Part.
ask	asked	asked
attack	attacked	attacked
bear	bore	borne
begin	began	begun
blow	blew	blown
break	broke	broken
burst	burst	burst
climb	climbed	climbed
come	came	come
do	did	done
drag	dragged	dragged
draw	drew	drawn
drink	drank	drunk
drown	drowned	drowned
freeze	froze	frozen
give	gave	given
go	went	gone
grow	grew	grown
hear	heard	heard
lead	led	led
ride	rode	ridden
ring	rang	rung
run	ran	run
see	saw	seen
show	showed	shown
shrink	shrank	shrunk
sing	sang	sung
speak	spoke	spoken
swing	swung	swung
take	took	taken
tear	tore	torn
throw	threw	thrown
use	used	used
wear	wore	worn
write	wrote	written

_____ 5. Sally and Richard have *asked* to occupy the seats.
_____ 6. I have *climbed* into one of the seats.
_____11. . . . the other schools that he has *gone* to.
_____21. My sister has *given* much time.
_____46. We have *written* to several colleges.
_____47. We have *begun* to read.
_____57. I had never *seen* so many people.
_____59. Our team *came* on the field.
_____65. He must have *frozen*.
_____67. We *sang* songs.
_____68. People *threw* confetti.
_____70. Mary has *asked* me to tell.

DIFFERENTIATE BETWEEN ADJECTIVES AND ADVERBS

11. Be careful to distinguish between adjectives and adverbs and to use the proper form. In general, adjectives may be changed to adverbs by the addition of -*ly*, although there are such exceptions as "good," an adjective, and "well," an adverb. An adverb is used if it modifies a verb, an adjective, or another adverb.

_____ 4. John intends to do his work *well*.
_____ 7. I can see *easily* now.
_____20. I am *surely* weak in grammar.
_____27. I shall consider the matter very *carefully*.
_____34. I'll be able to play basketball *well*.
_____38. She plays so *poorly*.
_____49. There are too many nice ones to choose one very *easily*.
_____60. The band played the college song very *soflty*.

12. Verbs pertaining to the senses and the verbs *to grow, to become,* are followed by an adjective unless they indicate action.

_____24. Our principal feels *bad*.
_____29. We never felt *sad*.
_____42. . . . perfume that smells very *sweet*.
          Other examples: Mary grew *hilarious*.
                  The flowers grow *quickly*.

WORDS CONFUSED

13. The following words are commonly confused:

    a. lie lay lain (to be in a stretched-out position)
       lay laid laid (to be placed in a recumbent position)
       He laid his hat on the table and lay down to rest.
    b. sit sat sat (to rest in a sitting position)
       set set set (to place in a position of rest)
       She set the basket in a corner and sat down to talk.
    c. let let let (to permit)
       leave left left (to abandon)
       The police let him go, and he left the city.
    d. can could (to be able or to be possible)
       may might (to be permitted)
       You may go if you can find someone to go with you.

e. a   (used before words beginning with a consonant)
   an   (used before words beginning with a vowel or vowel sound)
       an uncle, a hat, an onion, a cup.
f. there   (adverb)
   their   (pronoun)
   they're   (contraction of *they are*)
       They're going to buy their hats there.
g. to   (preposition, or sign of infinitive)
   two   (adjective or noun)
   too   (adverb)
       He has been too sick to go to school for the last two days.
h. teach   (to instruct or give knowledge)
   learn   (to acquire knowledge)
       He teaches quite effectively; as a result his pupils learn a great deal.

_____ 3. Mary, John, and Annabelle *sit* in the front row.
_____19. The teacher can't *teach* me English at all.
_____26. The principal won't *let* me drop chemistry.
_____33. She likes to *lie* around.
_____41. She wears such pretty clothes, *too.*
_____43. Mother won't *let* me have any perfume.
_____44. She said, though, that I *might* buy some next year.
_____48. There are almost *too* many nice ones.
_____52. Students have a better time *there.*
_____53. They have football games, *too.*
_____62. The substitutes *sat* down on the bench.
_____74. They have interesting courses *there.*

CAPITALIZATION

1. **First words.** Capitalize the first word of the following: (a) every sentence, (b) every line of poetry, (c) every complete grammatical statement (independent clause) following a colon, (d) every direct quotation. Do not capitalize the first word of a quotation that is only a fragment of a sentence, or the first word of an indirect quotation.

   a. This sentence illustrates the first rule.
   b. My heart leaps up when I behold
      A rainbow in the sky.
   c. The questions were as follows: What is an erg? What is a dyne?
   d. Annie said, "I think you should go to bed."
      "I think," Annie said, "you should go to bed."
      Annie said that you should go to bed.
      Stevenson called man "the disease of the agglutinated dust."

   _____ 2. She exclaimed, "What a beautiful lake!"

2. **Names of persons.** Capitalize the names of persons and the titles standing for the names of persons. Capitalize derivatives of these names. Do not capitalize the names of professions or professional ranks.

   _____ 6. "Tell me what Doctor Harris did," said Emily.
   _____ 7. "If that's all," John said, "we may as well go."
   _____ 12. Al Smith, the Democratic candidate, was defeated.

_____ 21. The ring is an heirloom; it belonged to Jenny Lind.

_____ 23. Esther, Jane, and Mary organized a girls' club.

_____ 28. Sinclair Lewis wrote these books.

_____ 34. He read Tennyson's famous poem, "In Memoriam."

_____ 35. A careful description of Captain Evans was given.

_____ 42. It's too bad Gerry can't go with us.

_____ 46. The various codes were submitted to General Johnson.

_____ 47. He said that he saw the Prince of Wales.

_____ 48. "Please come," she wrote, "Colonel Brown will be here."

_____ 49. Joe is not going, nor is Sally.

_____ 56. "You should talk to Professor Brown," she advised.

_____ 62. "That youngster," said Coach Jones, "will be a star."

_____ 63. It's raining hard, but Jim won't stay home.

_____ 71. You may take this note to Mr. Adams.

_____ 72. Joseph Conrad is the author of _Lord Jim_.

_____ 73. To be frank, she doesn't like Janice very well.

_____ 78. Mary, you may describe General Pershing's plan.

_____ 79. . . . to see what Mrs. Jones is wearing.

_____ 80. The play was almost over when John left.

3. **Names of places.** Capitalize the names of countries, states, cities, streets, buildings, mountains, rivers, oceans, or any word designating a particular location or part of the world. Capitalize derivatives of these names. Do not capitalize the points of the compass or such terms as street, river, ocean when not part of a name.

_____ 1. Are you going to Strassburg, Germany?

_____ 3. The Hudson, a river in New York, is very beautiful.

_____ 4. Do you expect to visit China or Ceylon?

_____ 5. Three weeks from now we'll be in Kansas City.

_____ 9. Why do so many people blame the Germans?

_____ 11. She lives at 25 Whittier Street, Dolby, Kentucky.

_____ 13. He attended Tate College; then he went to a law school.

_____ 14. My subjects include the following: history, English, and Latin.

_____ 17. He had started to Newberg; there was no retreat.

_____ 18. She intended to visit Mount Baker.

_____ 19. I think French a boring subject but like physics.

_____ 24. The letter was sent from Detroit.

_____ 30. If you see any American tourists, let me know.

_____ 32. John finished his Spanish; then he worked on biology.

_____ 37. We didn't have time to visit the Alps; still we saw almost every other part of Europe.

_____ 39. He claims that the government is as corrupt as in the days of Rome.

_____ 45. On Sunday we went fishing in Beaver Creek.

_____ 55. We saw the Capitol at Washington.

_____ 58. One of us must go to Lisbon.

_____ 60. You'll find it easier to go by way of Athens.

_____ 74. They went to Washington, to Oregon, and on to California.

_____ 76. We drove to St. Louis and then took a quaint old steamer down the Mississippi River.

4. **Names of organizations.** Capitalize the names of business firms, schools, societies, clubs, and other organizations. Capitalize derivatives of these names. Do not capitalize such words as *company, school, society,* when not part of a name.

_____ 12. Al Smith, the Democratic candidate, was defeated.
_____ 16. In the first place, the Ku Klux Klan was not legal.
_____ 26. Will the Socialist Party ultimately succeed?
_____ 38. His wife is a Presbyterian; he is a Baptist.
_____ 40. The National Railway Association should recognize that this type of engine will not pay.
_____ 41. The Lincoln School has been overcrowded for some time.
_____ 50. In other words, the General Electric Company refused my offer.
_____ 54. The Unemployed League will meet tomorrow.
_____ 59. . . . he wants to enter Harvard College next year.
_____ 67. He told me to meet him at the Seneca Hotel.
_____ 68. . . . she was elected to the Martha Washington Club.
_____ 69. . . . we'll put the money in the Chase Bank.
_____ 75. She resigned from the Missionary Society.

5. **Days, weeks, months, and so on.** Capitalize the days of the week, the months of the year, holidays, and church festivals. Do not capitalize the names of the seasons unless they are personified.

_____ 8. Friday, the tenth of June, was my birthday.
_____ 10. It was the Fourth of July, a national holiday.
_____ 24. The letter was sent from Detroit on August 8, 1933.
_____ 25. Christmas, Memorial Day, and Thanksgiving are holidays.
_____ 45. On Sunday we went fishing in Beaver Creek.
_____ 57. She said she played no card games during Lent.
_____ 64. June, July, and August are vacation months.
_____ 79. One goes to church on Easter.

6. **Titles.** Capitalize the first word and all other important words in titles (and subtitles and headings) of themes, magazines articles,[3] poems, books; of laws and governmental documents; of pictures, statues, musical compositions; and in trade names. Always capitalize the first and last words.

_____ 20. This poem is called "In the Cool of the Night."
_____ 27. I use Ipana; it is a good toothpaste.
_____ 28. Sinclair Lewis wrote these books: *Dodsworth, Babbitt,* and *Arrowsmith.*
_____ 33. "By a Waterfall" is a simple little piece to play.
_____ 34. He read Tennyson's famous poem, "In Memoriam."
_____ 36. She recommends Ajax for cleaning.
_____ 52. "I'm in a Hurry" is the name of an amusing short story.
_____ 53. You will like these movies: *Ben-Hur* and *Diary of Anne Frank.*
_____ 66. . . . you may have the Chevrolet.
_____ 70. I'll send you a subscription to the *Reader's Digest.*
_____ 72. Joseph Conrad is the author of *Lord Jim;* he also wrote *Victory.*

[3] In publishing bibliographies (as in this text) it is a frequently modern practice to capitalize only the first word of magazine titles. However, in publishing a magazine article its title is expected to follow the above rule.

PUNCTUATION

1. Use a period, question mark, or exclamation point at the end of a sentence.

———— 1. Are you going to Strassburg, Germany?
———— 2. She exclaimed, "What a beautiful lake!"
———— 4. Do you expect to visit China and Ceylon?
———— 9. Why do so many people blame the Germans?
———— 26. Will the Socialist Party ultimately succeed?
———— 58. One of us must go to Lisbon; which will it be?

2. Use a period after an abbreviation and after each initial.

———— 71. You may take this note to Mr. Adams.
———— 76. We drove to St. Louis.
———— 79. . . . to see what Mrs. Jones is wearing.

3. Use commas to set off parenthetic words, phrases, and clauses. That is, set off such elements as interrupt the sequence of the thought or do not form an essential part of the sentence. Among these are introductory words and phrases, interjections, words of address, appositives, loosely modifying phrases and clauses, and the like. Do not use superfluous commas. If in doubt, leave the comma out.

———— 3. The Hudson, a river in New York, is very beautiful.
———— 8. Friday, the tenth of June, was my birthday.
———— 10. It was the Fourth of July, a national holiday.
———— 12. Al Smith, the Democratic candidate, was defeated.
———— 22. The captain, our old friend, met us at the dock.
———— 34. He read Tennyson's poem, "In Memoriam."
———— 78. Mary, you may describe General Pershing's plan.

4. Use a comma to set off clearly introductory ideas at the beginning of a sentence or obviously added elements at the end.

———— 16. In the first place, the Ku Klux Klan was not legal.
———— 30. If you see any American tourists, let me know.
———— 36. She recommends Ajax for cleaning, since it is cheaper.
———— 50. In other words, the General Electric Company refused my offer.
———— 66. If it's really necessary, you may have the Chevrolet.
———— 68. Being capable and socially prominent, she was elected.
———— 70. I'll send you a subscription to the *Reader's Digest,* if you want it.
———— 73. To be frank, she doesn't like Janice very well.
———— 75. She resigned from the Missionary Society, thus losing many friends.

5. Use commas to separate a series of words, phrases, or clauses. In a series of more than two parts, grammarians usually ask that a comma precede the conjunction, although some style books suggest that the comma before the conjunction be omitted.

———— 14. My subjects include the following: history, English and Latin.
———— 23. Esther, Jane and Mary organized a girl's club.
———— 25. Christmas, Memorial Day and Thanksgiving are holidays.
———— 28. Sinclair Lewis wrote these books: *Dodsworth, Babbitt* and *Arrowsmith.*

_____ 39. He claims that the government is as corrupt as in the days of Rome, that there is no place for an honest man in politics, and that there is little hope for reform.

_____ 43. Oranges, lemons and grapefruit are citrus fruits.

_____ 64. June, July and August are vacation months.

_____ 65. He wants someone who is quick, who is ambitious, and who has had experience.

_____ 74. They went to Washington, to Oregon and on to California.

_____ 79. One goes to church on Easter to ease one's conscience, to wear one's new clothes, or to see what Mrs. Jones is wearing.

6. Ordinarily use a comma to separate clauses joined by the conjunctions *and, but, for, or, nor* if a change in subject takes place or if the clauses are long. Do not use a comma, however, if the subject is not changed or if it is not a clause that is joined.

_____ 15. They're ready, but we'll have to wait awhile.

_____ 19. I think French a boring subject but like physics.

_____ 31. He hurried on to the bank and asked for the president.

_____ 35. A careful description of Captain Evans was given, for he was an important witness in the trial.

_____ 47. He said that he saw the Prince of Wales, but no one believed him.

_____ 49. Joe is not going, nor is Sally.

_____ 55. We saw the Capitol at Washington, and then the driver took us home.

_____ 63. It's raining hard, but Jim won't stay at home.

_____ 67. He told me to meet him at the Seneca Hotel but he didn't appear.

_____ 76. We drove to St. Louis and then took a quaint old steamer down the Mississippi River.

7. Use commas to separate expressions like "he said" from a direct quotation. Indirect quotations should not be so separated.

_____ 2. She exclaimed, "What a beautiful lake!"

_____ 6. "Tell me what Doctor Harris did," said Emily.

_____ 7. "If that's all," John said, "we may as well go."

_____ 18. She said that she intended to visit Mount Baker.

_____ 29. "We are," said the speaker, "at the dawn of a new era."

_____ 44. She said that he would be glad to see you.

_____ 47. He said that he saw the Prince of Wales, but no one believed him.

_____ 48. "Please come," she wrote, "Colonel Brown will be here."

_____ 56. "You should talk to Professor Brown," she advised.

_____ 62. "That youngster," said Coach Jones, "will be a star next year."

_____ 69. "All right," he said, "we'll put the money in the Chase Bank."

8. Use commas to separate the parts of a date or an address.

_____ 1. Are you going to Strassburg, Germany?

_____ 11. She lives at 25 Whittier Street, Dolby, Kentucky.

_____ 24. The letter was sent from Detroit on August 8, 1933.

9. Use a semicolon between the clauses of a compound sentence when the clauses are closely related in thought and not joined by a conjunction. A semicolon is usually used where a period might be used, that is, between independent clauses.

———— 17. He started to Newburg; there was no retreat.
———— 21. The ring is an heirloom; it belonged to Jenny Lind.
———— 27. I use Ipana; it is a good tooth paste.
———— 38. His wife is a Presbyterian; he is a Baptist.
———— 40. The National Railway Association should recognize that this type of engine will not pay; it is out of date.
———— 51. Its hair is fine and soft; it's still just a puppy.
———— 58. One of us must go to Lisbon; which will it be?
———— 59. John makes high grades in mathematics; he wants to enter Harvard College next year.
———— 60. You'll find it easier to go by way of Athens; you'll save twenty miles.
———— 72. Joseph Conrad is the author of *Lord Jim;* he also wrote *Victory.*

10. Use a semicolon between clauses of a compound sentence when the second clause is introduced by *so, then, however, thus, hence, therefore, also, moreover, still, otherwise, nevertheless, accordingly, besides.*

———— 13. He attended Tate College; then he went to a law school.
———— 32. John finished his Spanish; then he worked on biology.
———— 37. We didn't have time to visit the Alps; still we saw almost every other part of Europe.
———— 61. I'm too tired to go out tonight; besides it's too cold.
———— 71. You may take this note to Mr. Adams; then drop these letters in the mailbox.
———— 77. I'll take you in the car; otherwise you'll be late.

11. Use a colon after a complete independent clause that formally introduces one of the following: a list or enumeration, a statement or question, or a long quotation.

———— 14. My subjects include the following: history, English and Latin.
———— 28. Sinclair Lewis wrote these books: *Dodsworth, Babbitt, and Arrowsmith.*
———— 53. You will like these movies: *Ben-Hur* and *Diary of Anne Frank.*

12. Use quotation marks to enclose all direct quotations and all parts of direct quotations that are divided.

———— 2. She exclaimed, "What a beautiful lake!"
———— 6. "Tell me what Doctor Harris did," said Emily.
———— 7. "If that's all," John said, "we may as well go."
———— 29. "We are," said the speaker, "at the dawn of a new era."
———— 48. "Please come," she wrote, "Colonel Brown will be here."
———— 56. "You should talk to Professor Brown," she advised.
———— 62. "That youngster," said Coach Jones, "will be a star next year."
———— 69. "All right," he said, "we'll put the money in the Chase Bank."

13. Use quotation marks to enclose the titles of poems, short stories, essays, chapters in books, or other parts of books, musical compositions, pictures, statues. Titles of books, movies, newspapers, pamphlets, periodicals, and poems of book length should only be underlined or italicized.

_____ 20. This poem is called "In the Cool of the Night."
_____ 28. Sinclair Lewis wrote these books: *Dodsworth, Babbitt,* and *Arrowsmith.*
_____ 33. "By a Waterfall" is a simple little piece to play.
_____ 34. He read Tennyon's poem, "In Memoriam."
_____ 52. "I'm in a Hurry" is the name of an amusing short story.
_____ 53. You will like these movies: *Ben-Hur* and *Diary of Anne Frank.*
_____ 70. I'll send you a subscription to the *Reader's Digest.*
_____ 72. Joseph Conrad is the author of *Lord Jim;* he also wrote *Victory.*

14. Use an apostrophe in contractions to indicate omitted letters.

_____ 5. . . . we'll . . .
_____ 7. . . . that's . . .
_____ 15. They're . . . we'll . . .
_____ 37. . . . didn't . . .
_____ 42. It's . . . can't . . .
_____ 51. . . . it's . . .
_____ 52. I'm . . .
_____ 54. . . . o'clock . . .
_____ 60. You'll . . . you'll . . .
_____ 61. I'm . . . it's . . .
_____ 63. It's . . . won't . . .
_____ 66. . . . it's . . .
_____ 67. . . . didn't . . .
_____ 69. . . . we'll . . .
_____ 70. I'll . . .
_____ 73. . . . doesn't . . .
_____ 77. I'll . . . you'll . . .

15. Use an apostrophe to indicate the possessive. When the singular or plural form does not end in *s,* add *'s.* When these end in *s,* place an apostrophe after the *s* if there is no new syllable in pronunciation. If a new syllable occurs, add *'s.* Possessive pronouns, *its, hers, his, yours, ours, theirs,* do not require the apostrophe.

_____ 23. Esther, Jane, and Mary organized a *girl's* club.
_____ 34. He read *Tennyson's* famous poem, "In Memoriam."
_____ 38. *His* wife is a Presbyterian; he is a Baptist.
_____ 51. *Its* hair is fine and soft; it's still just a puppy.
_____ 78. Mary, you may describe General *Pershing's* plan.
_____ 79. One goes to church on Easter to ease *one's* conscience, to wear *one's* new spring clothes, or to see what Mrs. Jones is wearing.
Other examples: Dickens' works
Jones's house

SENTENCE STRUCTURE

1. A sentence should express a complete and independent thought. Do not write as a sentence a group of words that are only part of a sentence.

Which of the following examples in the test did you miss? 6, 12, 21, 25, 26, 28, 33, 36, 39.

2. A sentence should not contain superfluous words that make the sentence cumbersome.

Which of the following examples in the test did you miss? 1, 13, 38.

3. A series of thoughts loosely strung together by conjunctions is weak and ineffective. Also avoid a series of short choppy sentences when expressing a closely unified idea.

Which of the following examples in the test did you miss? 3, 9, 16, 19.

4. The reference of phrases and modifiers should be unmistakably and immediately clear. Normally they should be next to the part modified.

Which of the following examples in the test did you miss? 4, 7, 8, 17, 22, 27, 30, 35.

5. The reference of a pronoun to its antecedent should be unmistakably and immediately clear. Pronouns should be close enough to their antecedents so that there is no possibility of misunderstanding.

Which of the following examples in the test did you miss? 2, 5, 10, 18, 20, 29, 37, 40.

6. Give parallel structure to those parts of a sentence that are parallel in thought.

Which of the following examples in the test did you miss? 11, 14, 15, 23, 24, 31, 32, 34.

SUMMARY OF PRINCIPLES VIOLATED MOST OFTEN

List below, as a series of phrases, the rules that you missed most often on these tests. These should form the primary basis for your remedial efforts.

PROGRAM FOR IMPROVEMENT

The preceding analysis probably shows that work on only a few rules will raise your percentile rank quite a few points. On the other hand, for many years you have been building your present language habits, so it will take definite and specific practice on your part to substitute correct language habits for these errors. Not only must you know a rule but you must also practice using it.

The following remedial suggestions are made:

1. Study the rules causing you the most difficulty.
2. Substitute the correct form for each of the errors that you have made.
3. Make a special effort to practice using the correct form in your everyday writing.
4. Regularly reread what you have written and look for instances in which these few rules occur; correct any errors.
5. Have your teachers indicate incorrect forms that you use in your writing; then proceed to correct them.
6. When in doubt use a source book on grammar.

Work hard in your English courses to remedy your difficulty. If your problem is extreme, you may wish to enroll in the special remedial English section that many colleges provide.

The primary consideration in improvement, however, is your own desire to improve; only this will lead you to be careful in your writing and to seek further practice.

Useful source books on grammar include:

Gorrell, R. M., and Laird, C., *Modern English Handbook*, 4th ed. Englewood Cliffs, N.J.: Prentice-Hall, 1967.
Hodges, J. C., and Whitten, M. E., *Harbrace College Handbook*, 6th ed. New York: Harcourt Brace & World, 1967.
Jordan, J. E., *Using Rhetoric*. New York: Harper & Row, 1965.
Kierzek, J. M., and Gibson, W. W., *Macmillan Handbook of English*, 4th ed. New York: Macmillan, 1960.
Opdycke, J. B., and Benedict, S., *Harper's English Grammar*, rev. ed. New York: Harper & Row, 1966.
Wykoff, G. S., and Shaw, H. L., *Harper Handbook of College Composition*, 3d ed. New York: Harper & Row, 1962.

B. Spelling

A student's occasional misspellings are important because their odd appearance distracts the reader's attention from the message and because people tend to judge the writer's cultural training on the basis of these errors. For example, many otherwise well-trained men have failed to obtain jobs because of misspellings in letters of application. Correct spelling is a skill that students should have learned before reaching college, but many of them have not learned them. Furthermore, spelling ability does not tend to increase during the college years unless specific remedial steps are taken.

On the other hand, there is a hopeful basis for improvement in the fact that a few "spelling demons" account for much of one's difficulty; learning these few words is a quick way to improve one's spelling. In one study in over 50 colleges of college students' spelling errors it was found that 90 words accounted for 30 percent of all misspellings, and 417 words accounted for over one-half of all misspellings of all of the students (286). Of course, the list that accounts for most of a particular student's spelling errors will be much smaller.

SELF-EVALUATION

A spelling test, based on the 228 most frequently misspelled words, as determined by combining several lists of common spelling errors, will be found in Appendix II on page 273–280. This test is difficult in the sense that it consists only of "spelling demons." On the other hand, since each word also fits the criterion of being frequently used, a student should be able to spell most of them correctly. (A student may omit learning any of the 228 words that he seldom, if ever, uses; looking them up in a dictionary takes less time.) When the test is completed, the key will be found on pages 299–302. Although the average freshman misses about 10 percent of these words, you should be able to spell all of those words that you use frequently.

To facilitate this study, use the space below to write the correct spelling of each of the words missed on this test.

You may also misspell other words that you use frequently. This is especially true of technical terms that are frequently used in your courses. Make a list below of these words that are misspelled in your papers during the school term.

PROGRAM FOR IMPROVEMENT

A hope that by often seeing words, as in frequent reading, you will cure your spelling difficulty is without research justification (366). You have to work at it.

Study the correct spelling of each of the preceding words you listed. The most effective study method is actually to try spelling these words; do not merely look at the list. Try visualizing the words (in every detail) on a flat surface in front of you; then look at the word to clarify any part that was not clearly visualized. Try spelling these words aloud or try writing them out. Above all, do not avoid these words in your everyday writing; make a special effort to use them and to spell them correctly. One theory concerning difficulty with spelling is that it is a result of disguised resistance to authority demands (430); however, this behavior actually does not hurt fathers, teachers, or society—only yourself.

Two additional ways to improve spelling have been suggested: locating the "hard spots" in words, and learning spelling rules. In many instances these methods have tended to involve more work than is necessary, but if they seem particularly applicable to many of your errors, it would be worthwhile for you to study this material further.

One analysis of spelling errors of college students showed that 90 percent of the misspelled words had only one hard spot (8). Thus, a misspelled word should not be considered entirely wrong. Each of your misspellings should be analyzed to find the letter combination that needs particular attention. Furthermore, two-thirds of college students' misspellings were found to represent phonetic substitutions (other letters with the same sounds) or phonetic renditions of mispronunciations. Be sure you know the correct pronunciation of the words you misspell, and pay particular attention to the places in the word that cause difficulty. Sometimes a little story or word game can be invented to help with these hard spots, e.g., remember the "sin" in "business."

The second approach is to learn spelling rules so as to have guides when spelling. The difficulty here is that most spelling rules have so many exceptions that many people feel it is easier not to bother, i.e., they just study the word in its correct form. The following seven rules, however, cover many spelling demons and have few exceptions (125). Many spelling errors are actually failures to follow rules of capitalization (see pages 185–187). If many of your spelling errors can be found in the following rules, these particular rules are well worth further study.

1. Most nouns form their plurals by adding s or es to the singular. Es is added to to make the word easier to pronounce.
   Examples: cars, cars
   pass, passes
   push, pushes
   porch, porches

2. Drop the final e before adding a suffix beginning with a vowel.
   Examples: ride, riding
   believe, believing

3. When final *y* is preceded by a consonant, change *y* to *i* before adding any suffix that does not begin with *i*.
   Examples: satisfy, satisfied, satisfying
   enjoy, enjoyable

4. *Q* is always followed by *u*.
   Examples: quiet, quick, quiver, quail

5. *I* before *e*
   Except after *c*
   Or when sounded as *a*
   As in *neighbor* and *weigh*
   Examples: diet, receive, neigh

6. The sound of *i* at the end of a word is usually spelled by the letter *y*.
   Examples: many, very, heavy, steady

7. With words of one syllable and with words accenting the last syllable and ending in one consonant preceded by one vowel, you double the final consonant when adding a suffix beginning with a vowel.
   Examples: fun, funny
   omit, omitted

Many words are used so infrequently that it is not worthwhile to learn to spell them. You occasionally may experience a block in spelling a word that you usually know. In such instances, reach for a dictionary or ask a friend. For further information on use of the dictionary, see Section C in Chapter 10.

Additional information on learning to spell, *e.g.*, the value of other rules and of knowledge of word roots can be found in the English handbooks listed earlier.

C. *Handwriting*

Experimental studies have shown that even though a teacher may endeavor not to count legibility of handwriting in his grading, actually he will give higher marks for the more legible writing (186). Legible handwriting helps to provide easier and more pleasant reading.

Many college students write so poorly (especially under pressure of speed in writing notes or quizzes) that instructors have difficulty in grading the papers. Two studies show that the average quality or legibility of college seniors' handwriting is *below* that of the average eighth-grader (164, 424). Indeed, a student may occasionally even be unable to read his own writing. The purpose of the following exercise is to show how you may locate your most serious writing faults and deal with them. It will demonstrate how the difficulties of a particular individual usually center around a few recurring errors.

Writing is intended to be read. In considering the quality of a piece of handwriting, and, still more, in considering what faults in it may be serious and need attention, the practical approach is to determine what features of that writing interfere with ease and accuracy in reading it.

The following chart shows the result of research in writing errors. A large number of samples of handwriting of children, college students, and adults were reviewed. The readers checked every place in which they had any difficulty (even though only momentary) in reading what had been written. The places checked were then returned to, and the illegibilities were analyzed and classified. These results were then brought together, and the most common illegibilities were determined. You will notice that certain general characteristics (such as crowding words together) cause trouble, but most difficulties are the result of writing one letter so that it looks like another: writing *d* like *cl*, *a* like *u*, or *r* like an undotted *i*. With this chart before you, you can easily locate and classify troublesome points in any piece of writing. Further experiment has shown that when such highly specific difficulties are located and effort is directed toward the elimination of the few most common illegibilities, improvement in handwriting is relatively easily achieved (215).

Error Analysis Chart[a]

Illegibility	Rater A	Rater B	Explanations
Words crowded			*Words crowded*—too little space between words, so that word divisions are not readily seen.
Too angular			
Rewriting			*Words broken*—breaks between parts of words so that word and syllable divisions are confused.
Words broken			
Loops long			*Loops long*—such letters as *y* and *g* reach down into the line below or *h* and *l* into the line above.
a like u			
a " o			*e closed*—*e* like undotted *i*.
a " ci			*l closed*—*l* like uncrossed *t*.
b " li			*h like p*—the main difficulty here is a prolongation of the main down-stroke of the *h*.
c " e			
c " i			*r like half n*—most likely in such combinations as *rr* like *n*.
d " ci			
e closed			*r like undotted i*—especially in such combinations as *ri* like *u*.
e too high			
g like y			*s indistinct*—incomplete forms coming at the end of a word.
h " li			
h " p			*t like l*—involves also omission or misplacement of cross bar.
h " b			
h " l			
i " e			
Dot misplaced			
k like h			
l closed			
l too short			
m like w			
n " u			
n " v			
o " a			
o " r			
o closed			
r like i			
r " s			
r half n			
r half u			
s indistinct			
s like r			
t " l			
Cross omitted			
Cross misplaced			
M like N			
W like U			
I like cl			
Other illegibilities			
Total			
Two most common			

[a] With slight modification, from S. L. Pressey and F. P. Robinson, *Laboratory Workbook in Applied Educational Psychology*, 3d ed., New York, Harper & Row, 1959. Used with permission.

SELF-EVALUATION

The self-evaluation of handwriting is simple.

1. Bring to class two samples of your handwriting that are at least 500 words in length and were written under ordinary conditions or under pressure of speed, as in writing a quiz or taking notes. Count the number of words from the beginning until you have 500; make a heavy cross after word 500. Have two other students who are not familiar with your writing read the material quickly; tell them to underline (not mark over) any letter, combination of letters, or place that caused even *momentary difficulty* in reading. (This project will be done in class.) The grader should keep in mind, however, that he is not to mark angularities, irregularities, peculiarities, or writing that makes the appearance unattractive or unusual as long as they do not interfere with reading. The analysis is for illegibility, not beauty. In case of doubt a place should not be marked. The marked places should represent real hindrances to easy reading.

2. In consultation with each reader, go over these marked places and determine in each instance what specific feature of your writing causes trouble in order that you may know what his difficulties in reading were. As you proceed make a tabulation mark on the Error Analysis Chart. Thus, if the first difficulty was *a* like *u*, put a mark beside this item; if the next illegibility was a result of crowding words together at the end of a line, put a tally mark after "words crowded"; if the next was another *a* like *u*, put another mark after this item. If you find an illegibility not listed in the chart, write it on one of the lines at the bottom of the chart, and put a tally mark after it.

3. Count the number of marks after each item and write these numbers to the right; then add in order to find the total number of your illegibilities and write this figure in the "total" row. Similarities in checking by the two raters should be convincing evidence that these particular illegibilities are generally a handicap.

4. Draw a circle around the figures for your two most frequent illegibilities. How many of your total illegibilities are a result of these two? Write the number in the row marked "two most common." If you were to cure yourself of these two most common faults, what proportion of the total number of your illegibilities would you dispose of?

5. In actual practice the handwriting of the average student would receive about 27 checks per 500 words. Student scribbling, however, is not a high standard toward which to aim. A much better goal is to try to write so that your handwriting causes little or no difficulty in reading. Illegibilities should be reduced to a minimum.

PROGRAM FOR IMPROVEMENT

Have you found that only a few letters are causing most of the difficulty? If so, a little care in forming these few letters will do a great deal toward improving your handwriting. You will have to try this in all writing situations, however, if you are to expect improvement in your everyday writing. Make it a regular practice to proofread your writing in order to correct illegibilities. Finally, have another person check later samples of your handwriting for illegibilities so that you may have a measure of improvement and a further indication of remaining errors.

The left-handed person often has particular difficulty with handwriting because progression from left to right is more difficult for him. Suggestions for improving handwriting of left-handed persons will be found in G. M. Blair, *Diagnostic and Remedial Teaching*, rev. ed., New York, Macmillan, 1956, pp. 316–318.

CHAPTER 12
Mathematics

Various attempts have been made to analyze which characteristics are most related to success or failure in mathematics; one procedure, noted in earlier chapters, is to give a great many different tests of aptitude, achievement, and personality and then to subject these findings to an elaborate factor analysis (71, 391, 414). The major variables found in mathematics achievement are ability to reason, attitude toward mathematics, and knowledge of basic mathematical processes. Further analysis shows that the ability to reason includes such aspects as intelligence, ability to manipulate relations, flexibility of thought, and ability to organize.

This ability to analyze or organize is in many respects similar to reading and, in fact, calls for reading ability (70). In one study when 499 high school and college students were asked to solve simple problems, such as "If 15 hens each lays 5 eggs per week for 4 weeks, what is the total value of the eggs at 6 cents each?," it was found that even some capable students stumbled in analyzing what arithmetic operations were to be carried out. It was concluded that "better training (a) in reading problems in order to sense relevant, irrelevant, or needed data, (b) in estimating reasonable answers, (c) in following a superior sequence of operations, and (d) in using abstract symbols might be expected to contribute to competence in problem solving" (69, p. 135).

Attempts to discover the personal characteristics of students who are good and poor at mathematics show that good mathematicians tend to be socially and intellectually mature and value theoretical matters (5). Students who were not good in mathematics were at the opposite end of the scale but were particularly characterized by negative attitudes toward mathematics (6, 100). These negative attitudes often had their origin in earlier traumatic experiences with attempts to learn mathematics, but these can be remedied by counseling (265).

The preceding points pertain to difficulties in taking mathematics courses.

Students also constantly run into the need for some mathematics in their other courses and sometimes have difficulty with them (or even seek to avoid such things as science courses) because of a negative attitude toward mathematics and some feeling that they just cannot do mathematical problems. One surprising finding is that many college students are not proficient in some quite elementary mathematical skills (152, 403). Arnold found that 10 percent of entering freshmen were unable to do a single one of 20 problems in long division, that 18 percent could not multiply common fractions, and that 20 percent could not divide decimal fractions (294). Inability to do well on a simple test like the one to follow is predictive of future difficulty with courses such as chemistry or physics (4, 196).

The value of trying to remedy difficulty with mathematical operations is shown by a study in which several hundred students scoring in the lowest third in a test, such as the following, came in voluntarily for only six sessions to remedy their difficulties (196). It was found that of those who scored 85 percent or better on a retest, none made below a C in chemistry that term. (Although there is a motivation factor in this latter result—those motivated enough to learn mathematics would also be motivated to learn chemistry—there is also good evidence that knowledge of basic mathematics is important in doing well in science courses.)

The central thesis in this chapter is that a few simple operations in arithmetic and in simple proportion are all that are necessary to handle problems in courses outside the mathematics department, including science courses.

SELF-EVALUATION

If there is a need for mathematics in any of your courses, you should take the following test so that you will know the areas in which you require improvement. This test is based on analyses of the mathematical skills that are most frequently used in college subjects and that teachers consider essential for work in their fields. Because of the bases for selection of the test items, a student should get every one correct. If a student misses both examples of a given process, he should give definite remedial attention to it. The key for this test is on page 287 in Appendix III.

PROGRAM FOR IMPROVEMENT

Any error made represents an item that you should know. Rather than being "altogether poor" in mathematics you have probably found that just a few processes are giving you difficulty. With such specific diagnostic information, your remedial efforts can be effectively focused on those particular difficulties. If you have great difficulty with this test or with other aspects of mathematics and these areas are necessary in your work, probably you ought to enroll in a basic mathematics course in order to obtain this background.

The following references also give helpful suggestions on how to carry out these mathematical operations and how to solve problems encountered in science laboratories.

Bernstein, A., and Wells, D. W., *Trouble-Shooting Mathematics Skills.* New York: Holt, Rinehart and Winston, 1963.

Frey, P. R., *Chemistry Problems and How to Solve Them*, 7th ed. New York: Barnes & Noble, 1968.

Miller, L. H., *Understanding Basic Mathematics*. New York: Holt, Rinehart and Winston, 1961.

Nielsen, K. L., *College Mathematics*. New York: Barnes & Noble, 1968.

Papay, J. J., *Basic Facts of College Mathematics*. New York: Crowell-Collier and Macmillan, 1965.

Sperling, A., and Stuart, M., *Mathematics Made Simple*, Rev. ed. New York: Doubleday, 1962.

Basic Skills in Mathematics

Percent right _____

(1) 448
     372
     981
     365
     ‾‾‾

(2) 484
     273
     189
     563
     ‾‾‾

(3)   27831
     − 9246
     ‾‾‾‾‾‾‾

(4)   73821
     − 6249
     ‾‾‾‾‾‾‾

(5)   2784
     × 385
     ‾‾‾‾‾‾

(6)   4287
     × 379
     ‾‾‾‾‾‾

(7) 17157 ÷ 86 _____

(8) 22989 ÷ 79 _____

(9) ⅝ + ⅕ _____

(10) ⅘ + ¾ _____

(11) 5⁄7 − ⅔ _____

(12) ⅚ − ¾ _____

(13) 4⁄7 × ¾ _____

(14) ⅖ × ¾ _____

(15) ⅓ ÷ 4⁄7 _____

(16) ⅗ ÷ ¾ _____

(17) 9.20 + 16. + .0071 + 1.275 + .7265 _____

(18) .0026 + 1.89 + .2478 + 86. + 1.002 _____

(19) 3. − 1.8306 _____

(20) 2. − 1.7058 _____

(21) 3.702 × .207 _____

(22) 1.008 × .074 _____

(23) .0036 ÷ 1.2 _____

(24) 3.05 ÷ .61 _____

(25) What percent is 5 of 8? _____

(26) What percent is 12 of 17? _____

(27) How is 20 percent written as a common fraction? _____

(28) How is 50 percent written as a common fraction? _____

(29) How is 20 percent written as a decimal fraction? _____

(30) How is 50 percent written as a decimal fraction? _____

(31–35) Write the squares of the following numbers from memory:

7 _____ 8 _____ 9 _____ 11 _____ 12 _____

(36) $1\frac{3}{4} \times 8 =$ _____

(37) $2\frac{1}{2} \times 16 =$ _____

(38) 20 percent of 50 = _____

(39) 110 percent of 10 = _____

Reduce these expressions to their simplest forms by cancellation and then express their answers as decimals to two places:

(40) $\dfrac{5 \times 7 \times 44}{50 \times 77} =$ _____

(41) $\dfrac{35}{560} \times \dfrac{48}{54} \times 20 =$ _____

(42) $\dfrac{.28 \times 5.6 \times 0.77}{1.1 \times 1.12 \times 140} =$ _____

(43) $\dfrac{0.45}{9} \times \dfrac{108}{1.05} \times \dfrac{.07}{1.2} =$ _____

In the following proportions, fill in the missing terms:

(44) $3/6 = ?/10$ _____

(45) $4/? = 6/12$ _____

(46) $4/2 = 12/?$ _____

(47) $?/15 = 12/36$ _____

The next three problems deal with simple relations in chemistry for which the following sample can act as a model. These are problems in proportion just like the ones above.

$C + \quad O_2 \quad \rightarrow \quad CO_2$
12    $2 \times 16 = 32$ $12 + 32 = 44$ (These numbers underneath show the atomic weights and resulting molecular weight of CO_2. The ratio of carbon entering CO_2 to the total weight produced is 12/44; that of O is 32/44.)

(48) If the reaction is begun with 36 grams of C, how much CO_2 will be produced?

That is, $\dfrac{12\,g}{44\,g} = \dfrac{36\,g}{?\,g}$ $\qquad\qquad ? =$ _____g

(49) How many g of O will be used to produce this? _____g

(50) If it is desired to produce 88 g of CO_2, how much C will be needed? _____g

CHAPTER 13
Looking ahead

The purpose of this final chapter is to make an inventory of your progress and to plan for whatever future work seems necessary. This cannot be a final attempt, since a single course cannot be expected completely to remedy the deficient attitudes, skills, and knowledge you may have developed over a period of many years. Thus far, you have had the following purposes in this course: (1) the development of an awareness of your various abilities and problems, (2) training in higher-level work skills, and (3) an initial attack to remedy deficiencies in, or adjust your plans to, your profile of abilities. Now there is need for a progress report upon which you can base your future efforts. Because training in how-to-study must be done in terms of specific problems, your diagnosis at the beginning of this course must now be changed in light of the work that you have accomplished.

Note also that if your present survey indicates the solution of some problem, such as reading rate, you still have to practice further in order to make this skill habitual and lasting.

What are some of the bases by which you may evaluate your present status?

1. A retest on some of the tests you took initially and on which you did poorly will indicate the extent of your gains and the present status of these problems.

2. These remeasured basic skills, though important, represent only a small part of what you have been working on this term. Also measure your improvement in the quality of your notebook and class papers, in your study habits, in your use of time, in your ability to concentrate, and in your ability to predict quiz questions and take tests.

3. You should include an evaluation of changes, if any, in your motivation for doing academic work.

4. Your conferences with your instructor or counselor about various problems also offer a good basis for the analysis of your present problems.

5. There are probably some traits on which you did not know your relative standing before taking this course. This new orientation should have assisted in your school adjustment.

Your problem in this project, then, is to (1) state your present status in terms of all these measures, (2) evaluate the gains you have made, and (3) outline the program of training that you plan to carry on after this course. You can best do this in an informal essay covering these points; it is to be handed in to the instructor not later than the last day of class before exam week.

Your instructor will be glad to go over your outline before you write this paper, and make pertinent suggestions and corrections.

If at a later time in your college program you need help with any aspect of the work that has been covered in this course, feel free to ask your present instructor for assistance.

Bibliography

1. ABPC releases survey report showing sales, 1952–1961. *Publishers' Weekly*, August 6, 1962, *182*, 48–49.
2. Abrams, A. G., The relation of listening and reading comprehension to skill in message structuralization. *Journal of Communication*, 1966, *16*, 116–125.
3. Adams, R. B., "The Phenomenon of Supernormal Reading Ability," in R. C. Staiger and C. Y. Melton, eds., *Twelfth Yearbook of the National Reading Conference*. Milwaukee: National Reading Conference, 1963, 133–142.
4. Adams, S., and Garrett, H. L., Scholastic background as related to success in college physics. *Journal of Educational Research*, 1954, *47*, 545–549.
5. Aiken, L. R., Jr., Personality correlates of attitude toward mathematics. *Journal of Educational Research*, 1963, *56*, 476–480.
6. Aiken, L. R., Jr., and Dreger, R. M., The effect of attitudes on performance in mathematics. *Journal of Educational Psychology*, 1961, *52*, 19–24.
7. ALA surveys reading in America. *Library Journal*, 1962, *87*, 524–525.
8. Alper, T. G., A diagnostic spelling scale for the college level: Its construction and use. *Journal of Educational Psychology*, 1942, *33*, 273–290.
9. Alper, T. S., and Korchin, S. J., Memory for socially relevant material. *Journal of Abnormal and Social Psychology*, 1952, *47*, 25–37.
10. Alpert, R., and Haber, R. N., Anxiety in academic achievement situations. *Journal of Abnormal and Social Psychology*, 1960, *61*, 207–215.
11. Ames, W. S., The development of a classification scheme of contextual aids. *Reading Research Quarterly*, 1966–1967, *2*, 57–82.
12. Anderson, I. H., Studies in the eye movements of good and poor readers. *Psychological Monographs*, 1937, *48*, 1–35.
13. Anderson, J. R., Do college students lack motivation? *Personnel and Guidance Journal*, 1954, *33*, 209–210.
14. Anderson, R. P., and Kuntz, J. E., The survey of study habits and attitudes in a college counseling center. *Personnel and Guidance Journal*, 1959, *37*, 365–368.
15. Anikeeff, A. M., The relationship between class absences and college grades. *Journal of Educational Psychology*, 1954, *45*, 244–249.
16. Arnold, H. F., The comparative efficiency of certain study techniques in fields of history. *Journal of Educational Psychology*, 1942, *33*, 449–457.
17. Arsenian, S., Own estimate and objective measurement. *Journal of Educational Psychology*, 1942, *33*, 291–302.
18. Athey, I., "Personality Factors and the Development of Successful Readers," in G. B. Schick and M. M. May, eds., *Fifteenth Yearbook of the National Reading Conference*. Milwaukee: National Reading Conference, 1966, 133–139.
19. Atkinson, J. W., "The Mainsprings of Achievement-Oriented Activity," in J. D. Krumboltz, ed., *Learning and the Educational Process*. Chicago: Rand McNally, 1965, 25–66.

20. Ausubel, D. P., The use of advance organizers in the learning and retention of meaningful verbal material. *Journal of Educational Psychology,* 1960, *51,* 267–272.
21. Ausubel, D. P., A subsumption theory of meaningful verbal learning and retention. *Journal of General Psychology,* 1962, *66,* 213–224.
22. Baird, L. L., The prediction of accomplishment in college: A study of achievement. *Journal of Counseling Psychology,* 1969, *16,* 246–253.
23. Baker, R. W., and Madell, T. O., Susceptibility to distraction in academically underachieving and achieving male college students. *Journal of Consulting Psychology,* 1965, *29,* 173–177.
24. Barch, Abram M., The relation of departure time and retention to academic achievement. *Journal of Educational Psychology,* 1957, *48,* 352–358.
25. Barton, W. A., Outlining as a study procedure. *Teachers College Contribution to Education,* 1930, no. 411.
26. Bear, R. M., and Odbert, H. S., Insight of older students into their knowledge of word meanings. *School Review,* 1941, *49,* 754–760.
27. Berdie, R. F., Personality changes from high school entrance to college matriculation. *Journal of Counseling Psychology,* 1968, *15,* 376–380.
28. Berg, Paul, "Reading in Relation to Listening," in O. S. Causey *Fourth Yearbook of the Southwest Reading Conference for Colleges and Universities.* Fort Worth, Tex.: Texas Christian University Press, 1955, 52–60.
29. Berg, P. C., "Flexibility in Reading," in J. A. Figurel, ed., *Proceedings of the Eleventh Annual Convention of the International Reading Association,* Part I, New York: Scholastic Magazines, Inc. 1967, *11,* 45–49.
30. Berg, P. C., and Rentel, V. M., Improving study skills. *Journal of Reading,* 1966, 9, 343–348.
31. Berger, A., "Controversial Issues Pertaining to Reading Rate," in G. B. Schick and M. M. May, eds., *Seventeenth Yearbook of the National Reading Conference.* Milwaukee: National Reading Conference, 1968, 18–24.
32. Berger, E. M., Willingness to accept limitations and college achievement. *Journal of Counseling Psychology,* 1961, *8,* 140–144.
33. Berger, E. M., Willingness to accept limitations and college achievement: A replication. *Journal of Counseling Psychology,* 1963, *10,* 176–178.
34. Berlyne, D. E., Conditions of prequestioning and retention of meaningful material. *Journal of Educational Psychology,* 1966, *57,* 128–132.
35. Berrien, F. K., Are scores increased on objective tests by changing the initial decision? *Journal of Educational Psychology,* 1940, *31,* 64–67.
36. Blaine, G. B., Jr., and McArthur, C. C., *Emotional Problems of the Student.* New York: Appleton-Century-Crofts, 1961.
37. Blake, W. S., Jr., Do probationary college freshmen benefit from compulsory study skills and reading training? *Journal of Experimental Education,* 1956, *25,* 91–93.
38. Blanton, W. L., and Peck, R. F., College student motivation and academic performance. *Educational and Psychological Measurement,* 1964, *24,* 897–912.
39. Bloom, B. S., Thought processes in lectures and discussions. *Journal of General Education,* 1953, *7,* 160–169.
40. Bloom, B. S., The 1955 normative study of the tests of General Educational Development. *School Review,* 1956, *64,* 110–124.
41. Bloom, B. S., and Broder, L. J., *Problem-Solving Processes of College Students.* Chicago: University of Chicago Press, 1950.
42. Blumenfeld, W. S., Franklin, R. D., and Remmers, H. H., Teenagers' attitudes toward study habits, vocational plans, religious beliefs, and luck. *Purdue Opinion Panel Poll Report,* 1962, *22,* whole no. 67 (11 pages).
43. Borglum, G., Memorandum to beginning students in French. *French Review,* 1959, *32,* 268–270.
44. Borow, H., The measurement of academic adjustment. *Journal of American Association of College Registrars,* 1947, *22,* 274–286.
45. Borow, H., *College Inventory of Academic Adjustment.* Palo Alto, Calif.: Stanford University Press, 1949.

46. Bowman, M. E., Some relationships between flexibility and reading gains at the college level. *Journal of the Reading Specialist*, 1966, *6*, 20–25.
47. Boyd, R., Rate of comprehension in reading among sixth form pupils in New Zealand schools. *The Reading Teacher*, 1966, *20*, 237–241.
48. Braam, L. S., Developing and measuring flexibility in reading. *Reading Teacher*, 1963, *16*, 247–251.
49. Braam, L. S., and Berger, A., Effectiveness of four methods of increasing reading rate, comprehension, and flexibility. *Journal of Reading*, 1968, *11*, 346–352.
50. Brethower, D. M., "Some Influences of 'Speed Set' on Rate of Comprehension During Testing," in D. M. Wark, ed., *Fifth Yearbook of the North Central Reading Association*. Minneapolis: National Central Reading Association, 1968, 93–103.
51. Briggs, Arvella, and Johnson, D. M., A note on the relation between persistence and achievement on the final examination. *Journal of Educational Psychology*, 1942, *33*, 623–627.
52. Briggs, Leslie, and Reile, Patricia, Should students change their initial answers on objective tests? More evidence regarding an old problem. *Journal of Educational Psychology*, 1952, *43*, 110–115.
53. Brooks, K., and Sister I. M. Wulftange, Listener response to oral interpretation. *Speech Monographs*, 1964, *31*, 73–79.
54. Brown, C. T., Studies in listening comprehension. *Speech Monographs*, 1959, *26*, 288–294.
55. Brown, F. G., Identifying the college dropouts with the Minnesota Counseling Inventory. *Personnel and Guidance Journal*, 1960, *39*, 280–282.
56. Brown, F. G., Study habits and attitudes, college experience, and college success. *Personnel and Guidance Journal*, 1964, *43*, 287–292.
57. Brown, F. G., and Dubois, T. E., Correlates of academic success for high-ability freshmen. *Personnel and Guidance Journal*, 1964, *42*, 603–607.
58. Brown, J. I., The objective measurement of listening ability. *Journal of Communication*, 1951, *1*, 44–48.
59. Brown, J. I., Evaluating student performance in listening. *Education*, 1955, *75*, 316–321.
60. Brown, J. I., "Reading Improvement Through Vocabulary Development: The CPD Formula," in G. B. Schick and M. M. May, eds., *Fifteenth Yearbook of the National Reading Conference*. Milwaukee, Wisc.: National Reading Conference, 1966, 197–202.
61. Brown, P., The relationship of attitude and reading comprehension to critical reading responses. *Dissertation Abstracts*, 1967, *27*, 3357–3358.
62. Brown, W. F., Abeles, N., and Iscoe, I., Motivational differences between high and low scholarship students. *Journal of Educational Psychology*, 1954, *45*, 215–222.
63. Brown, W. F., and Holtzman, W. H., *Survey of Study Habits and Attitudes Manual, Forms C and H*. New York: Psychological Corporation, 1967.
64. Brown, W. H., Vocational aspirations of seniors at North Carolina College: A follow-through study. *College and University*, 1955, *30*, 313–323.
65. Bruning, R. H., Effects of review and test-like events within the learning of prose materials. *Journal of Educational Psychology*, 1968, *59*, 16–19.
66. Brunkan, R. J., and Shen, F., Personality characteristics of ineffective, effective, and efficient readers. *Personnel and Guidance Journal*, 1966, *44*, 837–843.
67. Burton, D. L., "Teaching Students to Read Literature," in J. A. Figurel, ed., *Perspectives in Reading 2: Reading Instruction in Secondary Schools*. Newark, Del.: International Reading Association, 1964, 87–102.
68. Burtt, H. E., *Applied Psychology*, 2d ed. Englewood Cliffs, N.J.: Prentice-Hall, 1957.
69. Buswel, G. T., and Kersh, B. Y., Patterns of thinking in solving problems. *University of California Publications in Education*, 1956, *12*, no. 2, 63–148.
70. Call, R. J., and Wiggin, N. A., Reading and mathematics. *Mathematics Teacher*, 1966, *59*, 149–157.
71. Canisia, M., Mathematical ability as related to reasoning and use of symbols. *Educational and Psychological Measurements*, 1962, *21* 105–127.
72. Carmichael, L., and Dearborn, W. F., *Reading and Visual Fatigue*. Boston: Houghton-Mifflin, 1947.
73. Carpenter, W. W., and Fort, M. K., What effect do visitors have upon recitation? *Journal of Educational Research*, 1930, *22*, 50–53.

74. Carroll, Hazel Horn, "Word Attack and Vocabulary Development," in O. S. Causey, ed., *Third Yearbook of the Southwest Reading Conference for Colleges and Universities*. Fort Worth, Tex.: Texas Christian University Press, 1954, 100–103.

75. Carter, H. D., What are some of the basic problems in analysis of study techniques? *California Journal of Educational Research*, 1951, 2, 170–174.

76. Cartier, F. A., Comparison of overt and covert responding on a programmed lesson assigned as homework. *Journal of Programmed Instruction*, 1963, 2, 13–20.

77. Chahbazi, P., Analysis of Cornell Orientation Inventory items on study habits and their relative value in prediction of college achievement. *Journal of Experimental Education*, 1958, 27, 135–142.

78. Chamberlain, J. L., Jr., Some aids to teaching a spoken foreign language. *Modern Language Journal*, 1954, 38, 331–346.

79. Chandler, T. A., Reading disability and socio-economic status. *Journal of Reading*, 1966, 10, 5–21.

80. Check, J. F., and Rucinski, P., Study habits of college students. *College Student Survey*, 1967, 1, 49–54.

81. Christ, F. L., "Some University Students and Their Ideal Study Environment—as They See It!" in G. B. Schick and M. M. May, eds., *Sixteenth Yearbook of the National Reading Conference*. Milwaukee: National Reading Conference, 1967, 82–85.

82. Christensen, C. M., and Stordahl, K. E., The effect of organizational aids on comprehension and retention. *Journal of Educational Psychology*, 1955, 46, 65–74.

83. Clark, B., and Malone, R. D., Topographical orientation in naval aviation cadets. *Journal of Educational Psychology*, 1954, 45, 91–109.

84. Clark, P. M., "Examination Performance and Examination Set," in D. M. Wark, ed., *Fifth Yearbook of the North Central Reading Association*. Minneapolis: North Central Reading Association, 1968, 114–122.

85. Class, E. C., The effect of the kind of test announcement on students' preparation. *Journal of Educational Research*, 1935, 28, 358–361.

86. Cofer, C. N., On some factors in the organizational characteristics of free recall. *American Psychologist*, 1965, 20, 261–272.

87. Cole, C. W., and Miller, C. D., Relevance of expressed values to academic performance. *Journal of Counseling Psychology*, 1967, 14, 272–276.

88. Cole, Luella, *Improvement of Reading*. New York: Holt, Rinehart and Winston, 1938.

89. Colvin, C. R., Methods and materials in college reading programs: Pennsylvania revisited. *Journal of the Reading Specialist*, 1967, 7, 2–7.

90. Condon, J. T., Study habits and perceptions of desirable study space by California Community College students. *Dissertation Abstracts*, 1966, 27A, 896–897.

91. Cox, F. N., The prediction of success and failure in learning a foreign language. *Australian Journal of Psychology*, 1955, 7, 56–65.

92. Creaser, J. W., Factor analysis of a Study-Habits Q-Sort Test. *Journal of Counseling Psychology*, 1960, 7, 298–300.

93. Crites, J. O., and Semler, I. J., Adjustment, educational achievement, and vocational maturity as dimensions of development in adolescence. *Journal of Counseling Psychology*, 1967, 14, 489–496.

94. Dale, E., The time of our lives. *The Newsletter*, February 1969, 34, no. 5.

95. Dalton, P., Gliessman, D., Guthrie, H., and Rees, G., The effect of reading improvement on academic achievement. *Journal of Reading*, 1966, 9, 242–252.

96. Danskin, D. G., and Burnett, C. W., Study techniques of those superior students. *Personnel and Guidance Journal*, 1952, 31, 181–186.

97. Davis, F. B. "Measurement of Improvement in Reading Skill Courses," in E. P. Bliesmer and R. C. Staiger, eds., *Eleventh Yearbook of the National Reading Conference*. Milwaukee: National Reading Conference, 1962, 30–40.

98. Davis, F. B., Research in comprehension in reading. *Reading Research Quarterly*, 1968, 3, 499–545.

99. Dawes, R. M., Memory and distortion of meaningful written material. *British Journal of Psychology*, 1966, 57, 77–86.

100. Degnan, J. A., General anxiety and attitudes toward mathematics in achievers and under-achievers in mathematics. *Graduate Research in Education and Related Disciplines*, 1967, *3*, 49–62.

101. DeLong, G. H., *Relative Effectiveness of Six Methods of Teaching College Students How to Study*, Unpublished doctoral dissertation, Ohio State University, 1948.

102. DeSena, P. A., The effectiveness of two study habits inventories in predicting consistent over-, under-, and normal achievement in college. *Journal of Counseling Psychology*, 1964, *11*, 388–393.

103. Desiderato, O., and Koskinen, P., Anxiety, study habits, and academic achievement. *Journal of Counseling Psychology*, 1969, *16*, 162–165.

104. Devine, T. G., Listening. *Review of Educational Research*, 1967, 37, 152–158.

105. Dickinson, C., and Newbegin, B., Can work and college mix? *Personnel and Guidance Journal*, 1959, 38, 314–317.

106. Dixon, R. E., *The Effects of Different Types of Student Personnel Groupings on the Social Adjustment of College Students*, Unpublished doctoral dissertation, Ohio State University, 1948.

107. Dole, A. A., College students report on their use of time. *Personnel and Guidance Journal*, 1959, 37, 633–637.

108. Dostert, L. E., Foreign-language reading skill. *Journal of Chemical Education*, 1955, *32*, 128–132.

109. Dowell, R. L., and McNair, J., "Techniques and Procedures in Government Reading Programs," in O. S. Causey, ed., *Sixth Yearbook of the Southwest Reading Conference for Colleges and Universities*. Fort Worth, Tex.: Texas Christian Universtiy Press, 1957, 91–101.

110. Dressel, P. L., Factors involved in changing values of college students. *Educational Record*, 1965, *46*, 104–113.

111. Dudycha, G. J., An objective study of punctuality in relation to personality and achievement. *Archives of Psychology*, 1936, no. 204.

112. Duff, O. L., and Siegel, L., Biographical factors associated with acedamic over- and under-achievement. *Journal of Educational Psychology*, 1960, *51*, 43–46.

113. Duker S., *Listening: Readings*. New York: Scarecrow Press, 1966.

114. Eagly, A. H., Involvement as a determinant of response to favorable and unfavorable information. *Journal of Personality and Social Psychology*, 1967, 7 (monograph supplement).

115. Edgerton, H. A., A study of elimination of Ohio State University students in relation to intelligence. *Ohio College Association Bulletin "S,"* p. 107.

116. Eisner, S., and Rohde, K., Note taking during or after the lecture. *Journal of Educational Psychology*, 1959, *50*, 301–304.

117a. Elton, C. F., Patterns of change in personality test scores. *Journal of Counseling Psychology*, 1969, *16*, 95–99.

117b. Elton, C. F., and Rose, H. A., The face of change. *Journal of Counseling Psychology*, 1968, *15*, 372–375.

118. English, H. B., Welborn, E. L., and Killian, C. D., Studies in substance memorization. *Journal of General Psychology*, 1934, *11*, 233–259.

119. Entwisle, D. R., Evaluation of study-skills courses: A review. *Journal of Educational Research*, 1960, *53*, 243–251.

120. Eriksen, S. C., An experimental study of individual differences in scholastic motives. *Journal of Educational Psychology*, 1940, *31*, 507–516.

121. Eurich, A., The significance of library reading among college students. *School and Society*, 1932, *36*, 92–96.

122. Ewing, T. N., and Gilbert, W. M., Controlled study of effects of counseling on the scholastic achievement of students of superior ability. *Journal of Counseling Psychology*, 1967, *14*, 235–239.

123. Farnsworth, P. R., Seat preference in the classroom. *Journal of Social Psychology*, 1933, *4*, 373–376.

124. Fitch, M. L., Drucker, A. J., and Norton, J. A., Frequent testing as a motivating factor in large lecture classes. *Journal of Educational Psychology*, 1951, *42*, 1–20.

125. Foran, T. G., *The Psychology and Teaching of Spelling*. Washington, D.C.: Catholic Education Press, 1934.

126. Frase, L. T., Learning from prose material: Length of passage, knowledge of results, and position of questions. *Journal of Educational Psychology*, 1967, *58*, 266–272.

127. Frase, L. T., Some data concerning the mathemagenic hypothesis. *American Educational Research Journal*, 1968, *5*, 181–189.

128. Frase, L. T., Questions as aids to reading: Some research and theory. *American Educational Research Journal*, 1968, *5*, 319–332.

129. Freeburne, C. M., and Fleischer, M. S., The effect of music distraction upon reading rate and comprehension. *Journal of Educational Psychology*, 1952, *43*, 101–109.

130. Fretz, B. R., and Schmidt, L. D., Comparison of improvers and nonimprovers in an educational skills course. *Journal of Counseling Psychlogy*, 1967, *14*, 175–176.

131. Gaier, Eugene L., Student perceptions of factors affecting test performance. *Journal of Educational Research*, 1962, *55*, 561–566.

132. Geerlofs, M. W., and Kling, M., Current practices in college and adult reading programs. *Journal of Reading*, 1968, *11*, 517–520 and 569–575.

133. Gelso, C. J., How much do students study? *Journal of College Student Personnel*, 1967, *8*, 373–375.

134. Gelso, C. J., Some findings about student study patterns. *College Student Survey*, 1969, *3*, 49–54.

135. Gelso, C. J., and Rowell, D., Academic adjustment and persistence of students with marginal academic potential. *Journal of Counseling Psychology*, 1967, *14*, 478–481.

136. Gentry, I. A., Immediate effects of interpolated rest periods on learning performance. *Teachers College Contribution to Education*, 1940, no. 799.

137. Gifford, R., and Sommer, R., The desk or the bed? *Personnel and Guidance Journal*, 1968, *46*, 876–878.

138. Gladstein, G. A., Study behavior of gifted stereotype and non-stereotype students. *Personnel and Guidance Journal*, 1960, *38*, 470–474.

139. Gladstein, G. A., A new approach to identifying appropriate individual study behavior. *The School Review*, 1963, *71*, 158–169.

140. Golburgh, M. L., and Penney, J. T., A note on counseling underachieving college students. *Journal of Counseling Psychology*, 1962, *9*, 133–138.

141. Gough, H. H., Academic achievement in high school as predicted from the California Psychological Inventory. *Journal of Educational Psychology*, 1964, *55*, 174–180.

142. Gowan, J. C., Factors of achievement in high school and college. *Journal of Counseling Psychology*, 1960, *7*, 91–95.

143. Graesser, R. F., Guessing on multiple-choice tests. *Educational and Psychological Measurement*, 1958, *18*, 617–620.

144. Gray, W. S., and Rogers, B., *Maturity in Reading*. Chicago: University of Chicago Press, 1956.

145. Grayum, Helen S., Skimming in reading: A fine art for modern needs. *National Association of Secondary School Principals Bulletin*, 1955, *39*, no. 212, 26–34.

146. Greene, F. "Review of Research: Visual Discrimination," in D. M. Wark, ed., *Third and Fourth Yearbook of the North Central Reading Association*. Minneapolis: North Central Reading Association, 1965, 1–19.

147. Gruner, C. R., Kibler, R. J., and Gibson, J. W., A quantative analysis of selected characteristics of oral and written vocabularies. *Journal of Communication*, 1967, *17*, 152–158.

148. Hadley, L. S., Scholastic adjustment problems of the returning veterans. *Educational Research Bulletin*, 1945, *24*, 87–92.

149. Hafner, L. E., Using context to determine meanings in high school and college. *Journal of Reading*, 1967, *10*, 491–498.

150. Hall, W. E., and Robinson, F. P., An analytic approach to the study of reading skills. *Journal of Educational Psychology*, 1945, *36*, 429–442.

151. Hanawalt, N. G., and Tarr, A. G., The effect of recall upon recognition. *Journal of Experimental Psychology*, 1961, *62*, 361–367.

152. Hannon, H., The mastery of certain aspects of mathematics for general education by college students. *Journal of Educational Research*, 1957, *50*, 363–371.

153. Harrison, J. N., *The Relation of Student Expectancy Level to Improvement in a Study-Skills Course and in Counseling*, Unpublished doctoral dissertation, Ohio State University, 1966.

154. Haslam, W. L., and Brown, W. F., Effectiveness of study-skills instruction for high school sophomores. *Journal of Educational Psychology*, 1968, 59, 223–226.

155. Hay, J. E., and Lindsay, C. A., The working student: How does he achieve? *Journal of College Student Personnel*, 1969, 10, 109–114.

156. Hayden, L. A., "The Effect of Physical Fatigue on Reading Rate and Comprehension of College Athletes," in R. C. Staiger and C. Y. Melton, eds., *Twelfth Yearbook of the National Reading Conference*. Milwaukee: National Reading Conference, 1963, 202–205.

157. Helper, M. M., The effects of noise on work output and physiological activation. *USA Medical Research Laboratory Report*, 1957, no. 270.

158. Henderson, E. H., A study of individually formulated purposes for reading. *Journal of Educational Research*, 1965, 58, 438–441.

159. Henderson, M. T., Crews, A., and Barlow, J., A study of the effect of musical distraction on reading efficiency. *Journal of Applied Psychology*, 1945, 29, 313–317.

160. Hershberger, W. A., Self-evaluational responding and typographical cuing: Techniques for programming self-instructional reading material. *Journal of Educational Psychology*, 1964, 55, 288–296.

161. Hershberger, W. A., and Terry, D. F., Typographical cuing in conventional and programmed texts. *Journal of Applied Psychology*, 1965, 49, 55–60.

162. Hightower, Lenore A., *An Investigation of the Study Habits and Study Conditions of Women Students in a Domitory*, Unpublished master's thesis, Ohio State University, 1956.

163. Hill, G. E., The effect of changed responses on true-false tests. *Journal of Educational Psychology*, 1937, 28, 308–310.

164. Hill, G. E., The handwriting of college seniors. *Journal of Educational Research*, 1943, 37, 118–126.

165. Hill, W. R., Factors associated with comprehension deficiency of college readers. *Journal of Developmental Reading*, 1959, 3, 84–93.

166. Hill, W. R., "Studies of Student Readers and Their Implications for College Instruction," in O. S. Causey and E. P. Bleismer, eds., *Ninth Yearbook of the National Reading Conference*. Fort Worth, Tex.: Texas Christian University Press, 1960, 9–20.

167 Hill, W. R., "Influence of Direction upon Reading Flexibility of Advanced College Readers," In E. L. Thurston and L. E. Hafner, eds., *Thirteenth Yearbook of the National Reading Conference*. Milwaukee: National Reading Conference, 1964, 110–125.

168. Hinze, H. K., The individual's word associations and his interpretation of prose paragraphs. *Journal of General Psychology*, 1961, 64, 193–203.

169. Hoffman, A. C., Eye movements during prolonged reading. *Journal of Experimental Psychology*, 1946, 36, 95–118.

170a. Holland, J. L., The prediction of college grades from personality and aptitude variables. *Journal of Educational Psychology*, 1960, 51, 245–254.

170b. Holland, J. L., and Astin, A. W., The prediction of academic, artistic, scientific, and social achievement of undergraduates of superior scholastic aptitude. *Journal of Educational Psychology*, 1962, 53, 132–143.

171. Holmes, Eleanor, Reading guided by questions versus careful reading and rereading without questions. *School Review*, 1931, 39, 361–371.

172. Holmes, Jack A., "Speed, Comprehension and Power in Reading," in E. P. Bliesmer and R. C. Steiger, eds., *Eleventh Yearbook of the National Reading Conference*. Milwaukee: National Reading Conference, 1962, 6–14.

173. Horowitz, M. W., Organizational processes underlying differences between listening and reading as a function of complexity of material. *Journal of Communication*, 1968, 18, 37–46.

174. Horowitz, M. W., and Berkowitz, A., Listening and reading, speaking and writing: An experimental investigation of differential acquisition and reproduction of memory. *Perceptual and Motor Skills*, 1967, 24, 207–215.

175. Horrall, B. M., Academic performance and personality adjustment of highly intelligent college students. *Genetic Psychology Monographs*, 1957, *55*, 3–83.
176. Hovey, H. B., Effects of general distraction on the higher thought processes. *American Journal of Psychology*, 1928, *40*, 585–591.
177. Hultgren, D. D., "Rapid Reading: Problems, Parameters and Prospects (R2—3P)," in G. B. Schick and M. M. May, eds., *Seventeenth Yearbook of the National Reading Conference*. Milwaukee: National Reading Conference, 1968, 13–17.
178. Huntley, C. W., Changes in value scores during the four years of college. *Genetic Psychology Monographs*, 1965, *71*, 349–383.
179. Huntley, C. W., Changes in values during the four years in college. *College Student Survey*, 1967, *1*, 43–48.
180. Hvistendahl, J. K., The effect of subheads on reader comprehension. *Journalism Quarterly*, 1968, *45*, 123–125.
181. Ingram, C. O., How university freshmen read: A study of the dynamics of the reading process. *Dissertation Abstracts*, 1967, *28A*, 1210–1211.
182. Ironside, R. A., "Perception and Word Recognition in Workbooks at the College Level," in R. C. Staiger and C. Y. Melton, eds., *Twelfth Yearbook of the National Reading Conference*. Milwaukee: National Reading Conference, 1963, 63–72.
183. Irvin, F. S., Sentence completion responses and scholastic success or failure. *Journal of Counseling Psychology*, 1967, *14*, 269–271.
184. Izard, C. E., Personality change during college years. *Journal of Counsulting Psychology*, 1962, *26*, 482.
185. Jacobson, M. D., Reading difficulty of physics and chemistry textbooks. *Educational and Psychological Measurements*, 1965, *25*, 449–457.
186. James, H. W., The effect of handwriting upon grading. *English Journal*, 1927, *16*, 180–185.
187. James, N. E., Personal preference for method as a factor in learning. *Journal of Educational Psychology*, 1962, *53*, 43–47.
188. Johnston, J. O., and Calhoun, J. P., The serial position effect in lecture material. *Journal of Educational Research*, 1969, *62*, 255–258.
189. Jones, D. H., Training industrial executives in reading: A methodology study. *Journal of Applied Psychology*, 1965, *49*, 202–204.
190. Kahn, P., Time orientation and reading achievement. *Perceptual and Motor Skills*, 1965, *21*, 157–158.
191. Kamano, D. K., and Drew, J. E., Selectivity in memory of personally significant material. *Journal of General Psychology*, 1961, *65*, 25–32.
192. Karraker, R. J., Knowledge of results and incorrect recall of plausible multiple choice alternatives. *Journal of Educational Psychology*, 1967, *58*, 11–14.
193. Kershner, A. M., Speed of reading in an adult population under different conditions. *Journal of Applied Psychology*, 1964, *48*, 25–28.
194. Ketcham, C. A., Factors in the home background and reader self-concept which relate to reading achievement. *Dissertation Abstracts*, 1967, *28A*, 499.
195. Kingston, A. J., and White, W. F., The relationship of reader's self-concepts and personality components to semantic meanings perceived in the protagonist of a reading selection. *Reading Research Quarterly*, 1967, *2*, 107–116.
196. Kinzer, J. R., and Fawcett, H. P., The arithmetic deficiencies of college chemistry students. *Educational Research Bulletin*, 1946, *25*, 113–114.
197. Kirkendall, L. A., Factors inhibiting pupil questioning in class. *Journal of Educational Methods*, 1937, *16*, 359–362.
198. Kirkman, A. J., Command of vocabulary among university entrants. *Educational Research*, 1967, *9*, 151–159.
199. Klare, G. R., Mabry, J. E., and Gustafson, L., The relationship of patterning (underlining) to immediate retention and to acceptability of technical material. *Journal of Applied Psychology*, 1955, *39*, 40–42.
200. Knapp, R. H., and Garbutt, J. T., Variations in time descriptions and in achievement. *Journal of Social Psychology*, 1965, *67*, 269–272.
201. Knight, F. B., and Remmers, H. H., Fluctuations in mental production when motivation is the main variable. *Journal of Applied Psychology*, 1923, *7*, 209–223.

202. Koile, E. A., and Bird, D. J., Preferences for counselor help on freshman problems. *Journal of Counseling Psychology*, 1956, 3, 97–106.

203. Korn, H. A., "Personality Scale Changes from the Freshman Year to the Senior Year," in J. Katz, ed., *No Time for Youth: Growth and Constraint in College Students*. San Francisco: Jossey-Bass, 1968, 162–184.

204. Kraehenbuehl, J. O., *Study Facilities in College Dormitories*, Publication no. 232. New York: National Society for the Prevention of Blindness, 1937.

205. Krumboltz, J. D., and Weisman, R. G., The effect of overt vs. covert responding to programmed instruction on immediate and delayed retention. *Journal of Educational Psychology*, 1962, 53, 89–92.

206. Laffitte, R. G., Jr., "Analysis of Increased Rate of Reading of College Students," in R. C. Staiger and C. Y. Melton, eds., *Twelfth Yearbook of the National Reading Conference*. Milwaukee: National Reading Conference, 1963, 110–111.

207. Larsen, R. P., and Feder, D. D., Common and differential factors in reading and hearing comprehension. *Journal of Educational Psychology*, 1940, 31, 241–252.

208. Larsen, R. P., Wittenborn, J. R., and Giesecke, E. C., Factors contributing to achievement in the study of first semester college German. *Journal of Experimental Education*, 1942, 10, 265–271.

209. Lavin, D. E., *The Prediction of Academic Performance*. New York: Russell Sage Foundation, 1965.

210. Laycock, F., Significant characteristics of college students with varying flexibility in reading rate. *Journal of Experimental Education*, 1955, 23, 311–330.

211. Lebow, H., and Sweger, V., The developmental reading program at the secondary level. *Academic Therapy Quarterly*, 1966, 1, 185–187.

212. Lebow, H., and Sweger, V., The developmental reading program in the secondary school: Helping the college-bound student. *Academic Therapy Quarterly*, 1967, 2, 124–126.

213. Lehman, H. C., Does it pay to change initial decisions in a true-false test? *School and Society*, 1928, 28, 456–458.

214. Lehman, H. C., Motivation: College marks and the fraternity pledge. *Journal of Applied Psychology*, 1935, 19, 9–28.

215. Lehman, H. C., and Pressey, L. C., The effectiveness of drill in handwriting to remove specific illegibilities. *School and Society*, 1928, 27, 546–548.

216. Lehman, I. J., Changes in critical thinking, attitudes, and values from freshmen to senior years. *Journal of Educational Psychology*, 1963, 54, 305–315.

217. Levin, B. J., "The Flexibility of Reading Rate," in J. A. Figurel, ed., *Proceedings of the Twelfth Annual Convention of the International Reading Association*, 1968, 12, 596–602.

218. Levin, H., Understanding the reading process. *Report of the Thirty-first Educational Conference*, Educational Records Bureau, 1967, 127–133.

219. Levine, J. M., and Murphy, G., The learning and forgetting of controversial material. *Journal of Abnormal and Social Psychology*, 1943, 38, 507–517.

220. Lewis, J. W., A study of effectiveness of three methods of teaching one segment of elementary political science. *Journal of Experimental Education*, 1964, 33, 73–79.

221. Liberty, P. G., Pierson, J. S., and Burton, J. G., Cognitive and noncognitive aspects of reading ability. *Psychological Record*, 1964, 14, 349–353.

222. Liddle, W., An initial investigation of the Woods Reading Dynamics method. *Dissertation Abstracts*, 1966, 27, 985A.

223. Livingston, H., An investigation of the effect of instruction in general semantics on critical reading ability. *California Journal of Educational Research*, 1965, 16, 93–96.

224. Louttit, C. M., and Patrick, J. R., A study of students' knowledge in the use of the library. *Journal of Applied Psychology*, 1932, 16, 475–484.

225. Lowe, A. J., "State Survey of College Reading Improvement Programs," in R. C. Staiger and C. Y. Melton, eds., *Twelfth Yearbook of the National Reading Conference*. Milwaukee: National Reading Conference, 1963, 85–86.

226. Lowe, A. J., "Surveys of College Reading Improvement Programs: 1929–1966," in G. B. Schick and M. M. May, eds., *Sixteenth Yearbook of the National Reading Conference*. Milwaukee: National Reading Conference, 1967, 75–81.

227. Lowe, Mary L., and Crawford, C. C., First impressions versus second thoughts in true-false tests. *Journal of Educational Psychology*, 1929, 20, 192–195.

228. Lum, M. K. M., A comparison of under- and overachieving female college students. *Journal of Educational Psychology*, 1960, 51, 109–114.

229. Lundsteen, S., Critical listening—permanency and transfer of gains made during an experiment in the fifth and sixth grades. *California Journal of Educational Research*, 1965, 16, 210–216.

230. Lundsteen, S., "Listening, Reading, and Qualitative Levels of Thinking in Problem Solving," in J. A. Figurel, ed., *Vistas in Reading: Proceedings of the International Reading Association*, Part I, 1967, 11 450–454.

231. McAustin, S. D., A study in logical memory. *American Journal of Psychology*, 1921, 32, 370–403.

232. McClendon, P. I., An experimental study of the relationship between the note-taking practices and listening comprehension of college freshmen during expository lectures. *Speech Monographs*, 1958, 25, 222–228.

233. McClusky, H. Y., An experiment on the influence of preliminary skimming on reading. *Journal of Educational Psychology*, 1934, 25, 521–529.

234. McConihe, E. J., "The shifting scene in reading training at the college level," in G. B. Schick and M. M. May, eds., *Sixteenth Yearbook of the National Reading Conference*. Milwaukee: National Reading Conference, 1967, 86–91.

235. McCord, H., Background music: A possible aid in teaching adult reading improvement. *Journal of Developmental Reading*, 1961, 5, 60–61.

236. McCullough, C. M., The recognition of context clues in reading. *Elementary English Review*, 1945, 22, 1–5.

237. McDonald, A. S., Influence of a college reading improvement program on academic performance. *Journal of Educational Psychology*, 1957, 48, 171–181.

238. McDonald, A. S., "Factors Affecting Reading Test Performance," in O. S. Causey and E. P. Bliesmer, eds., *Ninth Yearbook of the National Reading Conference*. Fort Worth, Tex.: Texas Christian University Press, 1960, 28–35.

239. McDonald, A. S., "Flexibility in Reading," in J. Allen Figurel, ed., *Changing Concepts of Reading Instruction*, Proceedings of the International Reading Association, 1963, 81–84.

240. McDonald, A. S., Research for the classroom: Rate and reading flexibility. *Journal of Reading*, 1965, 8, 187–191.

241. McDougall, W. P., Differential retention of course outcomes in educational psychology. *Journal of Educational Psychology*, 1958, 49, 53–60.

242. McGann, Mary, Diagnostic testing and remedial teaching for common errors in mechanics of English made by college freshmen. *Journal of Educational Psychology*, 1947, 38, 499–503.

243. McGeoch, J., and McKinney, F., Retroactive inhibition in the learning of poetry. *American Journal of Psychology*, 1934, 46, 10–30.

244. MacIntosh, A., A study of factors associated with the stability of vocational goals in college students. *Dissertation Abstracts*, 1953, 13, 262.

245. McKeachie, W. J., and Hiler, W., The problem oriented approach to teaching psychology. *Journal of Educational Psychology*, 1954, 45, 224–232.

246. McKeachie, W. J., Pollie, D., and Speisman, J., Relieving anxiety in classroom examinations. *Journal of Abnormal and Social Psychology*, 1955, 50, 93–98.

247. Manuel, H. T., The use of parallel tests in the study of foreign language teaching. *Educational and Psychological Measurement*, 1953, 13, 431–436.

248. Marks, M. B., Improve reading through better format. *Journal of Educational Research*, 1966, 60, 147–151.

249. Marsh, Z. A., Economics of school heating and air conditioning. *Journal of Section, Heating, Piping and Air Conditioning*, 1958, 30, 157–160.

250. Marston, Albert R., and Marston, M. R., The effect of student participation in the construction of a multiple-choice achievement examination. *Journal of Educational Research*, 1965, 59, 105–107.

251. Mathews, C. O., Erroneous first impressions on objective tests. *Journal of Educational Psychology*, 1929, 20, 280–286.

252. Maxwell, M. J., "An Experimental Investigation of the Effect of Instructional Set and Information on Reading Rate," in E. L. Thurston and L. E. Hafner, eds., *Fourteenth Yearbook of the National Reading Conference*. Milwaukee: National Reading Conference, 1965, 181–187.

253. Maxwell, M. J., "Correlates of Concentration," in G. B. Schick and M. M. May, eds., *Fifteenth Yearbook of the National Reading Conference*. Milwaukee: National Reading Conference, 1966, 23–30.

254. Mayo, G. D., Effect of temperature upon technical training. *Journal of Applied Psychology*, 1955, 39, 244–246.

255. Meade, R. D., Achievement motivation, achievement, and psychological time. *Journal of Personality and Social Psychology*, 1966, 4, 577–580.

256. Mehler, J., Some effects of grammatical transformations on the recall of English sentences. *Journal of Verbal Learning and Verbal Behavior*, 1963, 2, 346–351.

257. Meyer, George, An experimental study of old and new types of examinations: II methods of study. *Journal of Educational Psychology*, 1935, 26, 30–40.

258. Miles, D. T., Kibler, R. J., and Pettigrew, L. E., The effects of study questions on college students' test performance. *Psychology in the Schools*, 1967, 4, 25–26.

259. Mitchell, C. C., The effects of non-verbal visual training and motivation on reading achievement and perception. *Dissertation Abstracts*, 1964, 24, 4818–4819.

260. Moe, I. L., "Reading Patterns among College Students," in R. C. Staiger and C. Y. Melton, eds., *Twelfth Yearbook of the National Reading Conference*. Milwaukee: National Reading Conference, 1963, 209–212.

261. Molsbergen, Mary Jane, *A Comparison of Students' Actual and Reported Work Methods*, Unpublished master's thesis, Ohio State University, 1954.

262. Morse, W. C., Ballantine, F. A., and Dixon, W. R., Studies in the psychology of reading. *University of Michigan Monographs in Education*, no. 4, 1951.

263. Morton, J., The effects of context upon speed of reading, eye movement, and eye-voice span. *Quarterly Journal of Experimental Psychology*, 1964, 16, 340–354.

264. Murphy, H. D., The effect of different locations of chapter summaries on immediate and delayed recall. *Dissertation Abstracts*, 1962, 23, 2014–2015.

265. Natkin, G. L., The treatment of mathematical anxiety through mediated transfer of attitude toward mathematics. *Dissertation Abstracts*, 1967, 27A, 4137.

266. Neal, C. M., The relationship of personality variables to reading ability. *California Journal of Educational Research*, 1967, 18, 133–144.

267. Newcomer, M., The Phi Beta Kappa student. *School and Society*, 1927, 25, 24.

268. Newman, S. E., Student vs. instructor design of study method. *Journal of Educational Psychology*, 1957, 48, 328–333.

269. Nichols, R. C., Personality change and the college. *American Educational Research Journal*, 1967, 4, 173–190.

270. Niple, M. L., *The Relationship of Different Study Methods to Immediate and Delayed Comprehension*, Unpublished doctoral dissertation, Ohio State University, 1968.

271. Oakland, J. A., The measurement of personality correlates of academic achievement in high school students. *Journal of Counseling Psychology*, 1969, 16, 452–457.

272. Oetting, E. R., Examination anxiety: Prediction, physiological response and relation to scholastic performance. *Journal of Counseling Psychology*, 1966, 13, 224–227.

273. Ofman, W., Evaluation of a group counseling procedure. *Journal of Counseling Psychology*, 1964, 11, 152–159.

274. Olson, A. V., Sanford, A., and Ohnmacht, F., Effectiveness of a freshman reading program. *Journal of Reading*, 1964, 8, 75–84.

275. Otterman, Lois M., The value of teaching prefixes and word roots. *Journal of Educational Research*, 1955, 48, 611–616.

276. Otto, W., Reactive inhibition as a contributor to school failure. *Journal of Special Education*, 1966, 1, 9–15.

277. Parker, J. P., Some organizational variables and their effect upon comprehension. *Journal of Communication*, 1962, 12, 27–32.

278. Patterson, H. O., "A Survey of Reading Improvement Programs in Industry," in O. S. Causey, ed., *Sixth Yearbook of the Southwest Reading Conference for Colleges and Universities.* Fort Worth, Tex.: Texas Christian University, 1957, 121–133.
279. Patterson, H. O., "Current Trends in Reading Improvement Programs in Industry," in R. C. Staiger and C. Y. Melton, eds., *Twelfth Yearbook of the National Reading Conference.* Milwaukee: National Reading Conference, 1963, 9–12.
280. Pauk, W., Study skills and scholastic achievement. *Reading Teacher,* 1965, *19,* 180–182.
281. Perry, W. G., Students use and misuse of reading skills: A report to the faculty. *Harvard Educational Review,* 1959, *29,* 193–200.
282. Peterson, H. A., Ellis, M., Toohill, N., and Kloess, P., Some measurements of the effects of reviews. *Journal of Educational Psychology,* 1935, *26,* 65–72.
283. Plant, W. T., Changes in ethnocentrism associated with a two-year college experience. *Journal of Genetic Psychology,* 1958, *92,* 189–197.
284. Plant, W. T., Longitudinal changes in intolerance and authoritarianism for subjects differing in amount of college education over four years. *Genetic Psychology Monographs,* 1965, *72,* 247–287.
285. Plant, W. T., and Minimum, E. W., Differential personality development in young adults of markedly different aptitude levels. *Journal of Educational Psychology,* 1967, *58,* 141–152.
286. Pollock, T. C., Spelling report. *College English,* 1954, *16,* 102–109.
287. Postman, L., Turnage, T. W., and Silverstein, A., The running memory span for words. *Quarterly Journal of Experimental Psychology,* 1964, *16,* 81–89.
288. Poulsen, Sten C., The relationship between study behavior of mathematics students and the examination marks gained after one year's study of pure mathematics at a university, Mathematics Education Project, Progress Report no. 1. Copenhagen: Danish Institute for Educational Research, 1969.
289. Poulton, E. C., British courses for adults on effective reading. *British Journal of Educational Psychology,* 1961, *31,* 128–137.
290. Powell, W. J., and Jourard, S. M., Some objective evidence of immaturity in underachieving college students. *Journal of Counseling Psychology,* 1963, *10,* 276–282.
291. Pressey, L. C., The permanent effects of training in methods of study on college success. *School and Society,* 1928, *28,* 403–404.
292. Pressey, L. C., and Pressey, S. L., *Essential Preparation for College.* New York: Holt, Rinehart and Winston, 1932.
293. Pressey, S. L., and Kuhlen, R. G., *Psychological Development Through the Life Span.* New York: Harper & Row, 1957.
294. Pressey, S. L., et al., *Research Adventures in University Teaching.* Bloomington, Ill.: Public School Publishing Company, 1929.
295. Pressey, S. L., Robinson, F. P., and Horrocks, J. E., *Psychology in Education.* New York: Harper & Row, 1959.
296. Preston, J. M., and Gardner, R. C., Dimensions of oral and written language fluency. *Journal of Verbal Learning and Verbal Behavior,* 1967, *6,* 936–945.
297. Preston, R. C., Improving the item validity of study habits inventories. *Educational and Psychological Measurements,* 1961, *21,* 129–131.
298. Preston, R. C., Ability of students to identify correct responses before reading. *Journal of Educational Research,* 1964, *58,* 181–183.
299. Preston, R. C., and Tufts, E. N., The reading habits of superior college students. *Journal of Experimental Education,* 1948, *16,* 196–202.
300. Randall, Helen, *A Study of Reading Efficiency Over Various Time Intervals and Under Different Work Conditions,* Unpublished master's thesis, Ohio State University, 1943.
301. Raph, J. B., Goldbert, M. L., and Passow, A. H., *Bright Underachievers.* New York: Bureau of Publications, Teachers College, 1966.
302. Ray, D. D., The permanency of gains made in a college reading improvement program. *Journal of Educational Research,* 1965, *59,* 17–20.
303. Ray D. D., and Martin, M. D., Gains in reading achievement. *Journal of Reading,* 1967, *10,* 238–242.
304. Reilly, Jean W., and Robinson, F. P., Studies of popularity in college: I. Can popularity of freshmen be predicted? *Educational and Psychological Measurements,* 1947, *7,* 67–72.

305. Reilly, Jean, W., and Robinson, F. P., Studies of popularity in college: II. Do dormitory arrangements affect popularity? *Educational and Psychological Measurements*, 1947, 7, 327–330.
306. Reiss, A. J., Jr., Occupational mobility of professional workers. *American Sociological Review*, 1955, 20, 693–700.
307. Robinson, F. P., Study skills of soldiers in ASTP. *School and Society*, 1943, 58, 398–399.
308. Robinson, F. P., Two quarries with a single stone. *Journal of Higher Education*, 1945, 16, 201–206.
309. Robinson, F. P., *Principles and Procedures in Student Counseling*. New York: Harper & Row, 1950.
310. Robinson, F. P., and Hall, P., Studies of higher-level reading abilities. *Journal of Educational Psychology*, 1941, 32, 241–252.
311. Rogers, G. W., *Lecture Listening Skills: Their Nature and Relation to Achievement*, Unpublished doctoral dissertation, Ohio State University, 1959.
312. Roossinck, E. P., Purposeful reading of science materials by scientists and children. *Dissertation Abstracts*, 1961, 21, 3382.
313. Rose, F. C., and Rostas, S. M., The effect of illumination on reading rate and comprehension of college students. *Journal of Educational Psychology*, 1946, 37, 279–292.
314. Rosen, C. L., Mechanical devices for increasing speed of reading. *Journal of Reading*, 1967, 10, 569–576.
315. Rothkopf, E. Z., Learning from written instruction materials: An exploration of the control of inspection behavior by test-like events. *American Educational Research Journal*, 1966, 3, 241–250.
316. Rothkopf, E. Z., Textual constraint as a function of repeated inspection. *Journal of Educational Psychology*, 1968, 59, 20–25.
317. Rothkopf, E. Z., and Bisbicos, E. E., Selective facilitative effects of interspersed questions on learning from written materials. *Journal of Educational Psychology*, 1967, 58, 56–61.
318. Russell, D., A conspectus of recent research on listening abilities. *Elementary English*, 1964, 41, 262–267.
319. Sage, E. H., Developmental scales for college freshmen. *Journal of Counseling Psychology*, 1968, 15, 381–385.
320. Salisbury, Rachel, Some effects of training in outlining. *English Journal*, college ed., 1935, 24, 111–116.
321. Samuels, S. J., Effect of word associations on reading speed, recall, and guessing behavior on tests. *Journal of Educational Psychology*, 1968, 59, 12–15.
322. Sassenrath, J. M., Anxiety, aptitude, attitude, and achievement. *Psychology in the Schools*, 1967, 4, 341–346.
323. Schroeder, P., Relationship of Kuder's conflict avoidance and dominance to academic accomplishment. *Journal of Counseling Psychology*, 1965, 12, 395–399.
324. Schutte, T. H., Students' estimates of their ability and achievement. *Journal of Educational Research*, 1929, 20, 394–396.
325. Seashore, R. H., Work methods: An often neglected factor underlying individual differences. *Psychological Review*, 1939, 46, 123–141.
326. Seibert, L. C., A series of experiments on the learning of French vocabulary. *Johns Hopkins University Study of Education*, 1932, no. 18 (106 pp.).
327. Serwer, B., and Levy, E. I., Group therapy as a part of a college-level study-skills program. *International Journal of Group Psychotherapy*, 1966, 16, 65–77.
328. Shaw, P., "Integration of Reading Instruction with 'Regular' College Offerings," in O. S. Causey, ed., *Tenth Yearbook of the National Reading Conference*. Milwaukee: National Reading Conference, 1961, 113–126.
329. Shaw, P., Teaching reading skills at college. *School and Society*, 1961, 89, 121–123.
330. Shenshev, L. V., Common aspects of mental processes in the mastery of mathematics and a foreign language. *Voprosy Psikhologii*, 1960, 4, 9–22.
331. Sherburne, J. W., *Problems and Outcomes of a College Remedial Program*, Unpublished Doctoral dissertation, Ohio State University, 1938.

332. Sherman, A. W., Jr., *An Investigation of Delayed Comprehension and Its Relationship to Other Aspects of Reading and to Academic Success*, Unpublished doctoral dissertation, Ohio State University, 1952.

333. Shuman, R. B., College dropouts: An overview. *Journal of Educational Sociology*, 1956, 29, 347–350.

334. Simons, J. S., Reasoning through reading. *Journal of Reading*, 1965, 8, 311–314.

335. Simpson, R. H., Those who influence and those who are influenced in discussion. *Teachers College Contribution to Education*, 1938, no. 748.

336. Singer, H., "Sub-strata Factor Patterns Accompanying Development in Power of Reading, Elementary Through College Level," in E. L. Thurston and L. E. Hafner, eds., *Fourteenth Yearbook of the National Reading Conference*. Milwaukee: National Reading Conference, 1965, 41–56.

337. Smith, H. K., The responses of good and poor readers when asked to read for different purposes. *Reading Research Quarterly*, 1967, 3, 53–83.

338. Smith, M. B., *Social Psychology and Human Values*. Chicago: Aldine, 1969.

339. Smith, D. E. P., and Wood, R. L., Reading improvement and college grades: A follow-up. *Journal of Educational Psychology*, 1955, 46, 151–159.

340. Snavely, Eloise, "A Study of Social and Experimental Factors Related to the Reading Abilities of College Freshmen," in O. S. Causey, ed., *Seventh Yearbook of the National Reading Conference for Colleges and Adults*. Fort Worth, Tex: Texas Christian University Press, 1958, 97–100.

341. Somerville, A. W., and Sumner, F. C., The persistence of vocational preference in successful individuals. *Journal of Psychology*, 1950, 30, 77–80.

342. Sommer, R., The ecology of privacy. *Library Quarterly*, 1966, 36, 234–248.

343. Sommer, R., The social psychology of cramming. *Personnel and Guidance Journal*, 1968, 47, 104–109.

344. Sones, A. M., and Stroud, J. B., Review, with special reference to temporal position. *Journal of Educational Psychology*, 1940, 31, 665–676.

345. Sopis, J., The relationship of self-image as a reader to reading achievement. *Academic Therapy Quarterly*, 1965–66, 1, 94–101, 113.

346. Sorin, M., and Gavilondo, L., Academic success in one school of a university. *Psicologia y Educacion*, 1965, 2, 27–41.

347. Spache, G. D., "Evaluation of eye movement photography in reading diagnosis and reading training," in O. S. Causey and E. P. Bliesmer, eds., *Ninth Yearbook of the National Reading Conference*. Fort Worth, Tex.: Texas Christian University Press, 1960, 98–106.

348. Spache, G. D., Is this a breakthrough in reading? *Reading Teacher*, 1962, 15, 258–262.

349. Spearman, L. H. O., A profile analysis technique for diagnosing reading disability. *Twentieth Yearbook of the National Council of Measurements in Education*, 1963, 75–86.

350. Spearritt, D., *Listening Comprehension: A Factorial Analysis*. Melbourne, Australia: G. W. Green and Sons, 1962.

351. Spielberger, C. D., The effects of manifest anxiety on the academic achievement of college students. *Mental Hygiene*, 1962, 46, 420–426.

352. Spielberger, C. D., and Weitz, H., Improving the academic performance of anxious college freshmen: A group counseling approach to the prevention of underachievement. *Psychological Monographs: General and Applied*, 1964, 78, whole no. 590, 13.

353. Spitzer, H. F., Studies in retention. *Journal of Educational Psychology*, 1939, 30, 641–656.

354. Sprinthall, N., A comparison of values among teachers, academic underachievers, and achievers. *Journal of Experimental Education*, 1964, 33, 193–196.

355. Stanley, J. C., Insight into one's own values. *Journal of Educational Psychology*, 1951, 42, 399–408.

356. Steinemann, J. H., Hooprich, E. A., and Anderson, E. H., Experimental evaluation of alternative methods for improving reading skills. *Proceedings of the Seventy-Fourth Annual Convention of the American Psychological Association*, 1966, 249–250.

357. Stevens, G. L., and Fulker, E. N., "Reading Improvement in Government." in O. S. Causey, ed., *Tenth Yearbook of the National Reading Conference*. Milwaukee: National Reading Conference, 1961, 1–8.

358. Stewart, L. H., Changes in personality test scores during college. *Journal of Counseling Psychology*, 1964, *11*, 211–220.

359. Stieg, L. F., Circulation records and the study of college-library use. *Library Quarterly*, 1942, *12*, 94–108.

360. Stordahl, K. E., and Christensen, C. M., The effect of study techniques on comprehension and retention. *Journal of Educational Research*, 1956, *46*, 561–570.

361. Taylor, R. G., Personality traits and discrepant achievement: A review. *Journal of Counseling Psychology*, 1964, *11*, 76–82.

362. Taylor, R. G., and Farquhar, W., Personality, motivation and achievement: Theoretical constructs and empirical factors. *Journal of Counseling Psychology*, 1965, *12*, 186–191.

363. Taylor, S. E., "An Evaluation of Forty-One Trainees Who Had Recently Completed the 'Reading Dynamics' Program," in E. P. Bliesmer and R. C. Staiger, eds., *Eleventh Yearbook of the National Reading Conference*. Milwaukee: National Reading Conference, 1962, 41–56.

364. Taylor, S. E., "A Study in Listening," in R. C. Staiger and C. Y. Melton, eds., *Twelfth Yearbook of the National Reading Conference*, Milwaukee: National Reading Conference, 1963, 189–201.

365. Taylor, S. E., Eye movements in reading: Facts and fallacies. *American Educational Research Journal*, 1965, *2*, 187–202.

366. Tegler, C. H., The effects of practice using auditory, visual, or a combination method in an attempt to increase the spelling ability of university students through reading. *Dissertation Abstracts*, 1967, 27A, 2458–2459.

367. Thalberg, S. P., An experimental investigation of the relative efficiency of the auditory and visual modes of presentation of verbal material. *Dissertation Abstracts*, 1964, *25*, 1017.

368. Thalberg, S. P., and Ellen, W., "A Comparison of Two Widely Different Methods of Teaching Reading Efficiency," in R. C. Staiger and C. Y. Melton, eds., *Twelfth Yearbook of the National Reading Conference*. Milwaukee: National Reading Conference, 1963, 112–117.

369. Thelen, M. H., and Harris C. S., Personality of college underachievers who improve with group psychotherapy. *Personnel and Guidance Journal*, 1968, *46*, 561–566.

370. Thoday, Doris, How undergraduates work. *Universities Quarterly*, 1957, *11*, 172–181.

371. Thompson, A. B. "Meeting the reading demands of literature," in J. A. Figurel, ed., *Proceedings of the Eleventh Annual Convention of the International Reading Association*, Part I, 1967, *11*, 104–106.

372. Tinker, M. A., Illumination standards for effective and easy seeing. *Psychological Bulletin*, 1947, *44*, 435–450.

373. Tinker, M. A., Recent studies of eye movements in reading. *Psychological Bulletin*, 1958, *55*, 215–231.

374. Tinker, M. A., Devices to improve speed of reading. *Reading Teacher*, 1967, *20*, 605–609.

375. Tobin, R. L., How much do they really understand? *Saturday Review*, May 13, 1967, *50*, 81–82.

376. Todd, F., Terrell, G., and Frank, C., Differences between normal and underachievers of superior ability. *Journal of Applied Psychology*, 1962, *46*, 183–190.

377. Topetzes, N. J., and O'Brien, C. C., Mechanics of expression at the graduate level. *Journal of Higher Education*, 1950, *21*, 380–381.

378. Torrance, P. E., and Harmon, J. A., Effects of memory, evaluative, and creative reading sets on test performance. *Journal of Educational Psychology*, 1961, *52*, 207–214.

379. Travers, R. M. W., *Educational Measurement*. New York: Macmillan, 1955.

380. Traxler, A. E. Rapid reading. *Educational Records Bulletin*, 1962, 82, 74–75.

381. Trela, T. M., Comparing achievement on tests of general and critical reading. *Journal of the Reading Specialist*, 1967, *6*, 140–142.

382. Trembly, D., Laws of learning general and specialized vocabularies. *Proceedings of the Seventy-Fourth Annual Convention of the American Psychological Association*, 1966, 229–230.

383. Tresselt, M. E., A preliminary study of factors in learning in a how-to-study course. *Journal of Psychology*, 1966, *64*, 91–93.

384. Troth, D. C., A ten-minute observation in the library. *School and Society*, 1929, 29, 336–338.

385. Trueblood, D. L., Selected characteristics of employed students in the Indiana University School of Business. *Journal of Educational Research*, 1956, 50, 209–213.

386. Tuddenham, R. D., Soldier intelligence in World Wars I and II. *American Psychologist*, 1948, 3, 54–56.

387. Tulving, E., The effect of alphabetical subjective organization on memorizing unrelated words. *Canadian Journal of Psychology*, 1962, 16, 185–191.

388. Van Parreren, C. F., and Schutte-Poen, W. C., Study habits of psychology students, *Nederlands Tijdschrift voor de Psychologie*, 1964, 19, 255–268.

389. Vernon, M. D., The improvement of reading. *British Journal of Educational Psychology*, 1956, 26, 85–93.

390. Vernon, P. E., The determinants of reading comprehension. *Educational and Psychological Measurements*, 1962, 22, 269–286.

391. Very, P. S., Quantitative, verbal, and reasoning factors in mathematical ability. *Dissertation Abstracts*, 1964, 25, 1371.

392. Vineyard, E. E., and Bailey, R. B., Interrelationships of reading ability, listening skill, intelligence, and scholastic achievement. *Journal of Developmental Reading*, 1960, 3, 174–178.

393. Votaw, D. F., A comparison of test scores of entering college freshmen as instruments for predicting subsequent scholarship. *Journal of Educational Research*, 1946, 40, 215–218.

394. Wagman, M., University achievement and daydreaming behavior. *Journal of Counseling Psychology*, 1968, 15, 196–198.

395. Wallach, M. A., and Wing, C. W., Jr., *The Talented Student*. New York: Holt, Rinehart and Winston, 1969.

396. Walsh, R. P., Engbretson, R. O., and O'Brien, B. A., Anxiety and test-taking behavior. *Journal of Counseling Psychology*, 1968, 15, 572–575.

397. Warga, R. G., Determination of an optimum time to teach freshmen students basic study skills. *Dissertation Abstracts*, 1966, 27A, 1675–1676.

398. Wark, D. M., "Reading Comprehension as Implicit Verbal Behavior," in G. B. Schick and M. M. May, eds., *Seventeenth Yearbook of the National Reading Conference*. Milwaukee: National Reading Conference, 1968, 192–198.

399. Washburne, J. N., The use of questions in social science material. *Journal of Educational Psychology*, 1929, 20, 321–359.

400. Waters, C. W., Construction and validation of a forced-choice over- and under-achievement scale. *Educational and Psychological Measurements*, 1964, 24, 921–928.

401. Watley, D. J., The Minnesota Counseling Inventory and persistence in an institute of technology. *Journal of Counseling Psychology*, 1965, 12, 94–97.

402. Watts, W. A., Lynch, S., and Whittaker, D., Alienation and activism in today's college-age youth: Socialization patterns and current family relationships. *Journal of Counseling Psychology*, 1969, 16, 1–7.

403. Weaver, H. B., The mathematical proficiency of students in psychology. *Journal of Educational Research*, 1957, 51, 261–270.

404. Weaver, W. W., and Bickley, A. C., Sources of information for responses to reading test items. *Proceedings of the Seventy-Fifth Annual Convention of the American Psychological Association*, 1967, 2, 293–294.

405. Weaver, W. W., and Kingston, A. J., Questioning in content reading. *Journal of Reading*, 1967, 11, 140–143, 150.

406. Webber, M. E., Studies of lighting and seeing for the student at home. *Illumination Engineering*, 1949, 44, 255–266.

407. Weber, R. J., Relationship of physical fitness to success in college and to personality. *Research Quarterly of the American Association for Health, Physical Education, and Recreation*, 1953, 24, 471–474.

408. Webster, H., Freedman, M. B., and Heist, P., "Personality Changes in College Students," in N. Sanford, ed., *The American College*. New York: John Wiley & Sons, 1962, 811–846.

409. Wedeen, S. U., A two-year basic skills study. *Journal of Reading*, 1967, 10, 231–237.

410. Weigel, R. G., and Weigel, V. M., The relationship of knowledge and usage of study skill techniques to academic performance. *Journal of Educational Research*, 1967, 61, 78–80.

411. Weiner, B., Motivation and memory. *Psychological Monographs: General and Applied,* 1966, *80,* no. 18 (22 pp.).
412. Weiss, D., Listening comprehension. *Reading Teacher,* 1967, *20,* 639–647.
413. Weitz, H., Clarke, M., and Jones, O., The relationship between choice of a major field of study and academic preparation and performance. *Educational and Psychological Measurement,* 1955, *4,* 64–70.
414. Werdelin, I., A synthesis of two factor analyses of problem solving in mathematics. *Didakometry,* 1966, *8,* 14.
415. Whiteley, J. M., and Hummel, R., Adaptive ego functioning in relation to academic achievement. *Journal of Counseling Psychology,* 1965, *12,* 306–310.
416. Wilbanks, W. A., Webb, W. B., and Tolhurst, G. C., A study of intellectual activity in a noisy environment. *USN School of Aviation Medical Research Report,* 1956, no. NM001 104 100, Report no. 1.
417. Williams, R. D., and Knox, G. W., A survey of dynamic principles governing memory. *Journal of General Psychology,* 1944, *30,* 167–179.
418. Williamson, E. G., The relationship of number of hours of study to scholarship. *Journal of Educational Psychology,* 1935, *26,* 682–688.
419. Willmore, Doloris J., A comparison of four methods of studying a college textbook. *Dissertation Abstracts,* 1967, *27,* 2413–2414.
420. Wilson, R. C., and Morrow, W. R., School and career adjustment of bright high achieving and underachieving high school boys. *Journal of Genetic Psychology,* 1962, *101,* 91–103.
421. Wittenborn, J. R., and Larsen, R. P., An empirical evaluation of study habits in elementary German. *Journal of Applied Psychology,* 1944, *28,* 420–430.
422. Wittenborn, J. R., and Larsen, R. P., A factorial study of achievement in college German. *Journal of Educational Psychology,* 1944, *35,* 39–49.
423. Wittroch, M. C., Effect of certain instructions upon conceptually mediated learning. *Journal of Educational Psychology,* 1963, *54,* 85–88.
424. Wixted, W. G., and Curoe, P. R. V., How well do college seniors write? *School and Society,* 1941, *54,* 505–508.
425. Wood, G., Mnemonic systems in recall. *Journal of Educational Psychology,* 1967, *58* (December monograph supplement).
426. Woolf, M. D., "Ego strength and reading disability," in E. L. Thurston and L. E. Hafner, eds., *Fourteenth Yearbook of the National Reading Conference.* Milwaukee: National Reading Conference, 1965, 73–80.
427. Wooster, G. F., *Teaching the SQ3R Method of Study: An Investigation of the Instructional Approach,* Unpublished doctoral dissertation, Ohio State University, 1954.
428. Wright, J. C., *A Study of High School Students' Insight into Their Problems and Resources,* Unpublished master's thesis, Ohio State University, 1944.
429. Wright, J. C., *An Investigation of the Nature of Comprehension Gained through Reading and Its Relationship to Other Aspects of Reading and to Academic Achievement,* Unpublished doctoral dissertation, Ohio State University, 1954.
430. Zimiles, H., and Konstadt, N., Orthography and authority: A study of cognitive-affective interaction. *Psychological Reports,* 1962, *10,* 623–626.

APPENDIX I
Quizzes on Chapters 2 Through 7

The keys are on pages 288–291.

The percent correct can be obtained by multiplying the number correct by five. Put this result on page 40.

Quiz on Part One of Chapter 2: SQ3R Method of Studying

1. Most study techniques of students tend to be inefficient.　　　　T　F

2. On a test of the main ideas in a selection, students get about what percent correct after reading the selection once? (1) 50%, (2) 75%, (3) 85%.　　　　_____

3. About what percent is remembered after two weeks of what was known right after reading a selection once? (1) 20%, (2) 40%, (3) 60%, (4) 80%.　　　　_____

4. Immediately rereading an assignment makes a bigger difference in the amount comprehended than just reading it once.　　　　T　F

5. If two comparable selections are printed, one with headings and the other with no headings, the typical student reads the former quite a bit better than the latter.　　　　T　F

6, 7. The text lists three kinds of cues provided in a course indicating what is important to learn, *e.g.,* textbook cues. Name the other two. _____
_____

8, 9. Give two example of textbook cues other than boldface headings. _____
_____

10. Analysis of the study skills of A students was the main source for building higher-level study skills.　　　　T　F

11. A preview of headings before reading a selection helps comprehension but does not affect rate of reading very much.　　　　T　F

12. Looking over a list of questions just before reading a selection will help in answering those questions later, but often has a bad effect on ability to answer other questions on the same selection.　　　　T　F

13. A few general questions should be formed at the start of a lesson rather than making up a long quiz.　　　　T　F

14. Questions prepared after reading a section demand an active answering rather than a mere reading.　　　　T　F

15. The best source of obtaining questions as one reads is _____

16. If a student gets tired while reading, the best place to stop momentarily is at the bottom of a page.　　　　T　F

17. Research shows that if college students are asked to read and take outline notes on one selection and just to read another selection, they will do much better when taking notes, even on the first trial.　　　　T　F

18–20. In taking what are known as "working notes":

　a. Complete sentences are written so the ideas can be understood later.　　　　T　F

　b. Each important point is jotted down as soon as a student comes to it in his reading.　　　　T　F

　c. It is better to use a shortened version of the wording in the text than to use the student's own wording.　　　　T　F

Quiz on Part Two of Chapter 2: SQ3R Method of Studying

1. Students tend to put off studying and then cram for an examination, because otherwise they would forget rapidly.　　　　　T　F

2. After reading, essential or main ideas tend to be better remembered than details.　　　　　T　F

3. Ability to learn and ability to remember are very similar; the student who learns the most from one reading will almost always be the one to remember the most several weeks after reading.　　　　　T　F

4. Giving the label "bad king" to a monarch you are reading about will tend to make you remember best which of his deeds?　(1) his good acts, (2) his bad acts, (3) will make no difference.　　_____

5–7. The text describes four methods of retarding forgetting. One way is the use of recitation; name the other three.　　_____

_____

_____

8. A study cited in the text showed that after reading a selection and using immediate recitation, the following average percent was remembered after two weeks.　(1) 20%, (2) 40%, (3) 60%, (4) 80%.　_____

9. After studying a lesson, the best time to do your first review is (1) immediately, (2) after about an hour, (3) the next day, (4) after a week, (5) right before an examination.　　_____

10. If you have to study two different subjects for an hour each, it is better to study straight through in order to get them done than to take a break of 10 minutes in between.　　　　　T　F

11–13. The text says that a higher-level reading skill should do four things for a student. One of these is increase speed of comprehending; what are the other three?　　_____

_____

_____

14–20. The following questions deal with details of the SQ3R method of study.

　b. Making a preview of the headings in a chapter should take less than a minute.　　　　　T　F

　c. Notes are written (1) in your own words from memory, (2) by jotting down the important phrases and sentences in the lesson.　_____

　d. Notes should be written down as soon as a student finds an important point.　　　　　T　F

　e. The first review step should take about 5 minutes.　　　　　T　F

　f. The recitation step is done (1) as soon as something important is found, (2) at the end of a headed section, (3) at the end of the lesson, (4) some time after reading the lesson.　_____

　g. Reading a section to answer a question helps in all three of these ways: increases interest or arouses curiosity, helps recall what is already known on the topic, and makes the important points stand out.　　　　　T　F

Quiz on Chapter 3: Other Applications of the SQ3R Method of Study

1–4. The following problems tend to occur when students use underlining as a study technique:

    a. They tend to underline too much.   T   F

    b. Afterwards it is difficult to see the organization of ideas.   T   F

    c. It does not usually check comprehension accuracy.   T   F

    d. It does not tend to fix ideas in your memory as well as note-
taking.   T   F

5–7. Four ways of going about underlining were recommended, *e.g.,*
wait until the end of a headed section. What were the other three
suggestions?   _____

                                             _____

                                             _____

8. The first step in reading a collateral assignment is to determine why
the assignment was made.   T   F

9. In reading a collateral assignment a student should read with one
question in mind until it is answered, then take another question and
read to answer it, and so on.   T   F

10. In collateral reading the recitation step is carried out at the end of a
chapter rather than after each headed section.   T   F

11. An English literature assignment should be read much as one would
read a novel from the library.   T   F

12–14. Which *three* of the following items are the more important outcomes of an English literature course? (1) the story of what happened, (2) what the characters were like, (3) what techniques of
writing the author used to obtain his effects, (4) what your reactions
are to the story, (5) what the author was like, (6) what the author's
intent was in writing the story.   _____

                                             _____

                                             _____

15. One purpose in reading English literature is to learn how to select
and appreciate good forms of aesthetic and emotional expression.   T   F

16. Authors of novels sometimes modify the characteristics of persons
and events primarily (1) so an actual person or place will not be
identified, or (2) so that a particular contrast will be more evident or
the plot movement enhanced.   _____

17. The main idea of every graph, table, or map in a text is important.   T   F

18. The two aspects of skill in reading nonverbal materials are: (a)
ability to determine what the main idea is, and (b) skill in reading the
graph or table to find the answer.   T   F

19. The text lists three sources or cues for finding out what a graph is
about. Two of them are: (a) the main trend of the lines in the graph,
and (b) the discussion in the text. What is the third source or cue?

                                             _____

20. In studying a diagram in zoology, which shows the process of circulation, a student should give less time to the reading step than to
the recitation step.   T   F

Quiz on Chapter 4: Effective Skill in Examinations

1. Three major divisions of examination skill were discussed in this chapter. Two of them are: (a) preparing for, and (b) taking examinations. What is the third division? _____

2. Time used for reviewing the night before a quiz should not be more than two hours so that plenty of sleep can be obtained.   T   F

3. In making quiz predictions a student should write out actual true–false, multiple choice, or essay questions.   T   F

4. It is possible to predict what most of the questions will be about on an examination.   T   F

5. The best way to review for a quiz is to take time quickly to reread all of the lessons.   T   F

6. It is usually easier to make A and B grades on an objective test than on an essay test.   T   F

7. In making plans for reviewing for final examinations it is better to plan several review sessions for each course than to have one long session.   T   F

8. The best way to combat emotional blocking on an examination is _____

9. In taking an examination the best way to keep from being rushed at the end is _____

10. Give an example of a "key word" in an essay question. _____

11. The first step in answering an essay question is _____

12. It is generally not worthwhile to number the points made in writing an essay question.   T   F

13. Generally, if one writes to the bottom of a page in answering an essay question, that is enough of an answer.   T   F

14. Illegible handwriting tends to decrease students' grades on essay tests.   T   F

15. It does not pay to guess on true–false examinations if the score is to be correct answers minus wrong answers.   T   F

16. In taking an objective test it pays to do the easy items first and then go back and answer the questions that caused the difficulty.   T   F

17. Adjective and adverb modifiers are important determinants in true–false examinations. What is the "modifier" in the preceding sentence? _____

18. The series of modifiers that include the word "some" would be

19. Research shows that it usually does not pay to change answers on objective tests.   T   F

20. The new types of examinations discussed in this chapter deal with better ways of measuring how well students learn the facts of a course.   T   F

Quiz on Chapter 5: Skills in Attack and Concentration

1. Research shows that after students are seated in a library they waste about one-fourth of the first 30 minutes of study.   T   F

2. When students read books under untimed conditions they read about (1) as fast, (2) 80 percent as fast, (3) 60 percent as fast as under timed conditions.   _____

3. The three steps in developing effective skill in time use are: setting up a time schedule, following the schedule until work habits develop, and applying conscious effort to work rules.   T   F

4. In filling out a time schedule the first thing to put down is study time.   T   F

5. A good time to study a particular course is just before or just after it meets as a class.   T   F

6. A good principle is to study the same course at the same time and at the same place every school day.   T   F

7. The most inefficiently used of the following times is usually (1) a vacant hour between classes, (2) from 4 to 6 P.M., (3) the hour after lunch, (4) from 10 to 11 P.M.   _____

8. Ease in getting down to work is more a matter of habit formation than of developing will power.   T   F

9. In studying it is better to wait until one feels like studying than to try studying at a set time when one does not feel like it.   T   F

10. The five major study conditions that affect ability to concentrate are: distractions, situations associated with other activities, study materials not convenient, poor lighting, and physiological conditions.   T   F

11. Research shows that, on the average, students who study in the library get (1) better, (2) no better, (3) poorer grades than those who study in their room.   _____

12. A study table should be cleared of everything but study materials and should face the wall.   T   F

13. It is least distracting to study with which of these background noises? (1) classical or mood music, (2) popular dance music, (3) popular songs, (4) television, (5) radio news.   _____

14. As good results can be obtained from dressing comfortably in pajamas and studying on a bed as can be obtained by keeping on one's street clothes and studying at a table or desk.   T   F

15. The three most important characteristics of good lighting are: adequate amount of light, even distribution of light, and use of a blue (daylight) bulb or fluorescent light.   T   F

16. None of these are considered good times to study: right after eating a meal, right after coming in out of cold weather, and after one's usual bedtime.   T   F

17–20. Four major factors in concentration were listed and discussed in this chapter. They are   _____

_____

_____

_____

Quiz on Chapter 6: Motivation to Study

1. Studies of over- and underachievers through use of tests of study habits and attitudes show that the former group differs from the latter group most in three areas: maturity, interest in getting an education, and efficiency.   T F

2. Comparisons of over- and underachievers through use of personality tests show that the latter group tends more often to be hostile, immature, and procrastinators.   T F

3. Comparisons of the same students as freshmen and later as seniors show that, in general, a college education tends to make people less authoritarian, more independent, and less stereotypic in their thinking.   T F

4. The great majority of college freshmen eventually graduate from college.   T F

5. What proportion of college students have below average scores on sociometry tests given in college?   (1) over one-half, (2) about one-half, (3) less than one-half.   _____

6. There is good research evidence that location of one's room in a dormitory has a marked effect on popularity in that dormitory.   T F

7. There seem to be two major factors in determining social acceptance: niceties of behavior and   _____

8. Talking about personal problems with a counselor is a help because it releases tensions and because   _____

9. Laziness is sometimes inherited.   T F

10. Some students dislike schoolwork because so many suggestions are made by someone in authority.   T F

11. Students often lack accurate insight into their own abilities.   T F

12. Very few eminent people changed their vocational choice after leaving high school.   T F

13. Good students complain (1) more, (2) as much, (3) less about schoolwork interfering with their social life than/as do average or poor students.   _____

14. Which one of these characteristics tends to be admired most by college students? (1) handsome, (2) kind, (3) well-dressed, (4) cooperative.   _____

15. In the experiment on working arithmetic problems, college students worked harder for the fraternity than they did for the professor.   T F

16. The grades of Phi Beta Kappa initiates tend to go down after they are initiated.   T F

17. Most adults like to read.   T F

18. The following steps help focus interests on schoolwork:
    a. Eliminate distractions in the study room.   T F
    b. Imagine immediate goals and work toward them.   T F
    c. Ask yourself questions about the lesson.   T F

Quiz on Chapter 7: Classroom Skills

1. Classroom skills are different from study skills and have to be taught separately.   T F

2–5. The four aspects of classroom skills discussed in the text are _____

_____

_____

_____

6. The most efficient seat location in a lecture class is (1) front, (2) middle, (3) back, (4) side.   _____

7–8. The two main purposes of lectures are   _____

_____

9. A typical lecture will usually contain 10 or more important ideas that are likely to be used on examinations.   T F

10–12. Name three kinds of cues that lecturers use to point out what is important in their lectures.   _____

_____

_____

13. If a student knows shorthand it is a good idea for him to take down as much of a lecture as he can in shorthand.   T F

14. Lecture notes should be kept in a large notebook so that large indentations and other organizational cues can be used.   T F

15. A few minutes should be used after a lecture to put notes into better organizational shape.   T F

16. Amount of participation in classroom discussion has been found to be related to classroom grades.   T F

17. On which one of these items will the most students nominate themselves on a "Guess Who" test?   (1) most afraid to discuss in class, (2) most likely to panic on an examination, (3) most disliked by the teacher, (4) knows the least in this class about this subject.   _____

18. A good principle in learning to participate in class discussion is to select the easiest class and start speaking today.   T F

19. Teachers dislike students putting on wraps or stacking books before the bell rings ending the class.   T F

20. Frequent absence, frequent tardiness, and lateness in turning in reports are all related to grades earned.   T F

APPENDIX II
Diagnostic Tests

Do not turn the page until the signal to begin reading is given.

A Test of Reading Ability for

Canadian History[1]

by FRANCIS P. ROBINSON and PRUDENCE HALL
The Ohio State University

Directions

1   The purpose of this test is to measure your ability to read school assignments. You
2 are to read the following history selection in your usual manner of reading assignments;
3 after 10 minutes of reading you will be asked to answer questions over the material
4 read. These questions will be of the type generally asked in class over such readings.
5   At the end of 3 minutes, 6 minutes, and 10 minutes of reading you will be asked to
6 "Mark." This means that you are to encircle quickly the number of the line that you
7 are reading (numbered as in the left-hand margin here) and then go on immediately
8 with your reading. At the end of 10 minutes you will be asked to stop reading and to
9 turn to the questions which follow.
10   Be accurate in noting the last line read, for *you will be expected to answer questions* over
11 all the material that you mark as having been read.

[1] Reprinted with permission of the copyright owner, F. E. Compton Company, division of Encyclopaedia Britannica, Inc., Chicago, Illinois.

The Stirring Story of Canada's Past

2   The story of Canada's past has, in some respects, an in-
3 terest and importance not always realized. From the stand-
4 point of geographical exploration, not only is it full of picturesque
5 and romantic detail, but it is the story of the opening up of
6 a considerable fraction of the land surface of the earth; and
7 from the standpoint of politics it is the story of a development
8 without parallel in previous history. In that "galaxy of free
9 nations" which has been well named the British Commonwealth
10 of Nations, it was Canada that first achieved the status of
11 a self-governing Dominion, that first reconciled colonial liberty
12 with the imperial tie. The American Revolution, by means
13 of which the 13 original British colonies in America gained
14 their independence, broke up the Old British Empire; the
15 Canadian Revolution—if one may apply that term to the long,
16 gradual, and peaceful process by which Canada has won self-
17 government—has not only *not* broken up the New British
18 Empire, but has probably strengthened in a peculiar degree
19 the vigorous racial bonds which bind it together.

21   *The first Europeans* to visit the shores of Canada were,
22 so far as we know, the Northmen. These daring seafarers
23 found their way to the northeast coast of North America, by
24 way of Greenland, about the year 1000. Their visits, however,
25 left no trace behind; and for practical purposes the discoverer
26 of Canada was John Cabot, an Italian merchant—sailor in the
27 service of the king, Henry VII of England, who sailed from
28 Bristol and touched at what is now Canadian soil in 1497—a
29 year before Columbus reached the South American mainland
30 on his third voyage. Cabot, like Columbus, was in search of
31 a sea-route to Asia; and when he did not find on the bleak
32 coasts of North America the oriental silks and spices which he
33 sought, he was bitterly disappointed. But though he did not
34 find silks and spices, he found something no less profitable
35 —the fish off the banks of Newfoundland. His son Sebastian,
36 on his return to Europe, went so far as to report that the
37 codfish were so numerous "they sumtymes stayed his shippes."
38 As a result, fishermen from European ports began to come
39 out to the Banks of Newfoundland and established a permanent
40 link.

41   SEARCH FOR NORTHWEST PASSAGE

42   Once it became clear that America was not Asia, the aim
43 of explorers came to be to find a way through to that "Western
44 Sea" which we call the Pacific Ocean. In this search they fol-
45 lowed, so far as Canada was concerned, two routes. The French
46 strove to push through by way of the St. Lawrence valley and
47 the Great Lakes; the English endeavored first to discover a
48 "Northwest passage" by way of Hudson Straits and the Arctic
49 Ocean. Both efforts were eventually crowned with success. In
50 1534 a French mariner named Jacques Cartier penetrated up
51 the St. Lawrence as far as Montreal. Two or three generations
52 later, in 1615, Samuel de Champlain, the founder of Quebec,

53 reached Lake Huron. Thence French missionaries and fur-
54 traders made their way into Lake Michigan and Lake Superior,
55 and into the country beyond. Between 1658 and 1660 two French
56 *coureurs-de-bois*, Radisson and Groseillers, penetrated as far west
57 as the Mississippi and the Great Plains; and in 1682 La Salle
58 followed the Mississippi to its mouth. Before French domination
59 in Canada had come to an end, in 1763, two of the sons of an in-
60 trepid western fur trader named La Verendrye had actually
61 sighted the foothills of the Rockies. When, therefore, Canada
62 passed into British hands, there remained only one stage of the
63 great process to be completed; and this was completed in 1793,
64 when Alexander Mackenzie, a partner of the famous North-West
65 Company, crossed the Rockies by the Peace River Pass and at
65 last reached the Pacific.
66 　　　Meanwhile, farther north, English sailors had been search-
67 ing for the "Northwest passage." In 1610 Henry Hudson had
68 penetrated into the inland ocean which still bears his name;
69 and the servants of the Hudson's Bay Company, which was
70 formed in 1670 to trade in the territories about Hudson Bay,
71 made some attempts to push farther westward. It was not
72 however, until the modern age of Arctic exploration that any
73 real progress was made. In 1847 Sir John Franklin, a British
74 naval officer who had explored a good part of the Arctic coast
75 of Canada, perished in the attempt to reach the Pacific by water;
76 and in the search for him ships coming from the Pacific met
77 ships from the Atlantic—thus demonstrating the existence of
78 the Northwest passage. Not until 1906, however, was it that
79 Roald Amundsen, a Norwegian explorer, finally achieved the
80 feat of bringing a ship all the way through from the Atlantic
81 to the Pacific.

82　　　　　　　SETTLEMENT AND DEVELOPMENT OF CANADA

83 　　　*The story of the colonization or settlement of Canada* can
84 merely be touched on here. The first colonists were French.
85 They settled mainly in Acadia (now Nova Scotia) and along
86 the St. Lawrence, though they established trading-posts as far
87 west as the Illinois River and the Great Plains. By the end of
88 the French rule in Canada their numbers had grown to more
89 than 60,000; and during the first years of the British rule it
90 looked as though Canada were destined to become predominantly
90 French.
91 　　　What gave Canada an English-speaking population was the
92 American Revolution. As a result of the Revolution, about 25,000
93 "United Empire Loyalists" were driven from their old homes,
94 and forced to take refuge in the wilds of Nova Scotia, New Bruns-
95 wick, and Upper Canada. This immigration was supplemented
96 later by successive waves of immigration both from the British
97 Isles and the United States; and, despite the fact that the original
98 French population multiplied with exceeding rapidity, it was
99 eventually outnumbered by the English-speaking elements. Not
100 only the Maritime Provinces and Ontario (Upper Canada), but
101 the Western Provinces have been settled mainly by people of

102 English-speaking stock. A colony of Scotch Highlanders was
103 founded in what is now Manitoba as early as 1812; and Van-
104 couver Island, on the Pacific coast, was erected into a crown
105 colony before the middle of the 19th century. The settlement of
106 the greater part of the Canadian West, however, has been a much
107 more recent matter. It has been only within the last half-century,
108 since the building of the first transcontinental railway and the
109 adoption of a vigorous immigration policy by the Canadian gov-
110 ernment, that the vacant spaces of the West have begun to fill up.

111 *The political history of the Canadian people*, in which
112 French, English, and other elements have thus been mingled,
113 has been full of interest. Though the French and the English
114 in Canada have had occasional sharp disagreements, there are
115 few countries in which peoples so different in language, religion,
116 and traditions have, on the whole, gotten along so well together.
117 And it is a remarkable fact that there is in existence in Canada
118 today a strong national feeling—a feeling not English-Canadian,
118 or French-Canadian, but all-Canadian.

119 There are few countries, moreover, whose annals present a
120 more remarkable illustration of the growth of self-government.
121 Not only during the period of French rule, but even under the
122 first 30 years of British rule, Canada was governed in an
123 arbitrary and despotic manner by officials sent out from the
124 mother country. The inhabitants had no voice in the control of
125 their own affairs. When, however, at the close of the American
126 Revolution the United Empire Loyalists—people who had been
127 accustomed in the American colonies to a fairly advanced type
128 of democratic government—flocked into Canada, a change be-
129 came necessary; and in 1791 the Canadians, both English and
130 French, were given popular assemblies composed of elected rep-
131 resentatives. These assemblies, unfortunately, were granted such
132 small powers that they became centers of a violent reform agita-
133 tion; and in 1837 the reformers, both in Upper and Lower
133 broke out in armed rebellion.

134 The upshot of this rebellion was that British statesmen
135 came to see that, so far at any rate as the domestic affairs of
136 Canada were concerned, Canadians had to be allowed to govern
137 themselves. Shortly afterwards, therefore, Canada was granted
138 what is known as "responsible government." In 1859 a tariff
139 barrier was raised against British goods; in 1862 Great Britain
140 began withdrawing troops and Canada took up the burden of its
141 own defense. In 1908 it asserted the right to exclude immigrants
142 from the British Isles. The World War hastened Canada's rise to
143 independent nationhood. The Canadian prime minister sat with
144 the imperial war cabinet in London, and the government firmly
145 denied Britain's right to requisition Canadian ships. The new
146 status of Canada and the other dominions as autonomous nations
147 of an imperial commonwealth was formally recognized by the
148 mother country. Canada was represented at the peace conference
149 after the World War, and became a member of the League of Na-
150 tions. It has its own ministers at Washington, Paris, and Tokyo,
151 and has the right to make treaties with foreign governments.

153   This development has been partly the result of another
154 movement in Canadian history—the movement toward confedera-
155 tion or national unity. Up to 1867 the British provinces in North
156 America were separated and disunited; but in that year Nova
157 Scotia, New Brunswick, Canada East (Quebec), and Canada
158 West (Ontario) agreed to unite in a confederation to be known
159 as the Dominion of Canada. An act establishing the Dominion
160 was passed by the British Parliament. Since 1867 the growth of
161 the Dominion has been phenomenal. In 1869 it acquired by pur-
162 chase the vast territories of the Hudson's Bay Company; and out
163 of these there was carved in 1870 the province of Manitoba, and
164 in 1905 the province of Saskatchewan and Alberta. In 1871 Brit-
165 ish Columbia, on the Pacific Coast, came into the Dominion; and
166 in 1873 Prince Edward Island, which had refused to come in in
167 1867, repented of its decision, and followed British Columbia's
168 example. Thus, within a few short years, Canada grew into a
169 serried row of self-governing provinces stretching from the At-
170 lantic to the Pacific. Newfoundland, including Labrador, alone
170 remains outside the Dominion.

170   POLITICAL HISTORY SINCE 1867

171   Alongside these outstanding features of Canadian history,
172 the details of the political history of the Dominion since 1867
173 are of only secondary importance, but they deserve perhaps a
174 brief description. The first administration of the Dominion was
175 that of Sir John Macdonald, a Conservative statesman who was
176 one of the most outstanding of the Fathers of Confederation. In
177 1873, Macdonald was driven from power as a result of the
178 "Pacific Scandal"—a scandal in connection with the building of
179 the Canadian Pacific Railway. He was succeeded by Alexander
180 Mackenzie, the leader of the Liberal party, who held office until
181 1878. In that year Macdonald was returned to power on a high
182 protectionist platform known as "the National Policy," and he
183 remained in power, the most loved and most hated of Canadian
184 politicians, until his death in 1891. For five years the con-
185 servative government he had headed then struggled on with-
186 out him, under a succession of prime ministers; but in 1896 it
187 was driven from power by the Liberals under Wilfrid (after-
188 wards Sir Wilfrid) Laurier, a French-Canadian Roman Cath-
189 olic. Laurier remained in office until 1911, when he was defeated
190 on the issue of reciprocity in trade with the United States.
191 A Conservative administration was then formed by Mr. (now
192 Sir) Robert Borden; and it was this administration, and a
193 "Unionist" coalition which succeeded it in 1917, that piloted
194 Canada through the World War. Sir Robert Borden resigned
195 in 1920, and his successor, Arthur Meighen, was defeated the
196 next year by the Liberals under William Mackenzie King with
197 a policy of low tariff and unified control of the government
198 railways. Mr. King remained in power until 1930, with one
199 brief break in 1926, when Mr. Meighen again became premier.
200 In 1926 also, Vincent Massey was named as Canada's first min-

201 ister to the United States. In 1930 discontent over the economic
202 situation brought the Convervatives into power, with Richard B.
203 Bennett premier. In 1935 the Liberals under King won a sweep-
204 ing victory, largely over the issues of unemployment relief,
205 lower taxes, and reciprocity with the United States.

206   HOW CANADA IS GOVERNED
207   To explain the system under which Canada is governed is
208 not easy. Superficially, the government of Canada resembles that
209 of the United States, on which it was to some extent modeled. In
210 each case, two distinct sets of political machinery were set up,
211 one central or federal, the other local or provincial, with a divi-
212 sion of powers between them. Just as among the 13 original
213 States of the American Union, so among the provinces of British
214 North America local jealousies and interests prevented a complete
215 union and compelled an arrangement under which each state or
216 province would have control of its own local affairs. In each case,
217 moreover, the federal senate or upper house was made the guard-
218 ian of the rights of the smaller states or provinces, which were
219 given in it especially generous representation. But here the
220 resemblance between the two systems ends. In its essential fea-
221 tures, the government of Canada is modeled on that of Great
222 Britain—a system so different from that of the United States
223 that the people of each country find it difficult to understand
224 the political institutions of the other. This difference arises
225 mainly from the fact that in Great Britain and Canada the execu-
226 tive government (that part of the government which carries out
227 the laws) is directly responsible to the legislature (that part of
228 the government which makes the laws) ; whereas in the United
229 States it is not.
230   *The political machinery of the Dominion* is composed of:
231 (1) a governor-general, who represents the Crown and is ap-
232 pointed by the king of Great Britain; (2) a cabinet of ministers,
233 headed by a prime minister, which corresponds almost exactly
234 with the British cabinet; and (3) a legislature or parliament
235 composed of two houses—an upper house termed the Senate,
236 which is, like the British House of Lords, not elected, but ap-
237 pointed, and a lower house termed the House of Commons, which
238 is modeled after the House of Commons at Westminster.
239   The governor-general, as the representative of the Crown,
240 is the nominal head of the government. Yet—and this is the
241 deceptive feature of the Canadian system—he has virtually
242 no powers of his own. In his official capacity he can do
243 nothing except on the advice of his Canadian ministers. He
244 has no veto on legislation, like the President of the United
245 States; even the speech he makes at the opening of parliament
246 is written by the prime minister. Formerly he served as
247 a sort of ambassador from the British government; but
248 since 1927 this function has been exercised by a high
249 commissioner.
250   It is the prime minister who is the real head of the gov-
251 ernment. He not only chooses the cabinet of ministers, or heads
252 of departments, and thus controls the carrying out of the laws;

253 he also very largely directs the making of the laws. This
254 is because he is, and must be, himself a member of parlia-
255 ment, who is in command of the confidence of the majority
256 of the House of Commons, the branch of the legislature that
257 enjoys the all-important function of voting money. He and
258 his cabinet sit in parliament and there render daily an account
259 of their stewardship. The President of the United States and
260 his cabinet do not sit in Congress, and during their term
261 of office cannot be removed by Congress, except by impeach-
262 ment; but the Canadian prime minister and his cabinet can
263 be forced to resign at any time merely by the passing in the
264 House of Commons of a vote of want of confidence. On the
265 other hand, so long as the Canadian cabinet continue to enjoy
266 the confidence of the House, they are practically masters of
267 the situation; and the prime minister, as head of the cabinet,
268 is little less than a dictator.
270   Of the two houses of parliament, the House of Commons
271 is by far the more important and powerful. In it sit nearly all
272 the cabinet ministers, and in it alone may bills be introduced
273 which require the expenditure of public money. On its good
274 will and support the very existence of the administration depends.
275 The Senate, on the other hand, unlike the Senate of the United
276 States, occupies in the constitution a distinctly inferior posi-
277 tion. It was intended mainly as a revising chamber, in which
278 hasty legislation passed by the lower house might be rejected
279 or amended; but its action in this respect has been somewhat
280 spasmodic. Owing to the fact that its members are appointed,
281 virtually for life, by the government of the day, and that each
282 government has been in the habit of appointing only its own
283 partisans, the Senate as a rule has been very subservient
284 toward the House of Commons when the party in power com-
285 mands a majority in both houses, and very obstructive when,
286 as usually happens after the advent to power of a new gov-
287 ernment, the dominant party in the House of Commons is in
288 a minority in the Senate. So unsatisfactory, indeed, has the
289 Senate proved that some observers have questioned whether it
290 performs any useful function in the Canadian system; and there
291 have been many proposals for its abolition or reform.

292   POWER OF THE DOMINION
293   Within the sphere assigned to it, the Dominion parliament
294 is supreme. Until 1931, the British government had, under the
295 British North America Act, which is the fundamental document
296 of the Canadian constitution, the power of disallowing Dominion
297 legislation; but this power had not been exercised for many
298 years, and in 1931 it was legally surrendered. The British North
299 America Act, it is true, can be amended only by the British par-
300 liament; but this is now done, almost as a matter of course, on
301 address from both houses of the Canadian parliament. For all
302 practical purposes, the only matters with which the Dominion
303 parliament is not competent to deal are those reserved exclusively
304 for the provincial legislatures. Powers not specifically conferred
305 on the provinces are reserved to the Dominion government.

306 The provincial constitutions are, some of them, survivals
307 of the days before confederation. In each province there is a
309 lieutenant-governor, who represents the Crown in the province
310 as the governor general does in the Dominion; though these
311 officials are appointed, not (as the governor-general is) by the
312 King directly, but by the Dominion government. In each case
313 the lieutenant-governor acts only on the advice of a provincial
314 cabinent, headed by a prime minister or "premier," and the cab-
315 inet is responsible to the representatives of the people. Quebec,
316 alone of all the provinces, has a legislature composed of two
317 houses—a Legislative Assembly elected by the people, and also a
318 Legislative Council of 24 members appointed by the lieutenant-
319 governor for life. In all the other eight provinces there is now
320 only a legislative assembly, those provinces which formerly had
321 an upper chamber having discarded it. Within the spheres as-
322 signed to them, these legislatures are supreme. They have even
323 complete oversight of the system of municipal government, which
324 is everywhere based on the principle of popular election; and
325 they determine the form of the provincial courts. Like the
326 United States, Canada has a Supreme Court for the whole coun-
327 try. The final court of appeal for Canada in the more important
328 cases is not, however, this court, but the Judicial Committee of
329 the Privy Council in England—a curious survival of Canada's
330 former colonial status. There are not a few Canadians who wish
331 to see appeals to this Judicial Committee abolished or restricted;
332 though there are many others in favor of the continuance of the
333 present arrangement, which has the advantage of giving Canada
334 a distinguished and impartial court of last resort far removed
335 from the stress and storm of Canadian politics. In general, it
336 must be said that if this and other slight limitations on Canadian
337 independence continue to exist, it is because the Canadian people
337 have willed that they should exist.
338 Education in Canada comes under provincial jurisdiction,
339 and its character differs therefore in different provinces. On the
340 whole, however, it is of a high standard. There are few coun-
341 tries of Canada's size which boast of so many universities;
342 and in most of the provinces school attendance is compulsory.
343 The existence side by side in Canada of French-speaking Roman
344 Catholics and English-speaking Protestants has introduced com-
345 plications into the educational system; and at the time of the
346 confederation both Ontario and Quebec had to accept "separate
347 schools"—schools, that is to say, that are Roman Catholic in
348 Protestant Ontario and Protestant in Roman Catholic Quebec.
349 In Ontario, moreover, difficulties have arisen from the fact that
350 the "separate school" supporters are both French and English
351 in point of language, whereas the official language of the province
352 is English. But these difficulties are not impossible of solution,
353 nor do they seriously affect the efficiency of the educational
354 system.

Do not look at the next three pages until after text is read.

Questions for Canadian History Reading Test

by FRANCIS P. ROBINSON and PRUDENCE HALL
The Ohio State University

Directions I

Note the number of the last line you had read at the end of 10 minutes. Turn this page and find the number in the left-hand margin which is just equal to, or just less than, this number. Draw a line across the page *under* the question thus numbered and then answer each of the questions down to this line.

After you have answered these questions, read *Directions II* and do what it requests.

Directions II

Write in below the three numbers which you encircled in the text at the end of 3 minutes, 6 minutes and 10 minutes of reading.

Rate of Reading .... $\left\{\begin{array}{l}\text{3-minute line} \underline{\hspace{2cm}} \\ \text{6-minute line} \underline{\hspace{2cm}} \\ \text{10-minute line}^2 \underline{\hspace{2cm}}\end{array}\right.$ | percentile |

Comprehension Accuracy: $\dfrac{\text{No. tried}}{\text{No. right}}$ .... =

% right	percentile

---

[2] This value for the 10-minute interval also equals the average number of words read per minute during this time.

In the left-hand margin there is a series of "line numbers." Find the number that is equal to, or just less than, the number of the last line you read. Mark this and do not answer questions beyond this point.

line

19 What two aspects of Canada's history are considered important in this selection? (1) wars (2) railroads (3) use of natural resources (4) exploration (5) politics (6) growth of trade and industry.

1. _____

2. _____

40 Who were the first Europeans known to visit Canada? (1) French (2) Spanish (3) Northmen (4) English (5) Italians.

3. _____

40 What did Sebastian Cabot report which caused others to come to Newfoundland? (1) silks and spices (2) furs (3) fish (4) natural resources.

4. _____

65 For what were both the English and French striving in America? (1) A water route to the Pacific Ocean (2) silks and spices (3) places to colonize.

5. _____

81 After each of the events in the right-hand column, write the number of the explorer associated with it.

   1. Amundsen   a. Followed Mississippi to Gulf.

6. _____

   2. Cabot

   3. Mackenzie   b. First brought ship from Atlantic to Pacific.

7. _____

   4. Champlain

   5. La Salle   c. Crossed Rocky Mountains and reached Pacific.

8. _____

81 The exploration of the water route around Northern Canada was carried on by the (1) French (2) Scandinavians (3) English (4) Portuguese (5) Italians.

9. _____

90 The French population that is in Canada is (1) spread rather evenly over the country (2) primarily in Eastern Canada (3) primarily in the Great Lakes region (4) primarily in Western Canada.

10. _____

90 In the early history of Canadian settlement, the dominant ethnic group was (1) English (2) French (3) people from the United States (4) Eskimos (5) Northmen.

11. _____

110 What changed Canada's ethnic composition? (1) legislation in the Mother country (2) American revolution (3) colonization from Europe (4) discovery of Northwest passage (5) foreign armed conquest.

12. _____

110 What two things encouraged Western expansion in Canada? (1) growth of lumber industry (2) building of transcontinental railway (3) adoption of a vigorous immigration policy (4) growth of mining (5) racial and religious strife in the East (6) overpopulation (7) better hunting in West (8) trade with the Indians.

13. _____

14. _____

118 The ethnic makeup of Canada makes loyalty primarily toward (1) England (2) France (3) United States (4) sharply divergent and toward several countries (5) national self-pride.

15. _____

line *(Continued)*

133 What served to precipitate the movement toward a more democratic government? (1) refugees from the American Revolution (2) tariff barrier against American goods (3) stationing of British soldiers in Canada (4) discovery of rich resources in Canada (5) taxation without representation.

16. _____

151 The Canadian Revolution differed from that of the United States chiefly in that it was (1) less successful (2) more gradual (3) had less national support (4) was concerned with entirely different issues.

17. _____

151 Canada has all the following rights without English control: representation at peace conferences, power to make treaties with other governments, and right to have ministers in foreign countries

18. T F

170 Which one of the following is not a part of Canada? (1) Quebec (2) Manitoba (3) Nova Scotia (4) Newfoundland (5) all of them are parts.

19. _____

170 United Government for Canada began about (1) 1700 (2) 1775 (3) 1812 (4) 1867.

20. _____

205 What are the two major political parties in Canada? (1) Liberals (2) Republicans (3) Tories (4) Socialists (5) Whigs (6) Conservatives (7) Democrats (8) Labor.

21. _____
22. _____

205 Which of the following have been the two main issues in Canadian politics? (1) national unity (2) government control of railroads (3) tariff and trade policy (4) national resources (5) war (6) England's policies.

23. _____
24. _____

229 Canada's government basically resembles that of which one of the following? (1) United States (2) Germany (3) Great Britain (4) not similar to any of these.

25. _____

238 Who represents the British Crown in Canadian government? (1) the governor-general (2) the high commissioner (3) the prime minister (4) ambassador from England.

26. _____

268 Which is the most powerful executive position? (1) the governor-general (2) the prime minister (3) Senate (4) the cabinet of ministers (5) the House of Commons.

27. _____

268 The head of the Canadian government

    (a) has more power in his government than the president has in ours.

28. T F

    (b) is a member of and meets with parliament.

29. T - F

    (c) has a definite term of office as in the U.S.

30. T F

    (d) can be removed only by a two-thirds vote of parliament

31. T F

292 Which house of parliament has the greater power? (1) Senate (2) House of Commons.

32. _____

292 The less important house of Parliament (1) still plays an important part in the government (2) is not very important and its elimination has been discussed.

33. _____

305 The Canadian government's actions can in a number of ways still be vetoed by the English government.

34. T F

337 The Canadians are rebellious against the English control which remains.

35. T F

337 The highest court of appeal is the (1) Supreme Court (2) Privy Council in England (3) the governor-general (4) prime minister.

353 Education is under federal jurisdiction and is remarkably uniform over Canada.

37. T F

353 What is meant by "separate schools"? (1) for boys and girls (2) for white and colored (3) for Catholic and Protestant (4) private and public.

38. _____

READING TABLES

Percent correct _____

TABLE II.1 **Table for Converting the Fraction** $\dfrac{\text{No. correct}}{\text{No. tried}}$ **into Percent correct**

Num-ber tried	Number correct																								
	10	11	12	13	14	15	16	17	18	19	20	21	22	23	24	25	26	27	28	29	30	31	32	33	34
10	100																								
11	91	100																							
12	83	92	100																						
13	77	85	92	100																					
14	71	79	86	93	100																				
15	67	73	80	87	93	100																			
16	63	69	75	81	88	94	100																		
17	59	65	71	76	82	88	94	100																	
18	56	61	67	72	78	83	89	94	100																
19	53	58	63	68	74	79	84	89	95	100															
20	50	55	60	65	70	75	80	85	90	95	100														
21	48	52	57	62	67	71	76	81	86	90	95	100													
22	46	50	55	59	64	68	73	77	82	86	91	95	100												
23	44	48	52	57	61	65	70	74	78	83	87	91	96	100											
24	42	46	50	54	58	63	67	71	75	79	83	88	92	96	100										
25	40	44	48	52	56	60	64	68	72	76	80	84	88	92	96	100									
26	38	42	46	50	54	58	62	65	69	73	77	81	85	88	92	96	100								
27	37	41	44	48	52	56	59	63	67	70	74	78	81	85	89	93	96	100							
28	36	39	43	46	50	54	57	61	64	68	71	75	79	82	86	89	93	96	100						
29	34	38	41	45	48	52	55	59	62	66	69	72	76	79	83	86	90	93	97	100					
30	33	37	40	43	47	50	53	57	60	63	67	70	73	77	80	83	87	90	93	97	100				
31	32	35	39	42	45	48	52	55	58	61	65	68	71	74	77	81	84	87	90	94	97	100			
32	31	34	38	41	44	47	50	53	56	59	63	66	69	72	75	78	81	84	88	91	94	97	100		
33	30	33	36	39	42	45	48	52	55	58	61	64	67	70	73	76	79	82	85	88	91	94	97	100	
34	29	32	35	38	41	44	47	50	53	56	59	62	65	68	71	74	76	79	82	85	88	91	94	97	100
	10	11	12	13	14	15	16	17	18	19	20	21	22	23	24	25	26	27	28	29	30	31	32	33	34

1. If a student gets 17 out of 21 questions correct, what percent does he have correct? 1. _____

2. If a student gets 13 out of 15 questions correct, what percent does he have correct? 2. _____

3. If a student gets 19 out of 21 questions corect, what percent does he have correct? 3. _____

4. $13\!\!/\!\!23$ is a larger fraction than $16\!\!/\!\!27$. 4. T F

5. $17\!\!/\!\!21$ is a larger fraction than $25\!\!/\!\!30$. 5. T F

6. What divided by 18 equals 78 percent? 6. _____

7. What divided by 24 equals 71 percent? 7. _____

TABLE II.2 Participation in Various High School Activities by Children from Different Socioeconomic Classes[a]

	Social class			
	Upper	Middle	Wage earners	Lower
Percentage distribution of student body	9	37	47	7
Percentage composition of student council	22	46	32	0
Percentage seldom missing or attending most:				
Evening plays and parties	89	56	12	0
High school dances	77	47	13	0
Games	94	75	44	0
No participation (%)	0	25	43	73
Number of cases	35	146	163	26

[a] From 295 and adapted from A. B. Hollingshead, *Elmtown's Youth*, New York, John Wiley, pp. 193–202.

8. Which social class has the most students? (1) upper, (2) middle, (3) wage earners, (4) lower.   8. _____

9. Which social class has the fewest members on the student council? (1) upper, (2) middle, (3) wage earners, (4) lower.   9. _____

10. Which social class has the greatest proportion of its own group on the student council? (1) upper, (2) middle, (3) wage earners, (4) lower.   10. _____

11. Students from which social class are most likely to attend various student activities? (1) upper, (2) middle, (3) wage earners, (4) lower.   11. _____

12. Students from which social class are least likely to attend various student activities? (1) upper, (2) middle, (3) wage earners, (4) lower.   12. _____

13. Most middle-class students "seldom miss or attend most" high school dances.   13. T F

14. In general, all students attend which one of these types of activities the most often? (1) evening plays and parties, (2) high school dances, (3) games.   14. _____

15. In each social class the order of frequency of attendance among the three types of school activities is the same.   15. T F

16. The purpose of this table is to show that the number of students in school from a particular social class is an important determinant of success in obtaining a seat on the student council.   16. T F

TABLE II.3 Percentage of University Students in 1923 and 1953, and Adults over 50 in 1953 (and Who Would Have Been College Students in 1923), Who Checked Certain Items as Wrong on the Pressey "XO" Tests[a]

	Men			Women		
	Junior-senior		Old	Junior-senior		Old
	1923	1953	1953	1923	1953	1953
Immodesty	70	40	86	80	47	70
Extravagance	61	25	65	55	32	63
Poolrooms	36	8	33	45	18	61
Overeating	68	46	63	65	30	58
Craps	60	16	45	61	29	40
Slang	43	11	45	48	21	39
Silliness	68	33	49	61	25	42
Flirting	47	11	24	56	19	35

[a] From 295 and adapted from S. L. Pressey, and A. W. Jones, 1923–1953 and 20–60 age changes in moral codes, anxieties and interests as shown by the "XO" tests, *Journal of Psychology* 1955, 39, 485–502.

17. The item most often thought wrong by men students in 1953 was   17. _____

18. The item most often thought wrong by both younger and older men's groups in 1953 was the same   18. T F

19. The item most often thought wrong by women students in 1923 was   19. _____

20. The item most often thought wrong by women students in 1923 and by older women in 1953 was the same   20. T F

21. In 1953 the young men and women on *every* item thought that it was less often wrong than did the older men and women.   21. T F

22. The item on which the greatest change took place for men between young 1923 and older 1953 was   22. _____

23. The item on which there was the greatest difference between the younger and older groups of women in 1953 was   23. _____

24. The older men and women in 1953 were more like students in 1923 in their attitudes than they were like students in 1953.   24. T F

25. On the basis of this table it would be expected that in 30 more years the students of 1953 would be more like themselves in 1953 than like the young students of 1983.   25. T F

READING CHARTS

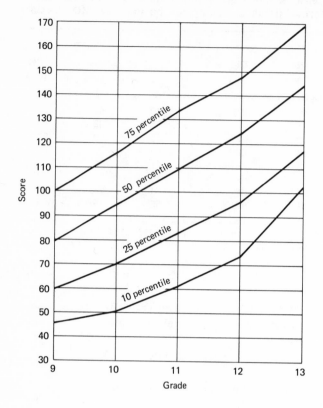

Percent right _____

Figure II.1. Increase in Iowa Silent Reading Test norms from grade 9 through grade 13. (Based on publisher's norms.)

Use Figure II.1 to answer questions 1–6.

1. The average score during the freshman year in college is:
   1. _____

2. At which grade is the most marked gain shown in reading ability?
   2. _____

3. On this test, the person at the 10th percentile of college freshmen is midway between the average student of what two grades?
   3. _____

4. Which part of the distribution of readers shows the greatest change on entering college? (1) highest quarter, (2) average, (3) lowest quarter, (4) lowest 10 percent.
   4. _____

5. There is a greater difference within the middle 50 percent of 12th graders (75th percentile–25th percentile) than there is between the average 12th grader and the average 9th grader.
   5. T F

6. The most marked change in one year is made in what year at what level?
   6. _____

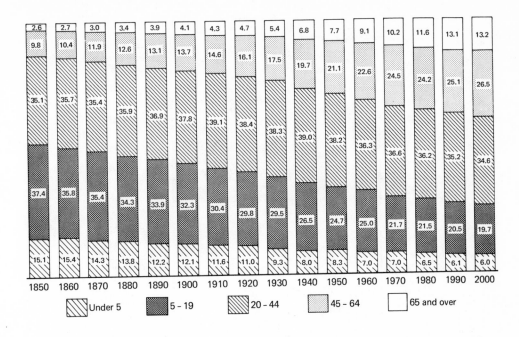

Figure II.2. Percent distribution of total population by age, United States 1850 to 2000. (Based on U.S. Census enumerations and estimates by the Bureau of the Census.)

Use Figure II.2 to answer questions 7–13.

7. This graph indicates that the Census Bureau believes that the total population will remain just about the same size through the year 2000.

7. T F

8. What is the first decade that the percent 65 and over became greater than the percent 5 years and younger?

8. _____

9. What is the first decade that the group 45–64 became greater than the group 5–19?

9. _____

10. What age group maintains the most stable proportion of the total population?

10. _____

11. The estimated decreasing proportion 19 and under in the decades ahead is probably due primarily (1) to smaller family sizes these days, or (2) to increased numbers living to older ages.

11. _____

12. What was the last decade in which over one-half of the population was less than 20 years of age?

12. _____

13. No single age grouping ever equalled 50 percent or more of the population during the decades listed.

13. T F

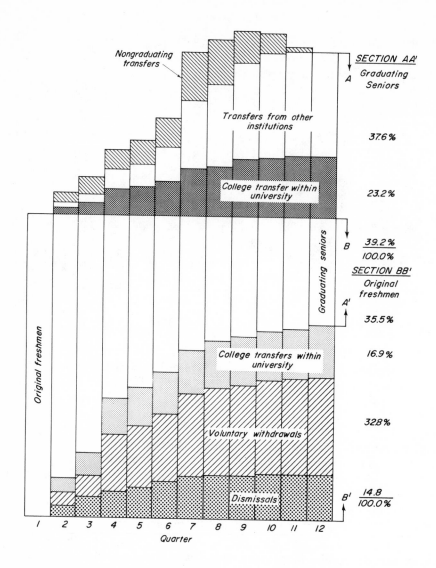

Figure II.3. The academic history of students who enter and who graduate from a college in a university. (Adapted from R. D. Bennett, Ohio State University, mimeographed report.)

Use Figure II.3 to answer questions 14–20.

14. What percent of entering freshmen graduate in the same college?   14. _____

15. The greatest number of voluntary withdrawals takes place at the end of which quarter?   15. _____

16. There were more dismissals than there were withdrawals.   16.   T   F

17. The time of greatest change in the original class is at the end of which quarter?   17. _____

18. The time of greatest increase in incoming transfers is at the beginning of which quarter?   18. _____

19. More students are dismissed from school at the time of their senior year than at any other year.   19.   T   F

20. More than one-half of the class graduating from this college is made up of students who entered this college as freshmen.   20.   T   F

Percent right _____

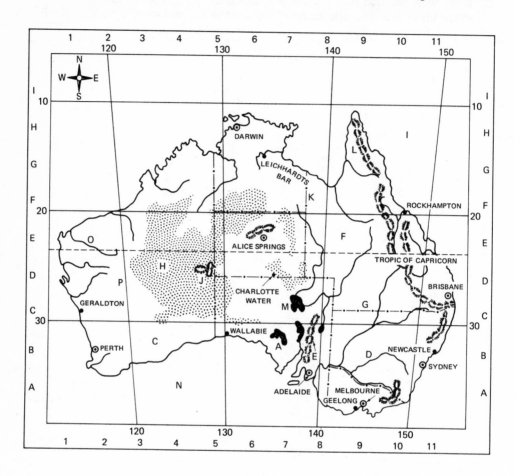

Use the above map to answer questions 1–22.

1. What letters indicate borders of states?

1. _____

2. How many capital cities are there on this map?

2. _____

3. What town is located at 1–C?

3. _____

4. What town is located at 6–E?

4. _____

5. What letters represent desert?

5. _____

6. What letter represents a group of mountains almost surrounded by desert?

6. _____

7. Which coast (north, south, east, or west) could be called mountainous?

7. _____

8. Is Darwin on the north, south, east, or west coast?

8. _____

9. Is Darwin or Melbourne closer to the equator?

9. _____

260   *Appendix II*

10. Is Alice Springs east or west of Wallabie?   10. _____

11. What town is located directly on one of the latitude lines?   11. _____

12. What town is located directly on one of the longitude lines?   12. _____

13. What letters indicate lakes?   13. _____

14. What letters indicate the ocean?   14. _____

15. What letters indicate rivers?   15. _____

16. What town is located on a river and on the coast?   16. _____

17. What direction is the equator from this country?   17. _____

18. What town is farthest south?   18. _____

19. What town is farthest west?   19. _____

20. Is Alice Springs in the torrid zone or the temperate zone?   20. _____

21. If one inch equals 600 miles (| 1″ = 600 mi. |) on this map, about what would be the greatest distance of this country from east to west?   21. _____

22. About what would be the greatest distance from north to south?   22. _____

MATHEMATICAL FORMULAS

Directions

Place the letter of the best answer in the space provided. (Note: The purpose of this test is to measure your ability to manipulate values in formulas. For this reason some of the formulas do not represent actual physical events; hence you cannot depend upon your knowledge of physics to answer the questions.)

1. $f = ws$ where f = force, w = weight, s = speed. In the case of a one-ounce bullet that hits an object with the same force as a two-ounce bullet, the value of s in the formula is (a) halved, (b) doubled, (c) squared, (d) equal.
1. _____

2. $d = vt$ where d = distance, v = velocity, t = time. Where the values of d and v are both doubled, the value of t (a) remains the same, (b) is also doubled, (c) is halved, d) is squared.
2. _____

3. $rt = mv^2$ where r = radius, t = tension on string, m = mass of whirling object, v = velocity. An object at the end of a string is whirled around one's head. If the length of the string is doubled and the velocity remains the same, what happens to the value of t? (a) doubled, (b) halved, (c) quadrupled, (d) almost doubled.
3. _____

4. $V_1 P_1 = V_2 P_2$ where V_1 = original volume, P_1 = original pressure, V_2 = second volume, and P_2 = second pressure. If the value of P_2 is twice that of P_1, the value of V_2 is how large in relation to V_1? a) double, (b) half, (c) quadruple, (d) squared.
4. _____

5. $P = haDg$ where P = pressure at outlet, h = height of water above outlet, a = area of outlet, D = density of liquid, and g = force of gravity. The pressure at the outlet of identical containers completely filled with different liquids will vary with (a) volume, (b) height, (c) area, (d) density.
5. _____

6. $E = vDgh$ where E = energy lost by drop of liquid, v = velocity of drop, D = density of drop, g = force of gravity, and h = height drop falls. If two drops of the same size fall under identical conditions but lose different amounts of energy, they must have differed in respect to (a) their densities, (b) the velocity of fall, (c) the height fallen, (d) the effect of gravity.
6. _____

7. $2v = gt^2$ where v = velocity, g = gravity, and t = time. For the velocity of one object to be 4 times as great as that of a second object, when the effects of gravity are constant, the value of t must be (a) halved, (b) doubled, (c) quadrupled, (d) squared.
7. _____

8. $2v = gt^2$ where v = velocity, g = gravity, and t = time. Where the value of g remains constant, doubling the value of v has what effect on the value of t? (a) halved (b) doubled, (c) about 1½ times, (d) about quadrupled.
8. _____

9. $E = \frac{1}{2}mv^2$ where E = energy, m = mass, and v = velocity. When the velocity is doubled, the value of E is (a) halved, (b) doubled, (c) squared, (d) quadrupled.
9. _____

10. $V = \sqrt{K/D}$ where V = velocity of sound, K = a constant unchanging value, and D = density of air. As the density of air is doubled, what change occurs in velocity of the sound? (a) de-

creases more than ½, (b) decreases ½, (c) decreases less than ½, (d) stays the same.

10. _____

11. $t = \sqrt{2d/a}$ where t = time, d = distance, and a = acceleration. If the value of a remains unchanged while the value of d is doubled, what change occurs in the value of t? (a) decreases about ½, (b) doubles in value, (c) increases about ½, (d) decreases less than ½.

11. _____

English Survey Test[3]—Form A

By S. L. PRESSEY
Ohio State University

No. lines right _____ **Percentile** _____ **Date** _____

GRAMMAR TEST

Directions

In each line of the passage below, four words are underlined. In most of the lines, *one* of these underlined words is grammatically incorrect. Disregard punctuation; assume that it is correct.

Make your answer to each line in one of the following ways: (1) when there is an error, write the correct form of this wrong word on the line at the left. (2) When you are sure that there is no error in the line, write a "0" to the left. (3) If you do not know what the correct form is, or if you are uncertain whether or not there is an error, leave the line at the left blank.

Look over the examples below. Then begin at once. Work rapidly. You will have 25 minutes in which to complete this section. The key for correcting this test is on pages 294–295.

Example

were	There was money, bonds, and other valuable papers
to	in the safe. The boys were anxious too see the inside.

1. _____ It is the first day of school; each of we
2. _____ pupils greet the teacher. We have already taken
3. _____ our seats. Mary, John, and Annabelle set in the
4. _____ front row. John intends to do his work good this
5. _____ year. Sally and Richard have ask to occupy seats
6. _____ near the window. I have clumb into one of the seats in
7. _____ the front row. I can see easy now.
8. _____ Miss McDonald, our new teacher, has told
9. _____ each one to do their part. We accomplish more if
10. _____ there is cooperation between us. Jack don't remember
11. _____ the other schools that he has went to. Mary is two
12. _____ years older than I. Neither Martha nor John are
13. _____ younger than I. The teacher wanted to know whom my
14. _____ father was. I told her his name and who I was living
15. _____ with. Each of us were told to register. Algebra and
16. _____ geometry has been easy for me; so I chose more math-

[3] Used with the permission of the Ohio State Department of Education.

17. _____ ematics. The greater part of the curriculum are

18. _____ English subjects, which is very uninteresting.

19. _____ The teacher can't learn me English at all.

20. _____ Verbs make my head ache. I am sure weak in grammar.

21. _____ My sister has gave much time to her lessons. Martha,

22. _____ my older sister, don't go to school. The weakest

23. _____ part of our school are the materials in the labora-

24. _____ tories. Our principal feels badly about the lack

25. _____ of funds. The price of supplies are high. Perhaps

26. _____ the principal will leave me drop chemistry. I shall

27. _____ consider the matter very careful.

28. _____ Neither Jane nor I were able to play basketball

29. _____ last year. However, we never felt sadly

30. _____ about it for we could not help it. Basket-

31. _____ ball and baseball is what I am going to take this

32. _____ year. Jane don't want to play games because she is

33. _____ lazy. She likes to lay around and read too much to

34. _____ suit me. Soon I'll be able to play basketball good

35. _____ and then she will be sorry. Most of us has a very

36. _____ good time playing baseball. Jane is taller than me

37. _____ and she used to play baseball better than me, but

38. _____ she plays so poor now that no one wants her on

39. _____ their team. I wish I were as pretty as Jane, though.

40. _____ She is fourteen, like Mary and I, and she has curly

41. _____ black hair. She wears such pretty clothes to. She

42. _____ has some perfume that smells very sweetly. Mother

43. _____ won't leave me have any perfume. She said, though

44. _____ that I could buy some next year.

45. _____ When we graduate from high school us girls

46. _____ are going to the same college. We have wrote to

47. _____ several colleges and have began to read all about

48. _____ the different ones. There are almost to many nice

49. _____ ones to choose one very easy. A few like women's

50. _____ colleges better than co-educational colleges. Most

51. _____ of us prefers the schools where both boys and girls

52. _____ may attend because students have a better time their.

53. _____ They have football games, to. I saw a football game

54. _____ once at Hopewell College. The price of the tickets

55. _____ were two dollars and seventy-five cents. We surely

56. _____ had a good time. There was about 30,000 people there.

57. _____ I had never saw so many people in one place. Every-

58. _____ one shouted as loud as they could when our team

59. _____ come on the field. Between halves the band played

60. _____ the college song very soft while everyone sang.

61. _____ Then the teams came back and each player took their

62. _____ position on the field. The substitutes set down on

63. _____ the bench. The referee, like the other officials, were

64. _____ dressed in white linen knickers. His sleeves

65. _____ were rolled up. He must have froze because it was

66. _____ very cold. Everyone was happy when our team won

67. _____ the game. We sung songs and cheered as we followed

68. _____ the band out of the stadium. People throwed confetti

69. _____ everywhere. Mary, as well as the other girls, have

70. _____ ask me to tell about this game over and over again.

71. _____ No one in our crowd have seen a big game except me.

72. _____ There is several reasons why we want to go to

73. _____ Hopewell College. Our teacher told Mary and I

74. _____ that they have interesting courses their. To tell

75. _____ the truth, the curriculum don't matter so much to us.

76. _____ Either dramatics or athletics are going to be my

77. _____ specialty. There is several things to choose from.

78. _____ I think that sports is the best part of any school.

79. _____ Everybody don't agree with me, however. Mary prefers

80. _____ athletics, like Frances and I.

CAPITALIZATION AND PUNCTUATION TEST

Capitalization: **No. lines correct** _____ **Percentile** _____
Punctuation: **No. lines correct** _____ **Percentile** _____

Directions

All the capitals and punctuation marks have been omitted from the sentences below, except the capital at the beginning of each sentence and the period at the end.

Look over these sentences carefully. Whenever you find a word which should be capitalized, write the letter which should be a capital on the line at the left of the sentence. Sometimes several capitals are needed in one sentence; you will then write several letters on the line at the left. In some sentences no words need to be capitalized. When this is true, leave the line blank. If you are uncertain, it is generally best to omit a capital.

Also, insert in the places in each sentence where they are needed such punctuation marks as you think should be added. You may change a period to an exclamation point or question mark when desirable, but do not cut a sentence into two or more short sentences. In some sentences, no punctuation marks are needed. When in doubt it is best to omit a mark. Make all marks large enough to be seen readily.

Study the examples below and then begin at once. Work rapidly. You will have 25 minutes in which to complete this section. The key for correcting these tests is on pages 295–298.

Example

    S S V D   Do you like s. s. van dine's mystery stories?

      I   Just imagine how frightened i was!

1. _____ Are you going to strassburg germany.
2. _____ She exclaimed what a beautiful lake.
3. _____ The hudson a river in new york is very beautiful.
4. _____ Do you expect to visit china or ceylon.
5. _____ Three weeks from now well be in kansas city.
6. _____ Tell me what doctor harris did said emily.
7. _____ If thats all john said we may as well go.
8. _____ Friday the tenth of june was my birthday.
9. _____ Why do so many people blame the germans.
10. _____ It was the fourth of july a national holiday.
11. _____ She lives at 25 whittier street dolby kentucky.
12. _____ Al smith the democratic candidate was defeated.
13. _____ He attended tate college then he went to a law school.
14. _____ My subjects include the following history english and latin.
15. _____ Theyre ready but well have to wait awhile.
16. _____ In the first place the ku klux klan was not legal.
17. _____ He had started to newburg there was no retreat.
18. _____ She said that she intended to visit mount baker.
19. _____ I think french a boring subject but like physics.
20. _____ This poem is called in the cool of the night.

21. _____ The ring is an heirloom it belonged to jenny lind.
22. _____ The captain our old friend met us at the dock.
23. _____ Esther jane and mary organized a girls club.
24. _____ The letter was sent from detroit on august 8 1933.
25. _____ Christmas memorial day and thanksgiving are holidays.
26. _____ Will the socialist party ultimately succeed.
27. _____ I use ipana it is a good tooth paste.
28. _____ Sinclair lewis wrote these books dodsworth babbitt and arrowsmith.

29. _____ We are said the speaker at the dawn of a new era.
30. _____ If you see any american tourists let me know.
31. _____ He hurried into the bank and asked for the president.
32. _____ John finished his spanish then he worked on biology.
33. _____ By a waterfall is a simple little piece to play.
34. _____ He read tennysons famous poem in memoriam.
35. _____ A careful description of captain evans was given for he was an important witness in the trial.
36. _____ She recommends ajax for cleaning since it is cheaper and just as good.
37. _____ We didnt have time to visit the alps still we saw almost every other part of europe.
38. _____ His wife is a presbyterian he is a baptist.
39. _____ He claims that the government is as corrupt as in the days of rome that there is no place for an honest man in politics and that there is little hope for reform.
40. _____ The national railway association should recognize that this type of engine will not pay it is out of date.
41. _____ The lincoln school has been overcrowded for some time.
42. _____ Its too bad that gerry cant go with us.
43. _____ Oranges lemons and grapefruit are citrous fruits.
44. _____ She said that he would be glad to see you.
45. _____ On sunday we went fishing in beaver creek.
46. _____ The various codes were submitted to general johnson.
47. _____ He said that he saw the prince of wales but no one believed him.
48. _____ Please come she wrote colonel brown will be here.
49. _____ Joe is not going nor is sally.
50. _____ In other words the general electric company refused my offer.
51. _____ Its hair is fine and soft its still just a puppy.
52. _____ Im in a hurry is the name of an amusing short story.
53. _____ You will like these movies ben-hur and diary of anne frank.

54. _____ The unemployed league will meet tomorrow at seven oclock.
55. _____ We saw the capitol at washington and then the driver took us home.
56. _____ You should talk to professor brown she advised.

57. _____ She said she played no card games during lent.
58. _____ One of us must go to lisbon which will it be.
59. _____ John makes high grades in mathematics he wants to enter harvard college next year.
60. _____ Youll find it easier to go by way of athens youll save twenty miles.
61. _____ Im too tired to go out tonight besides its too cold.
62. _____ That youngster said coach jones will be a star next year.

63. _____ Its raining hard but jim wont stay at home.
64. _____ June july and august are vacation months.
65. _____ He wants someone who is quick who is ambitious and who has had experience.
66. _____ If its really necessary you may have the chevrolet.
67. _____ He told me to meet him at the seneca hotel but he didn't appear.
68. _____ Being capable and socially prominent she was elected to the martha washington club.
69. _____ All right he said well put the money in the chase bank.
70. _____ Ill send you a subscription to the readers digest if you want it.
71. _____ You may take this note to mr adams then drop these letters in the mailbox.
72. _____ Joseph conrad is the author of lord jim he also wrote victory.
73. _____ To be frank she doesnt like janice very well.
74. _____ They went to washington to oregon and on to california.
75. _____ She resigned from the missionary society thus losing many friends.
76. _____ We drove to st louis and then took a quaint old steamer down the mississippi river.
77. _____ Ill take you in the car otherwise youll be late.
78. _____ Mary you may describe general pershings plan.
79. _____ One goes to church on easter to ease ones conscience to wear ones new spring clothes or to see what mrs jones is wearing.
80. _____ The play was almost over when john left.

TEST ON SENTENCE STRUCTURE

No. right *times 2* _____ **Percentile** _____

Directions

Each of the following paragraphs contains three statements. One of these violates some rule of good sentence structure; it is poorly expressed or not clear. Write the number of the *wrong* statement in each paragraph, in the parentheses at the left. Do not change or mark on any sentence. Look over the example. Then begin at once. Work rapidly. You will have 15 minutes in which to complete this section. The key for this test is on page 299.

Example

1. (1) (1) The man with the pipe sitting on the bank. (2) The man with the pipe is sitting on the bank. (3) The man sitting on the bank has a pipe.

1. ( ) Where is he? (2) Where is he at? (3) Where has he gone?
2. ( ) (1) The grocer offered me a job, but I refused it. (2) The grocer said that I could work for him Saturdays, but I refused it. (3) The grocer offered me work on Saturdays, but I refused his offer.
3. ( ) (1) I saw your uncle. The one from Dayton. (2) I saw your uncle who lives in Dayton. (3) I saw your uncle, the one from Dayton.
4. ( ) (1) While reading a book, I was startled by the telephone ringing. (2) While reading a book, the telephone rang. (3) While I was reading a book, the telephone rang.
5. ( ) (1) Jane was nervous when Nancy called to her. (2) When Nancy called to Jane, she was nervous. (3) Nancy was nervous when she called to Jane.
6. ( ) (1) His brother is very strong. (2) He has a brother who is very strong. (3) He has a brother is very strong.
7. ( ) (1) Riding down the street in a car they passed John who was afoot. (2) Walking down the street we met John in a car. (3) Walking down the street John passed us in his car.
8. ( ) (1) He had a revolver in his desk, which he had carried in the army. (2) In his desk he had a revolver which he had carried in the army. (3) In the army he had carried the revolver which he now had in his desk.
9. ( ) (1) I got this book from Tom, who got it from Mary. (2) Since this book has left the store it has been first Tom's and then Mary's. (3) This is the book which I got from Tom, who secured it from Mary, who purchased it at the store.
10. ( ) (1) John raced down the field, which was 110 yards long. (2) John ran the full length of the field, which made him a hero. (3) John, who is our best player, raced down the field.
11. ( ) (1) Helen prefers Mary to Jane. (2) Helen likes Mary better than Jane does. (3) Helen likes Mary better than Jane.
12. ( ) (1) Cheering wildly as the team came on the field, all ready for the game. (2) The crowd cheered wildly as the team came on the field. (3) Cheering wildly, we rushed the bleachers.
13. ( ) (1) Chinning is when you pull yourself up to a rod. (2) Chinning is pulling yourself up to a rod. (3) Pulling yourself up to a rod is called chinning.
14. ( ) (1) I like football better than basketball. (2) A game of tennis gives more exercise than a ride in an automobile. (3) Playing tennis is better exercise than to ride in an automobile.

270   *Appendix II*

15. ( ) (1) It is a novel which has great merit and which should be read by all. (2) *A Tale of Two Cities* is a novel of great merit and which should be read by all. (3) *A Tale of Two Cities* is a fine novel which should be read by all.
16. ( ) (1) We went to the city and saw a show. We had a good time. (2) After going to the city and seeing a show, we came home. (3) We went to the city and we saw a show, and we came home, and we had a good time.
17. ( ) (1) We took an airplane because it was the quickest means of travel. (2) Wanting to get there quickly, an airplane was taken. (3) To get there quickly we took an airplane.
18. ( ) (1) The boys fumbled in the third quarter. This fumble caused us to lose the game. (2) The boys fumbled in the third quarter, which caused us to lose the game. (3) The game was lost when the boys fumbled in the third quarter.
19. ( ) (1) He ran home. He told his mother. She came out. We were severely scolded. (2) He ran home and told his mother. She came out and scolded us severely. (3) John having gone home and told his mother, we were severely scolded.
20. ( ) (1) John spoke to the man, and he was very cross. (2) John spoke crossly to the man. (3) John spoke to the man, who was very cross.
21. ( ) (1) A lesson which was too long and which should not have been assigned. (2) The lesson, which was too long, should not have been assigned. (3) The lesson was too long and should not have been assigned.
22. ( ) (1) He arose late and ate no breakfast. (2) Having arisen late, no breakfast was served. (3) He ate no breakfast because he had arisen late.
23. ( ) (1) The summer being very dry, and all the creeks dried up. (2) Because the summer was very dry all the creeks dried up. (3) The summer was very dry. All the creeks dried up.
24. ( ) (1) We finished the problem at noon; then we called the teacher. (2) We finished the problem at noon and called the teacher. (3) We finished the problem at noon and calling for the teacher.
25. ( ) (1) Ann is a cute child. Who is always getting into trouble. (2) Ann is a cute child, but she is always getting into trouble. (3) Ann is a cute child who is always getting into trouble.
26. ( ) (1) After the car stopped we stepped out. (2) We stepped out. The car having stopped. (3) The car stopped. We stepped out.
27. ( ) (1) She joined the party, reserved and quiet. (2) The party which she joined was a reserved and quiet affair. (3) She joined the party, but was reserved and quiet.
28. ( ) (1) Although he read everything he could, he acted as if he were compelled to do it. (2) He read everything as if he were compelled to do so. (3) Reading everything he could, as if he were compelled to do so.
29. ( ) (1) John was talking about that man. (2) That is the man whom John was discussing. (3) That is the man; he was just discussing him.
30. ( ) (1) Tom was sorry because he was too late. (2) Tom was too late, and he was sorry. (3) Tom was sorry, being too late.
31. ( ) (1) He is a student who is popular, but who is always in trouble. (2) That student is popular, but always troublesome. (3) He is a popular student, but who is always in trouble.
32. ( ) (1) Everyone is welcome, and you do not have to contribute. (2) Everyone is welcome, and no one has to contribute. (3) You are welcome; you do not have to contribute.

33. ( ) (1) She thought of only one person. Her brother, who was ill. (2) She thought of only one person, her brother. (3) Her brother, the one who was ill, is coming.

34. ( ) (1) I like a good novel—one which portrays strong characters and which thrills the reader. (2) I like a good novel—one which portrays strong characters and in reading the book you are thrilled. (3) I like novels which are thrilling and which portray strong characters.

35. ( ) (1) James, sitting on the platform, was looking at the audience. (2) There was James, looking at the audience sitting on the platform. (3) There was James, sitting on the platform and looking at the audience.

36. ( ) (1) If she is better tomorrow we will go. (2) We do not expect to go. Unless she is better tomorrow. (3) We do not expect to go unless she is better tomorrow.

37. ( ) (1) The ball which he had just purchased was thrown into the gutter. (2) He threw the ball which he had just purchased into the gutter. (3) He threw the ball into the gutter which he just purchased.

38. ( ) (1) Mother was ill. That was why I was absent. (2) The reason I was absent was because Mother was ill. (3) I was absent because Mother was ill.

39. ( ) (1) We will keep going regardless of anything. (2) Whether we win or lose, we will go on. (3) Whether we win or lose; whether we fail or succeed.

40. ( ) (1) A long lesson was assigned before Christmas, which made us angry. (2) A long lesson assigned before Christmas made us angry. (3) A long lesson was assigned before Christmas. This assignment made us angry.

Test of Words Commonly Spelled Incorrectly

No. correct out of 228 _____   **Percent right** _____

This is a self-administering test of spelling and has no time limit. You are to write out the spelling of each of the words listed below.

The sound of each word is indicated at the left by a crude phonetic method (exactly correct pronunciations are not always indicated and a few times the correct spelling is used to indicate how the word sounds); the middle column gives a definition of each word; and you are to write the correct spelling of each word, thus sounded and defined, in the space at the right-hand side.

A good way "to take" this test is to decide what the word is in terms of the first two columns and then, disregarding the first two columns, sound the word as you spell it. A dash over a letter, _e.g.,_ "ā," indicates that it has a "long" sound, _i.e.,_ sounded as in saying the alphabet.

The key for correcting this test is on pages 299–302.

How word sounds	Definition	Spelling
1. ab sense	to be away	_____
2. āk	to pain	_____
3. all together	without exception	_____
4. a fect	to influence	_____
5. ak si dent ily	without intention	_____
6. ak sept	to approve	_____
7. a cross	on the other side of	_____
8. add vize	to warn	_____
9. a comma date	to adapt to	_____
10. all red i	previously	_____
11. ān jell	celestial being	_____
12. a mung	in the midst of	_____
13. all ways	at all times	_____
14. all most	nearly	_____
15. ang gull	sharp corner	_____
16. a per ate us	machine	_____
17. auks ill er i	helping	_____
18. ath let ick	good at sports	_____
19. are gu ment	dispute	_____
20. a tack t	assaulted	_____
21. a pier unce	external show	_____
22. ath leet	football player	_____

How word sounds	Definition	Spelling
23. be leave	to accept as true	_____
24. ba lense	equilibrium	_____
25. be gin ing	at the start	_____
26. biz nes	commercial enterprise	_____
27. ben i fit	for the sake of	_____
28. by sickle	vehicle with two wheels	_____
29. come er shell	related to industry	_____
30. ch owes	to have selected in the past	_____
31. care actor	reputation, sum of one's characteristics	_____
32. chain ja bull	varying	_____
33. kal end er	table of days and months	_____
34. care actor i stick	typical, distinctive	_____
35. kol ledge	university, school	_____
36. ch ooze	to select	_____
37. chēf	leader	_____
38. sir ten	sure	_____
39. cap ten	officer in army	_____
40. come ing	approaching	_____
41. krit i size	to find fault	_____
42. korse	school subject	_____
43. kon vēn yent	near at hand	_____
44. komp li ment air i	given to flattering remarks	_____
45. komp li ment	flattering remark	_____
46. come pair i tiv lee	relatively	_____
47. come it ē	group of people	_____
48. kon shence	feeling of obligation to do right	_____
49. kon she en chus	faithful, exact	_____
50. kon troll	govern, direct	_____
51. kon shus	aware of	_____
52. kon spick you us	prominent, easily seen	_____
53. de sēēve	mislead	_____

How word sounds	Definition	Spelling
54. dē side	to conclude	————————
55. deaf a nit	limited, fixed	————————
56. duz	form of verb "to do"	————————
57. dis a point	to not fulfill expectation	————————
58. dis a pier	to go from sight	————————
59. de vel up	to form, expand	————————
60. de vel up ment	formation, expansion	————————
61. de scribe	to relate, depict	————————
62. des send	to go down	————————
63. die ning	eating	————————
64. dis sip lin	to punish	————————
65. dock ter	medical person	————————
66. de pen dunt	not self-sustaining	————————
67. doe nt	contracted form of "do not"	————————
68. eks is tense	to be	————————
69. eks pier ē ense	to live through an event	————————
70. eks er size	exertion, to run, play games	————————
71. eks ek ū tiv	administrator	————————
72. eks sept	to leave out	————————
73. ē nuff	adequate	————————
74. ē quip t	furnished	————————
75. em a grunt	person from a country	————————
76. em bear us ment	to feel uncomfortable	————————
77. em bear us	to make uncomfortable	————————
78. e fekt	result of a cause	————————
79. el ij a bull	qualified to be chosen	————————
80. fas sin ate	to hold attention	————————
81. feb you wary	second month of the year	————————
82. fine ul ē	at last	————————
83. four mer li	previously	————————
84. four di	spell "40"	————————
85. full fill	to satisfy, to carry out	————————

How word sounds	Definition	Spelling
86. frend	person that likes you	_____
87. great full	to have gratitude	_____
88. grēv us	heavy, distressing	_____
89. gram er	language form	_____
90. guv urn er	head of a state	_____
91. ges	to judge at random	_____
92. hugh mer us	funny	_____
93. hope ing	desire for something	_____
94. hear	at this place	_____
95. hear	to sense sounds	_____
96. hair us	to worry by repeated attacks	_____
97. ear resist a bull	overpowering	_____
98. its	contracted form of "it is"	_____
99. i me grunt	person coming into a country	_____
100. i mēd i et li	right away	_____
101. i maj in	to form a mental image	_____
102. in deep end ent	free from external control	_____
103. in ti rest ing	exciting	_____
104. judge ment	belief, opinion	_____
105. jew dish al	pertaining to a court	_____
106. new	past tense of verb meaning to have information about	_____
107. lab ra tor i	place for experiments	_____
108. lād	past tense of verb meaning "to place upon"	_____
109. led	past tense of verb meaning "to show the way"	_____
110. lee zure	time outside of work	_____
111. lie berry	place for books	_____
112. lew z	not to win	_____
113. lew se	to be free from	_____
114. litter a ture	books, writing	_____
115. lie sense	official permit	_____

How word sounds	Definition	Spelling
116. man age ment	those in charge	_____
117. ment	past tense of "to mean"	_____
118. miss spell	to spell incorrectly	_____
119. mis cheev us	to cause annoyance	_____
120. more gage	a debt on property	_____
121. mi nut	$\frac{1}{60}$th of an hour	_____
122. nessy sary	something that must be	_____
123. notice a bull	conspicuous	_____
124. nīn teen	spell "19"	_____
125. twen tea	spell "20"	_____
126. knee se	daughter of one's sister or brother	_____
127. O.K. shun	the time for	_____
128. O.K. shun a lee	now and then	_____
129. aw per toon i ti	chance	_____
130. ō mish un	left out	_____
131. offen	happen frequently	_____
132. ō clock	time of day	_____
133. ō mit ed	left out	_____
134. ō cur d	happened	_____
135. pair a lel	extending in same direction	_____
136. prob bub lee	likely	_____
137. pro seed	to begin or go forward	_____
138. pro fes er	college teacher	_____
139. praw fess i	prediction (noun)	_____
140. purr man ent	continue without change	_____
141. purr miss a bull	allowable	_____
142. percy vear	to keep trying at something	_____
143. pick nick ing	lunch outdoors	_____
144. pre seed	to go ahead of	_____
145. pose esh un	to have with one	_____
146. plan ing	scheming, devising	_____
147. plan d	schemed, devised	_____

How word sounds	Definition	Spelling
148. peace	a part of	_____
149. preh fur unce	greater liking for	_____
150. pre fur d	had greater liking for	_____
151. priv i ledge	a right or immunity	_____
152. preh purr ā shun	state of readiness	_____
153. prince a pull	head of a school	_____
154. prince a pull	fundamental truth	_____
155. preh jew dis	opinion against	_____
156. par la ment	governing body	_____
157. part ner	associate	_____
158. purr form	to do, accomplish	_____
159. purr haps	possibly	_____
160. kwan ti tea	amount, sum	_____
161. kwī et	without noise	_____
162. kwīt	entirely, positively	_____
163. rē a li	actually	_____
164. re seat	acknowledgment of payment	_____
165. ri them	movement marked by regular recurrence	_____
166. rye m	poetry	_____
167. re spon sa bull	trustworthy	_____
168. re speck full lee	regardful for	_____
169. rep i ti shun	repeating	_____
170. rē lij us	godly, pious	_____
171. rē leave	to free from burden	_____
172. wreck ō mend āshun	good suggestion	_____
173. wreck ō mend	to suggest as good	_____
174. wreck og nīz	identify, to know	_____
175. rē sēv	to accept	_____
176. sal ar i	wage	_____
177. se purr ate	to divide, take away	_____
178. seas	to take, grab	_____
179. sek ri tary	stenographer	_____

How word sounds	Definition	Spelling
180. sked yule	time table, catalogue	———————————
181. seen	view, part of a play	———————————
182. sin sear lee	genuinely, honestly	———————————
183. shine ing	reflecting light	———————————
184. sim i ler	being alike	———————————
185. shep urd	a tender of sheep	———————————
186. s peach	talk, oration	———————————
187. sof a more	second year in college	———————————
188. skill full	expert	———————————
189. stay shun ery	writing material	———————————
190. stay shun ery	stay in one place	———————————
191. sh your	with certainty	———————————
192. stop ing	ceasing of movement	———————————
193. stud ē ing	to read lessons	———————————
194. suck ses	to attain a goal	———————————
195. sue purr seed	to be in place of	———————————
196. sue purr in ten dent	head of school system	———————————
197. stop t	to have ceased moving	———————————
198. sir prize	unexpected	———————————
199. sill i bull	part of a word	———————————
200. tare if	tax on imports	———————————
201. th air	opposite of here	———————————
202. th air	belonging to them	———————————
203. th air	contraction of "they are"	———————————
204. th air four	for that reason	———————————
205. threw	to be done with	———————————
206. to	also	———————————
207. two gether	in company with	———————————
208. tra jed i	fatal or mournful event	———————————
209. to	spell "2"	———————————
210. to elf	spell "12th"	———————————
211. try z	he attempts	———————————

How word sounds	Definition	Spelling
212. true lee	genuinely, honestly	_____
213. un nessy sary	useless, needless	_____
214. un till	to the time that	_____
215. use ing	employing	_____
216. witch	interrogative or relative pronoun	_____
217. hole	all of	_____
218. wi men	persons of female sex	_____
219. weth er	state of the atmosphere	_____
220. Wens day	4th day of week	_____
221. wear	at or in what place	_____
222. wry ting	what one has composed	_____
223. use you lee	commonly, ordinarily	_____
224. vil un	scoundrel	_____
225. vil edge	small town	_____
226. woe nt	contraction of "will not"	_____
227. wood	form of verb "will"	_____
228. rīt	to compose a letter	_____

APPENDIX III
Keys

11. F

12. T

13. F

14. T

15. A

16. C

17. A

18. E

19. H

20. 2

21. F

22. 1958
23. T

24. 4

25. T

26. F

27. I

28. E

29. F
30. G

31. C

32. H

33. D

LIBRARY INFORMATION
(pages 133–138)

1. 3
2. 4
3. 1
4. 2
5. 5

6. T
7. T

8. F

9. F

10. T

LIBRARY INFORM. *(Cont.)*

34. h
35. f
36. d
37. a
38. c
39. k
40. j
41. l

42. T

43. T

44. T

45. T

46. F

47. F

48. T

49. 3

50. 1

51. F
52. T

53. 1

54. T
55. 2

56. T

57. T

58. 1

59. T

60. 1

61. 3

62. T

GENERAL VOCABULARY TEST
(pages 167–169)

1. (2)
2. (3)
3. (3)
4. (5)
5. (1)
6. (2)
7. (4)
8. (1)
9. (5)
10. (3)
11. (3)
12. (1)

GEN. VOCAB. *(Cont.)*

13. (4)

14. (1)

15. (3)

16. (2)

17. (3)

18. (5)

19. (4)

20. (3)

21. (5)

22. (5)

23. (2)

24. (3)

25. (1)

26. (5)

27. (4)

28. (3)

29. (3)

30. (4)

31. (1)

32. (4)

33. (1)

34. (5)

35. (5)

36. (2)

37. (1)

38. (4)

39. (2)

40. (5)

41. (3)

42. (4)

43. (5)

44. (5)

45. (1)

46. (4)

47. (5)

48. (3)

49. (2)

50. (3)

51. (1)

52. (3)

53. (1)

54. (2)

55. (4)

56. (5)

DICTIONARY TEST
(pages 170–173)

1. T

2. T

3. T

4. F

5. F

6. T

7. T

8. T
9. T

10. F
11. F

12. T

13. T
14. F

15. T

16. F

17. F

18. 18

19. F

DICTIONARY (*Cont.*)

20. rigid

21a. 1

b. 5

MATHEMATICS

(pages 205–206)

1. 2166

2. 1509

3. 18,585

4. 67,572

5. 1,071,840

6. 1,624,773

7. 199.5

8. 291.00

9. 33/40

10. 1 11/20

11. 1/21

12. 1/12

13. 3/7

14. 3/10

15. 7/12

16. 4/5

17. 27.2086

18. 89.1424

19. 1.1694

20. .2942

21. .766314

22. .074592

23. .003

24. 5.

25. 62.5 percent

26. 70.59 percent

27. 1/5

28. 1/2

29. .20

30. .50

31. 49

32. 64

33. 81

34. 121

35. 144

36. 14

37. 40

38. 10

39. 11

40. .40

41. 1.11

42. .007

43. .30

44. 5

45. 8

46. 6

47. 5

48. 132

49. 96

50. 24

CHAPTER 2, PART ONE QUIZ
(page 231)

1. T
2. 1

3. 1

4. F

5. F

6, 7. lecture cues
    examination cues

8, 9. italics, summary paragraphs,
    numbered points, and so on

10. F

11. F

12. F

13. T

14. T

15. headings
16. F

17. F

18–20a. F

    b. F

    c. F

CHAPTER 2, PART TWO QUIZ
(page 232)

1. T

2. T

3. F

4. 2

5–7. interest and intent to remember,
    select major points and key
    phrases, distributed learning

8. 4

9. 1

10. F

11–13. select what to learn, fix ideas in
    memory, efficient exam review

14–20a. recite
    b. T

    c. 1

    d. F

    e. T
    f. 2

    g. T

CHAPTER 3 QUIZ
(page 233)

1–4. a. T
    b. T
    c. T
    d. T

5–7. think what main point is, under-line only a phrase, use marks to make underlining into an outline in book

8. T

9. F

10. T

11. F

12–14. 3, 4, 6

15. T

16. 2

17. T
18. T

19. legend of graph

20. T

CHAPTER 4 QUIZ
(page 234)

1. use of returned exam

2. T

3. F

4. T

5. F

6. F

7. T

8. predict exam questions
9. schedule time per page or question

10. outline, list, compare, and so on
11. jot down outline
12. F

13. F

14. T

15. F

16. T

17. important

18. all, most, some, none
19. F

20. F

CHAPTER 5 QUIZ
(page 235)

1. T

2. 3

3. T

4. F
5. T

6. T

7. 1

8. T

9. F

10. T

11. 1

12. T

13. 1

14. F

15. F

16. T

17–20. work skills, study conditions, time habits, motivation

CHAPTER 6 QUIZ
(page 236)

1. T

2. T

3. T

4. F

5. 1

6. F

7. worth of person

8. counselors know patterns that maladjustments take

9. F
10. T

11. T
12. F

13. 3

14. 4

15. T

16. F

17. T
18–20a. T
     b. T
     c. T

CHAPTER 7 QUIZ
(page 237)

1. T

2–5. listening to lectures, discussing in class, classroom manners, conferences with teachers

6. 1

7, 8. elaborate on important points in assignments, add new important points

9. F

10–12. uses numbers in listing points, puts topic on board, repeats point, makes summary statements, etc.

13. F

14. T

15. T

16. T

17. 1

18. T

19. T

20. T

CANADIAN HISTORY
(pages 250–252)

1. 4
2. 5
3. 3
4. 3
5. 1
6. 5
7. 1
8. 3
9. 3
10. 2
11. 2
12. 2
13. 2
14. 3
15. 5

CAN. HIST. (Cont.)

16. 1

17. 2

18. T

19. 4

20. 4

21. 1 or 6
22. 6 or 1

23. 2 or 3
24. 3 or 2

25. 3

26. 1

27. 2

28. T
29. T
30. F
31. F

32. 2

33. 2

34. F

35. F

36. 2

37. F

38. 3

READING TABLES
(pages 253–255)

1. 81 percent

2. 87 percent

3. 90 percent
4. F
5. F
6. 14
7. 17

READING (Cont.)

8. 3

9. 4

10. 1

11. 1

12. 4

13. F

14. 3

15. F

16. F

17. overeating

18. F

19. immodesty

20. T

21. T

22. flirting

23. poolrooms

24. T

25. T

CHARTS
(pages 256–259)

1. 145
2. 13
3. 10 and 11

4. 4

5. T

6. 13, 10th percentile

14. 35.5 percent
15. 3d

7. F

16. F

17. 3d

8. 1960

18. 7th

9. 1970

10. 20–44

11. 2

12. 1860   19. F

13. T   20. F

SKILLS IN MAP READING
(pages 260–261)

1. GK
2. 7
3. Geraldton
4. Alice Springs
5. BH

6. J

7. East
8. North
9. Darwin

10. East
11. Rockhampton
12. Wallabie
13. AM
14. IN
15. DO
16. Rockhampton
17. North
18. Geelong
19. Geraldton
20. Torrid zone

21. about 2550 mi.
22. about 1900 mi.

MATHEMATICAL FORMULAS 10. c
(pages 262–263)

11. c

1. b

2. a

3. b

4. b

5. d

6. a

7. b

8. c

9. d

**ENGLISH SURVEY TEST—
GRAMMAR**
(pages 264–266)

Rule	Answer
1. (9)	us
2. (7)	greets
3. (13)	sit
4. (11)	well
5. (10)	asked
6. (10)	climbed
7. (11)	easily
8.	0
9. (8)	his
10. (6)	doesn't *or* does not
11. (10)	gone
12. (1)	is
13. (9)	who
14. (9)	whom
15. (7)	was
16. (1)	have (had)

17. (5)	is
18. (8)	are
19. (13)	teach
20. (11)	surely
21. (10)	given
22. (6)	doesn't *or* does not
23. (5)	is
24. (12)	bad
25. (2)	is
26. (13)	let
27. (11)	carefully
28. (1)	was
29. (12)	sad
30.	0
31. (1)	are
32. (6)	doesn't *or* does not
33. (13)	lie
34. (11)	well
35. (7)	have
36. (9)	I
37. (9)	I
38. (11)	poorly
39. (8)	his (her)
40. (9)	me
41. (13)	too
42. (12)	sweet
43. (13)	let
44. (13)	might
45. (9)	we
46. (10)	written
47. (10)	begun
48. (13)	too
49. (11)	easily
50.	0
51. (7)	prefer
52. (13)	there
53. (13)	too
54.	0

55. (2)   was
56. (4)   were
57. (10) seen
58. (8)   he
59. (10) came
60. (11) softly
61. (8)   his
62. (13) sat
63. (3)   was
64.   0
65. (10) frozen
66.   0
67. (10) sang
68. (10) threw
69. (3)   has
70. (10) asked
71. (7)   has
72. (4)   are
73. (9)   me
74. (13) there
75. (6)   doesn't *or* does not
76. (1)   is
77. (4)   are
78. (5)   are
79. (7)   doesn't *or* does not
80. (9)   me

CAPITALIZATION
(pages 267–269)

	Rule	Answer
1.	(3)	S G
2.	(1)	W
3.	(3)	H N Y
4.	(3)	C C
5.	(3)	K C
6.	(2)	D H E
7.	(2)	J
8.	(5)	J
9.	(3)	G
10.	(5)	F J
11.	(3)	W S D K
12.	(2, 4)	S D
13.	(3)	T C
14.	(3)	E L
15.		—
16.	(4)	K K K
17.	(3)	N
18.	(3)	M B
19.	(3)	F
20.	(6)	I C N

	Rule	Answer
21.	(2)	J L
22.		—
23.	(2)	J M
24.	(3, 5)	D A
25.	(5)	M D T
26.	(4)	S P
27.	(6)	I
28.	(2, 6)	L D B A
29.		—
30.	(3)	A
31.		—
32.	(3)	S
33.	(6)	W
34.	(2, 6)	T I M
35.	(2)	C E
36.	(6)	A
37.	(3)	A E
38.	(4)	P B
39.	(3)	R
40.	(4)	N R A
41.	(4)	L S
42.	(2)	G
43.		—
44.		—
45.	(3, 5)	S B C
46.	(2)	G J
47.	(2)	P W
48.	(2)	C B
49.	(2)	S
50.	(4)	G E C
51.		—
52.	(6)	H
53.	(6)	B H D A F
54.	(4)	U L
55.	(3)	C W
56.	(2)	P B
57.	(5)	L
58.	(3)	L

CAP. (Cont.)

59. (4)	H C	
60. (3)	A	
61.	—	
62. (2)	C J	
63. (2)	J	
64. (5)	J A	
65.	—	
66. (6)	C	

67. (4)	S H	
68. (4)	M W C	
69. (4)	C B	
70. (6)	R D	
71. (2)	M A	
72. (2, 6)	C L J V	
73. (2)	J	
74. (3)	W O C	

75. (4)	M S	
76. (3)	S L M R	
77.	—	
78. (2)	G P	
79. (2, 5)	E M J	
80. (2)	J	

PUNCTUATION
(pages 267–269)

Note: Comma underlined thus $_{\text{,}}$ is optional; the sentence is correct either with or without the mark.

The total score in punctuation is the total number of lines in which correct punctuation marks *and no others* have been inserted (except as certain alternatives are allowed as indicated by the marks in parentheses). If the student has only three of four punctuation marks needed on a line or if he has all the punctuation and adds a mark, no credit is given. The total possible score is thus 80 points.

Rule	Answer
1. (1, 8)	strassburg, germany?
2. (12, 1, 7)	exclaimed, "what lake!"
3. (3)	The hudson, a york, is
4. (1)	ceylon?
5. (14)	we'll
6. (12, 7)	"Tell did,"
7. (14, 12, 7)	"If that's all," john said, "we go." (that's said,)
8. (3)	Friday, the june,
9. (1)	germans?
10. (3)	july, a
11. (8)	street, dolby, kentucky.
12. (3)	Al smith, the candidate,
13. (10)	college; then
14. (11, 5)	following: history, english, and latin.
15. (14, 6)	They're ready, but we'll
16. (4)	place, the
17. (9)	newburg; there (started; to)
18. (7)	(No punctuation needed)
19. (6)	(No punctuation needed)
20. (13)	called "in night."

PUNCTUATION (*Cont.*)

21. (9)   heirloom; it
22. (3)   captain, our friend, met
23. (15, 5)   Esther, jane, and girls'
24. (8)   8,1933
25. (5)   Christmas, memorial day, and
26. (1)   succeed?
27. (9)   ipana; it
28. (13, 11, 5) books: *dodsworth, babbitt,* and *arrowsmith.* (books; "dodsworth," "babbitt," and "arrowsmith.")
29. (12, 7) "We are," said the speaker, "at era."
30. (4)   tourists, let
31. (6)   (No punctuation needed)
32. (10)   spanish; then
33. (13)   "By a waterfall" is
34. (15, 3, 13) tennyson's poem, "in memoriam."
35. (6)   given, for

36. (4)   cleaning, since

37. (14, 10) didn't alps; still

38. (15, 9)   presbyterian; he
39. (5)   rome, that politics, and

40. (9)   pay; it

41.   (No punctuation needed)
42. (14)   It's can't
43. (5)   Oranges, lemons, and
44. (7)   (No punctuation needed)
45.   (No punctuation needed)
46.   (No punctuation needed)
47. (7, 6)   wales, but
48. (12, 7) "Please come," she wrote, "colonel here."
49. (6)   going, nor
50. (4)   words, the
51. (15, 14, 9) soft; it's
52. (14, 13) "I'm hurry"
53. (13, 11) movies: *ben hur* and *diary of anne frank.* (movies, "ben hur" and "diary of anne frank.")
54. (14)   tomorrow, at o'clock.
55. (6)   washington, and
56. (12, 7) "You brown," she

PUNCTUATION (Cont.)

57.   (No punctuation needed)
58. (1, 9)   lisbon; which be?
59. (9)   mathematics; he

60. (14, 9)   You'll athens; you'll
61. (14, 10)   I'm tonight; besides it's
62. (12, 7)   "That youngster," said coach jones, "will year." (said, "coach year.")
63. (14, 6)   It's hard, but jim won't
64. (5)   June, july, and
65. (5)   quick, who ambitious, and

66. (14, 4)   If it's necessary, you
67. (14, 6)   didn't
68. (4)   prominent, she

69. (7, 12, 14) "All right," he said, "we'll bank."
70. (14, 13, 4) I'll *reader's digest,* if("reader's digest,")
71. (2, 10)   mr. adams; then

72. (13, 9)   *lord jim;* he *victory.* ("   ")
73. (14, 4)   frank, she doesn't
74. (5)   washington, to oregon, and
75. (4)   society, thus
76. (6, 2)   st.

77. (14, 10)   I'll car; otherwise you'll
78. (15, 3)   Mary, you pershing's
79. (15, 5, 2) one's conscience, to one's clothes, or mrs.

80.   (No punctuation needed)

SENTENCE STRUCTURE
(pages 270–272)

Rule		Answer	

Rule	Answer
1. (2)	2
2. (5)	2
3. (3)	1
4. (4)	2
5. (5)	2
6. (1)	3
7. (4)	3
8. (4)	1
9. (3)	3
10. (5)	2
11. (6)	3
12. (1)	1
13. (2)	1
14. (6)	3

15. (6)	2
16. (3)	3
17. (4)	2
18. (5)	2
19. (3)	1
20. (5)	1
21. (1)	1
22. (4)	2
23. (6)	1
24. (6)	3
25. (1)	1
26. (1)	2
27. (4)	1
28. (1)	3
29. (5)	3
30. (4)	3
31. (6)	3
32. (6)	1

33. (1)	1
34. (6)	2
35. (4)	2
36. (1)	2
37. (5)	3
38. (2)	2
39. (1)	3
40. (5)	1

SPELLING TEST
(pages 273–280)

1. absence
2. ache
3. altogether
4. affect
5. accidentally
6. accept
7. across
8. advise
9. accommodate
10. already
11. angel
12. among
13. always
14. almost
15. angle
16. apparatus
17. auxiliary
18. athletic
19. argument
20. attacked
21. appearance
22. athlete

23. believe
24. balance
25. beginning
26. business
27. benefit
28. bicycle
29. commercial
30. chose

31. character
32. changeable
33. calendar
34. characteristic
35. college
36. choose
37. chief
38. certain
39. captain
40. coming
41. criticize (*or* criticise)
42. course
43. convenient
44. complimentary
45. compliment
46. comparatively
47. committee

48. conscience
49. conscientious
50. control
51. conscious
52. conspicuous
53. deceive

54. decide
55. definite
56. does
57. disappoint
58. disappear
59. develop (*or* develope)
60. development (*or* developement)
61. describe
62. descend
63. dining
64. discipline
65. doctor
66. dependent
67. don't
68. existence
69. experience
70. exercise
71. executive
72. except
73. enough
74. equipped
75. emigrant
76. embarrassment
77. embarrass
78. effect
79. eligible
80. fascinate
81. February
82. finally
83. formerly
84. forty
85. fulfil (*or* fulfill)

SPELLING *(Cont.)*

86. friend
87. grateful
88. grievous
89. grammar
90. governor
91. guess
92. humorous (*or* humourous)
93. hoping
94. here
95. hear
96. harass
97. irresistible
98. it's
99. immigrant
100. immediately
101. imagine
102. independent
103. interesting
104. judgment (*or* judgement)
105. judicial

106. knew
107. laboratory

108. laid

109. led
110. leisure
111. library
112. lose
113. loose
114. literature
115. license (*or* licence)

116. management
117. meant
118. misspell
119. mischievous
120. mortgage
121. minute
122. necessary
123. noticeable
124. nineteen
125. twenty

126. niece
127. occasion
128. occasionally
129. opportunity
130. omission
131. often
132. o'clock
133. omitted
134. occurred
135. parallel
136. probably
137. proceed
138. professor
139. prophecy
140. permanent
141. permissible
142. persevere
143. picnicking
144. precede
145. possession
146. planning
147. planned

148. piece
149. preference
150. preferred
151. privilege
152. preparation
153. principal
154. principle
155. prejudice
156. parliament
157. partner
158. perform
159. perhaps
160. quantity
161. quiet
162. quite
163. really
164. receipt

165. rhythm
166. rhyme
167. responsible
168. respectfully
169. repetition
170. religious
171. relieve
172. recommendation
173. recommend
174. recognize
175. receive
176. salary
177. separate
178. seize
179. secretary

180. schedule
181. scene
182. sincerely
183. shining
184. similar
185. shepherd
186. speech
187. sophomore
188. skillful (*or* skilful)
189. stationery
190. stationary
191. sure
192. stopping
193. studying
194. success
195. supersede
196. superintendent
197. stopped
198. surprise
199. syllable
200. tariff
201. there
202. their
203. they're
204. therefore
205. through
206. too
207. together
208. tragedy
209. two
210. twelfth
211. tries

212. truly
213. unnecessary
214. until
215. using

216. which
217. whole
218. women
219. weather
220. Wednesday
221. where
222. writing
223. usually
224. villain
225. village
226. won't
227. would
228. write

Index